Conflicting Theories of Instruction

Conceptual Dimensions

Zvi Lamm

Hebrew University of Jerusalem

McCutchan Publishing Corporation
2526 Grove Street
Berkeley, California 94704

ISBN 0-8211-1112-4
Library of Congress Catalog Card Number 76-9238

FOREWORD

"Good teaching"—in the whole world of education nothing else is the object of such endless search and yearning. Despite all the other variables, everyone knows that it is the "good teacher" who finally makes all the difference.

And yet, despite decades of research, good teaching remains bafflingly difficult to identify, to define, or to prescribe. Through at least the first half of this century the search centered chiefly on the question of methods. Back of this was something like a faith that—to paraphrase Plato—"In Heaven there is laid up for us" a perfect pattern of teaching practices. To the extent that a teacher employed those practices, ran the unspoken premise, he could be "good."

Common sense itself belied the belief. Every experienced supervisor knew teachers who seemed to do all the right things—and yet made sticky messes of their classrooms. Even laymen remembered all their lives a few teachers who did everything wrong—and were great. Late in his career A. S. Barr, who undoubtedly devoted more years than anyone else to the quest, wrote wryly that he had found a lot of things that did not work. Though many still cling to the old faith, the cold fact is that the perfect body of practices has never been found.

It never will be found, said a new generation of researchers, because teaching is a deeply personal thing, and what works for one teacher may only mean failure to another. The center of attention must be the person within the teacher. What a teacher *is*, one study group hypothesized, is more important than anything he *does*. The autonomous professional, trained in a broad array of teaching skills but freely following his own inner mandates, is the nearest guarantee we have of good teaching. After years of study, Arthur W. Combs became a leading proponent of the view that the effective teacher is, above all else, a mature person who has learned to use his own self as a teaching instrument. It is a position that encourages the use of superior practices, but it relies primarily upon the trained intuition of the teacher to choose among them.

Comes now Zvi Lamm, who builds further upon the conception of the autonomous professional, adding the resources of systematic logic to his intuitive making of choices. Especially in this time of turmoil in our schools, when alternative models struggle in a confusing competition for acceptance—but, in a deeper sense, at *any* time—there can be no one pattern of instruction, simply because the teaching-learning complex has so many dimensions. There cannot even be one linear logic to determine all teaching activities. Differing logics flow from different dimensions and, in turn, generate a complex interplay of many, sometimes conflicting, patterns of activity. More than ever before, the good teacher must be able to peer into the heart of every situation through each of its multiple facets and adapt his teaching to his trained judgment of what he sees.

To produce that combination of sharp multivariant analysis with appropriate action selected from multiple possibilities is the basic purpose of this book.

Fred Wilhelms

PREFACE

The school has not lacked detractors in any period of its history. What distinguishes our own period from previous periods is the fact that no one seems prepared to defend it any longer. The school as we know it has apparently reached the end of one more stage in its history.

There is much evidence to indicate that this is so. The structure, content, and methods of the conventional school and all that stems from them are being reexamined in contemporary educational research, and the stability once characteristic of daily educational activities has not existed for some time. School administrators, teachers, parents, and pupils are concerned about the present situation. This is clearly a period of transition from the school as we have known it to an institution of a different kind whose characteristic patterns of activity have not yet crystallized.

Many alternatives to the conventional school are now emerging, and it is impossible to predict which of the proposed alternatives will prevail or, indeed, if the one that will eventually prevail has yet been proposed. A general agreement concerning a number of basic assumptions on which the new school will be founded seems to be emerging. The road from these basic assumptions to the crystallization of daily patterns of activity in the school is, however, a long one, and most of it is still in front of us. For the present, we must live with an institution in which everything once regarded as fixed and permanent is being called into question, and for whose place many new patterns of activity are competing. Furthermore, the interconnections are not always clear, and they do not invariably unite into an effective and harmonious whole.

This situation is not easy for the teacher. He has to function with the knowledge that what he does today may be considered wrong tomorrow, and even today there is no agreement about the best way of doing things. But the present situation need not necessarily lead to confusion and despair. It can also be stimulating and exciting. Change affects different people in different ways: some gather their resources and strengthen their wills; others give up the struggle and sink into apathy. Differences in personality are not, however, the only factor influencing the teacher's reactions to change. Professional training is also important.

In the prevailing state of affairs there is no substitute for the ability of the teacher to bring autonomous professional considerations to bear on the teaching situation. Where the situation is relatively static, the teacher can sometimes rely on the school's traditional way of doing things, on his own intuitions and his past experience as a pupil, or even on a rigid and authoritarian structure in the school. In conditions of accelerated change he must be able to assess the alternative patterns of activity open to him in order to be able to choose among them. He must, in other words, be capable of acting independently on the basis of valid professional considerations.

The professional reasoning of the teacher must always, in the nature of classroom situations, refer to all the dimensions of educational activity at once, beginning with ultimate goals and ending with the most specific techniques of instruction. In a fluid and unstructured situation, such as presently prevails, a teacher who is unable to diagnose the problem and choose the appropriate measures for dealing with it will be lost. This situation makes it impossible to equip him with a set of rules because the circumstances in which he must put them into practice are likely to have changed even before he begins to operate, and none of the instructions he has received will prove adequate to the situation.

This book is intended to develop the teacher's ability to bring professional considerations to bear on the teaching situation. It presents the teacher with the basic dimensions of instruction together with the possible patterns of activity in each dimension and the interconnections among them. The interconnections among patterns of activity in the various dimensions of instruction are generated by different logics, each of which generates a different type of teaching. In this book an attempt is made to identify the types of instruction and the logics that give rise to them.

Teaching activities whose justification stems from different logics are often mutually exclusive and usually neutralize each other. Teachers who are unaware of this often wonder why their hard and devoted labors do not lead their pupils toward the goals they have set for them. The reason may be that the efforts they have expended on one set of activities have invalidated the achievements obtained by a previous, contradictory set of activities.

Many factors are at work in the process of creating the new school, but the one indispensable factor is the autonomic teacher—the teacher who is able to bring autonomous professional considerations to bear on the teaching situation. This book is an attempt to contribute to the emergence of the new school by helping the teacher advance toward autonomy and by equipping him to act as an agent of change.

CONTENTS

ONE   The Logic of the School and the Logics of Instruction

Three hundred years ago Comenius pointed out the essential weakness of the school — its dominant verbalism. Yet the school has remained a temple to the word. Later Rousseau attacked the authoritarianism of the school for interfering with the development of children. Yet the school remains, to this day, an institution dependent on authority, and it operates by means of authority. Pestalozzi's ardent desire to create an atmosphere of love in the school, too, was lost, and the competitive achievement orientation he strove to modify seems to have grown even more intense. Robert Owen's ideas concerning the desired relationship between learning and doing in the school, like those of G. Kerschensteiner and John Dewey a hundred years later, have been incorporated in the school system only to the extent that they serve as a caricature of the original intent. Such has also been the fate of Spenser's ideas concerning the rationalization of the curriculum and of the reforms attempted by M. Montessori, O. Decroly, J. Korczak, and A. S. Neill, critics of the school in recent generations. Nor has scientific research had any real influence on the school system, despite the enormous prestige enjoyed by science in our day and despite the fact that teachers and educationists generally accept the relevant findings of scientists.

That the school has been able to withstand criticisms leveled against it for hundreds of years, as well as the many attempts made to improve it, may well rouse feelings of curiosity, not to say amazement. During the same period other social institutions have undergone many radical transformations. The state, the economy, even the family, are no longer what they were in the past, but the school stands firm. It continues to resist, as it has in the past, all the factors working to change it.

This resistance is usually passive. Reformers occasionally succeed in changing some aspect of the curriculum, a method of instruction or the organization of the learning group, and their reforms are hailed as presaging a new era in education after generations of stagnation. It soon becomes clear, however, that any change is more illusory than real. Then the excitement subsides, the "reform" or "experiment" is forgotten, and the school returns to its former state. Such reforms and experiments do, however, leave some traces. Here and there are remnants of self-organization among pupils, directed and supervised by teachers; here and there pupils work on individual self-work sheets as proof that someone once tried to satisty the child's need for spontaneous activity; here and there, completely isolated from "academic" subjects, of course, handicraft lessons remind us that educationists once strove to combine learning with doing; here and there a school newspaper, mainly the effort of a teacher, testifies to the memory of projects based on pupil initiative; here and there a play put on by well-drilled pupils in honor of some gala occasion marks the grave of erstwhile intentions to provide children with opportunities for self-expression. The school, at its hard, resistant core, remains what it has always been, albeit underneath a fashionable camouflage of slogans — self-rule, self-work, promote initiative, provide opportunities for self-expression, among others — emptied of all content. The slogans are no more than fossilized relics of intentions that were never realized and of temporary arrangements that never took root.

There is, perhaps, no field in which the school's stubborn resistance to change is more apparent than in that concerned with methods of instruction. The verbal method still dominant in education has been severely criticized for several generations, not only by psychologists but also by teachers and inspectors; even those who do not actively criticize it do not seem particularly eager to defend it. Yet research conducted in the United States in 1966 (three hundred years after the time of Comenius) showed that from two-thirds to three-quarters of classroom time is taken up with the teacher's talking, and the remaining time is used for activities that are also mainly verbal.[1] This finding led two other researchers to examine the changes that have taken place in this area over the past decades. They studied the available literature on the classroom behavior of teachers and examined the results of research dealing with instruction in an attempt to discover the extent to which theories demanding that pupils be active, which have been current in educational circles for several decades, have actually influenced teachers' patterns of behavior. They concluded that the "studies that have been reviewed show a remarkable stability of classroom verbal behaviour patterns over the last half century, despite the fact that each successive generation of educational thinkers, no matter how else they differed, has condemned the rapid-fire, question-answer pattern of instruction."[2] Research into other aspects of instruction produced similar findings:

Shortly after the turn of the century arguments for breaking down the massive uniformity of instruction gained support with the appearance of instruments for measuring human abilities. With the increasing sophistication of psychometric tools it has become clear that students differ not only in intelligence but in creativity and in at least 80 elements of intellect (Guilford). It also became clear that great differences between competence and performance are possible, and that inequalities in intellect, physical ability, and social behavior, great in childhood, increase as students move through the grades. Dramatically, it could be shown that among 80 ninth graders reading and mathematics test scores ranged from Grades 3 and 4 to college sophomore and junior levels (pp. 30-33). Yet graded mass teaching continues.[3]

The history of attempts to eradicate predominantly verbal instruction or to increase individualized instruction in the school shows quite clearly it was not the opposition of teachers, parents, or educational authorities that prevented the desired changes from taking place. It is true that the prospect of change or innovation usually arouses opposition, if only temporarily, among these groups, as it also often does among the pupils themselves. But even in cases where the projected change has been accepted by everyone concerned (as in the case of individual differences, which no one denies should be considered in teaching), nothing changes. This paradoxical situation has led many would-be reformers of the school system to despair of the possibility of change. It apparently "would be easier to disband the armies and navies of the world than the forces which administer our educational systems. They must be left to die a natural death," writes Herbert Read,[4] while Reimer goes even further and ascribes the present state of the school to the fact that it is already dead.[5] What, then, actually prevents the reform of the school system? What is the true source of power that successfully rejects all attempts to change and improve?

The school does not function according to the logics of instruction. It operates in accord with the needs inherent in its own structure, not the needs of instruction. Because schools have a long past but a short history, their structure was determined long ago, according to the needs of an earlier society and an image of what constituted a good education at that time. The needs of society and the educational ideals of men have changed more than once since then, but the structure of the school and the modes of operating derived from it remain unchanged. In order to understand the logic of the school, which determines its mode of operating, it is necessary first to understand its structural foundations, and, in order to understand these, we must turn our attention to the social circumstances and the images in the minds of men at the time the school became an institution.

The Origin of the School

The school was established to aid the socialization of members of the privileged classes into traditional societies. In other words, the structure of the school was determined by three needs: to provide an instrument of *socialization,* to train those destined for positions of *leadership* in society, and to maintain the values and ideologies of *traditional* societies.

The first of these needs meant that society established and maintained schools in order to transmit to members of the younger generation behavior (in the widest sense, modes of thinking and feeling, manners, occupational skills, and so forth) considered desirable. This does not mean, however, that all the functions of socialization were delegated to the school or that family, religious, and other social institutions were released from educational roles. The school was intended to play a complementary role in areas where the family and other institutions were unable to advance the socialization of the children, primarily in the areas of imparting knowledge. Although the distribution of roles among family, religious, and other institutions and the school was never strictly defined, it was quite clear. Imparting knowledge to the younger generation was, and has remained, the role of the school.

The second of the needs determining the structure of the school stemmed from its role in training the elite. During the greater part of its existence the school has been a selective institution. It was not open to everyone, and those to whom it was open were obliged to compete fiercely for status. Those initially trained by the school were mainly destined for religious leadership. Nor did all training for leadership necessitate the services of the school. The aristocracy of the Middle Ages, for example, did not usually need the school to train its sons for elitist positions in society. And other socialization roles not connected in some way with training for leadership were generally delegated to other institutions. The guilds of the Middle Ages, where apprentices were taught especially skills, are a good example of socialization for nonleadership roles outside the school. In time the school opened its doors to those not destined to fulfill leadership roles, a change that might have been expected to lead to changes in structure. This did not, however, occur. The school continued to operate as though its sole function was the training of youths for positions of leadership. It is not surprising, therefore, that children from poor and deprived families did not generally profit from schooling. Not only did they fail to assimilate the values of the ruling classes, but failure to do so became an additional burden for them. The school as an institution has, from its beginnings, always strengthened the strong and weakened the weak.

The third need affecting the character of the school was that of perpetuating the values and the ideologies of traditional societies, which encouraged a preference for the past over the present and the future. The school has always displayed an excessive concern for preserving traditional forms, as well as a deep suspicion of change. This conservatism, bequeathed to the school by traditional society, is responsible for several basic characteristics that have been preserved to this day and continue to affect the school directly. The characteristics most decisive for the school's structural development were conceptions of childhood, youth, and the nature of knowledge, as well as the role of knowledge in individual life that were current during the formative period in its history and crystallized over time.

"Childhood is one of the great discoveries of the eighteenth century," writes a student of the family in our day,[6] and this discovery may have taken place even later. W. Hugo, writing in the nineteenth century, claimed: "Columbus only discovered America; it was I who discovered the child."[7] Before childhood was "discovered," it was perceived as a period with no distinguishing characteristics of its own, to be exploited in preparation for adult life. Efficient exploitation of childhood meant suppressing the natural needs of the child. Children were not allowed to play, laugh, fantasize, chatter, or otherwise participate in activities considered frivolous because this was considered a "waste of time." Laws of development governing childhood and its unique needs were not recognized during the period when the school became an institution, and this lack of recognition has had profound and lasting effects on its structure. The school was an institution designed from its inception to "prepare children for life," that is, to mold their personalities in accord with models of existing roles. Schools were supposed to "make" children into men, mainly by a process of "addition." The child was a little man who needed to have his mind (and body) "added to" in order to become a proper man. The school was established to add systematically to children's minds by imparting knowledge, as knowledge was interpreted by those who established the school. We must, of course, distinguish between the social function fulfilled by knowledge at this time and the role it played in the lives of the many individuals who sought truth and tried to find answers to troublesome questions. If, during this period, men broadened their knowledge about the world and themselves, it was not because of, but despite, the role played by knowledge in society, which was to ensure the privileged positions held by members of the upper classes. Although this interpretation of knowledge and its possible functions in human life were those proposed by philosophers, the schools did teach philosophical theories, and many teachers believed in them. The difference was that the school interpreted knowledge in terms of the zeitgeist, and what emerged, first and foremost, constituted a status symbol. Knowledge distinguished between the educated and the ignorant, the elite and the common man, with all that this implied concerning the social status of the man belonging to either of the two groups. This became, then, the sole function that knowledge taught in schools was expected to play in society. The struggle for existence depended, instead, on traditional knowledge handed down from father to son without any reference to the school. What was taught in the school had nothing to do with how men earned their bread, solved their social problems, or educated their children. People went to school in order to secure their place in one of the privileged groups of their society. What they learned at school was not designed to help them solve their problems; it was to show that they belonged to an educated group, which gave them the right to lead society, or at least to associate with those who did.

To understand why there is so much indoctrination, brainwashing, emotional pressure, preaching, and persuasion in our schools today, remember that the school, from its inception, was designed to support the socialization of children for positions of leadership in traditional societies and that it has not yet freed itself from patterns of behavior designed to serve this goal. Even in the earliest days of the school it was difficult, if not impossible, to present a rational case, open to criticism and argument, that could excuse the axiomatic truths, prejudices, and superstitions that the school undertook to impart to its pupils. If pupils cannot subject what they are taught to rational examination or exercise independent judgment concerning it, tl.en indoctrination and exhortation are the only alternatives left, and the early school developed patterns of behavior appropriate to the performance of these functions and has never relinquished them. The same methods once employed to impart habits of obedience to superiors, submission to authority, and belief in the privileges of certain classes in society or nations in the world are now used to teach the pupils in our schools the essentials of mathematics and history, literature and physics. These subjects are presented to the pupil as collections of truths that he must accept whether or not he understands them, whether or not he believes them.

To understand why schools continue to maintain a system of marks and tests, and to "measure" the achievements of pupils day in and day out, despite the many findings of psychologists clearly implying the error of such proceedings, remember that the school was intended, from its inception, to act as a machine for winnowing out the "best" and preparing them for leading positions in society. Competition is so integral to its structure that the school cannot exist without it. Schools that have attempted to eliminate marks and tests have soon been forced to restore them in one disguise or another. It is not the process of instruction that demands these methods, and it is certainly not the pupil (unless he has been influenced by the school). It is the school itself, its very structure, that cannot do without the pressure it exerts on its pupils by means of marking and testing.

To understand why school curricula, after all the reforms that have been carried out on them, are still so similar to what they have always been, remember that it is tradition, not change and development, that has always been valued by the school. The school, constructed on the lines of a historical museum, preserves and exhibits all that has ever been considered valuable in the societies of the past.

To understand why the organization of school classes is based on the pupils' age group, despite practical and theoretical proofs that this procedure is irrelevant and harmful, recall the image of childhood that guided the school's creators: children enter the first grade and "ascend" from one class to another on their way to eventual adulthood. At each stage of this ascent, that is, each class, they are supposed to acquire a fixed amount of knowledge. If, at any specific stage of the ascent, the child fails to acquire the requisite amount of knowledge, he must retrace his steps, or repeat a class.

To understand why the school demands rote learning of material that should rather be used as a tool to think with, consider the status of knowledge in the society where the school was founded. The idea that dominated, and still dominates, the school was that there were certain things a person *must* know; they are essential for social survival, and there are no substitutes. When this is the status of knowledge, any means leading to acquisition seems justified, and, although mechanical repetition of learned material is no longer considered an achievement worthy of the name, the school regards it as being essential. The ability of the pupil to repeat what he has heard from his teacher or to read what is in his textbook is the minimum achievement that the school demands from him. In order to ensure this minimum achievement, the school employs methods that prevent it from attaining goals that are more desirable, even by its own definition. If knowledge is regarded primarily as subject matter to be transmitted to the pupil as an object is transmitted from hand to hand, its effect on the pupil when he receives it, if he indeed receives it, is of secondary importance. Whether what a pupil learns is meaningful to him, whether he internalizes it, whether he simply remembers it by mnemonic techniques, or whether he is prepared to put it to use in situations different from those in which he first encountered it — none of these are important considerations when the school is considering methods of instruction. The school has undertaken the task of imparting knowledge, and impart knowledge it does, to the best of its ability.

Thus it is that any examination of the basic characteristics of the school leads straight to the beginnings of the school as an institution, when its structure was determined. This structure may have suited the requirements of society then, but the requirements of society have changed.

The Changing Need

Schools that educate people to maintain the status quo and keep society static are no longer needed. Schools must, instead, enable people to change society by developing all of its facets, and existing schools do not educate for life in a changing society.[8]

Nor is it feasible to support schools that select the "best" and devote themselves to cultivating this group to the exclusion of others. Schools must support the development of all pupils and advance them as far as they can go. Modern society needs more people capable of performing complex tasks that demand extensive training for proper performance than any society in the past. This need is no less urgent because education, more than birth, is now the key to social status. People know that, if the school fails to provide their children with a proper education, they are doomed. Social harmony is impossible if the road to social advance by means of education is not open.

Socialization based on the needs of modern society bears no resemblance whatsoever to that based on the needs of traditional societies. This is especially true in the intellectual field, which is the school's main concern. Few things are more worthless, even harmful, to modern society or the individual living in it than the way most schools stuff information into the heads of their pupils, reflecting an era when knowledge meant knowing the right answers to questions, but imparting information continues to be the main activity of schools.[9] In the computer age knowledge has value only as it enables the individual to pose relevant questions and to detect problems; knowledge that enables him to give conventional answers to conventional questions is not adequate. Intellectual development in our time and in light of the needs of contemporary society means developing the ability to think independently and daringly, imaginatively as well as systematically, remaining open to the lessons of experience. It must not be bound by conventions. Information readily available today in the form of printed matter and computer "memories" at last frees the human brain to perform a function more worthy of it than that of storing facts.

Schools can no longer be satisfied with performing socialization functions, either. Even if these were fulfilled in a manner most calculated to meet the requirements of modern society, which they certainly are not, such a function would be inadequate. Because changes have taken place in society in recent generations, the school is expected to perform a growing number of functions, many of which were fulfilled by other social agencies — family, community, religious — in the past. In addition to serving as an agent of *socialization,* the school is also expected to serve as an agent of *acculturation* and *individuation.* Acculturation is the process by which the individual gradually internalizes the principles and values of his culture. By these criteria he later assesses norms and behaviors current in society in order to choose those appropriate to his own views, beliefs, conscience, aesthetic sense, and so forth — all of which in turn stem from the culture he has internalized. Individuation is the process by which the unique personality of the individual is developed. While socialization, especially in traditional societies, works toward establishing uniform models of social roles, individuation strives for differentiation between individuals in order to realize the unique potential of each. The school generally supports acculturation, at least to some extent (although not with any great success where children have a cultural background different from that of the school). As for individuation, however, insofar as the school has any influence at all, that influence is negative. The school sees its pupils mainly as groups (grade one or grade two, bright or dull, advanced or backward). It does not relate to what is specific and unique in the individual pupil.

The failure of the school is due to its excessive stability. It has not adapted to changes taking place around it, and it has rejected all attempts to change its structure. Why is this so?

The Unchanging Schools

To show that the school has not changed and that its structure stems from the needs of a society that no longer exists is one thing; to try to discover why is another. Historians have worked hard to show all the changes that have taken place in the school over the generations. They have described changes in curricula, in methods of instruction, in class organization, and in other areas, but they do not recognize how meaningless these changes were from the educational point of view, how much harm the petrification of the school has done society, culture, and individuals. Our concern is not historical, but we must describe, however briefly, those factors leading to the petrification of the school that are relevant to our discussion.

First, no professional body solely responsible for the school ever arose. Teachers should have constituted such a body, but we need only compare them with doctors and their status in medicine, actors and directors and their status in the theater, or clerics and their status in the church in order to see that school was never the business of teachers in the same sense that medicine was the business of doctors; the theater, of actors; and churches, of clerics. Medicine was advanced by doctors forced to conduct a running battle against prejudice and against social institutions with a vested interest in prejudice. The theater was advanced by the efforts of people working in it. Educational theories, however, were largely propounded by people outside the school. Comenius was a theologist; Rousseau, a writer, philosopher, and ideologist; Herbart, a psychologist and philosopher; Dewey, a philosopher; and Montessori, Decroly, and Korczak, doctors. This phenomenon caused Piaget to inquire: "Why is pedagogy so little the work of pedagogues?"[10] We do not seek to answer this question here, nor even to examine Piaget's answer. It is sufficient to recognize that the school was never ruled by a professional body of teachers who held themselves solely responsible for it. Who, then, was responsible?

The answer to this question leads to the identification of a second factor responsible for the petrification of the school. No body ever held itself continuously responsible for the school. What happened in schools was always affected by pressure from outside social forces that viewed the school as an instrument to be used in achieving goals. Politicians and ideologists used it. Clerics used it. Businessmen used it. Not one of these groups was much concerned with the primary function of the school, which was to educate people. Those primarily concerned with the quality of education provided by the school, that is, parents and children, were always too weak to counteract social pressures and ensure conditions needed to perform educational functions properly. As for teachers, not only were they too weak to represent the specific interests of the school vis-à-vis society, but it is also doubtful if, during most of their history, they were intellectually capable of resisting the blandishments of outside agencies invading territory ostensibly theirs. For generations the school was victimized by those who used it to further their own ends and ignored educational goals entirely, and there was no force strong enough to place the needs of the developing human personality at the center of the school's activities. The school remained inert, the existing structure being supported by the interests of the social institutions that required its services. And it was this support of the social institutions that gave the school great stability, the very stability that prevented necessary reforms and improvements or the emergence of a new institution capable of fulfilling the educational functions *expected* of the school with greater success.*

The school, which took shape as a stable institution in response to social pressures that have disappeared, is still structured to meet needs that no longer exist. No force has yet been strong enough to change its rigid structure and adapt it to existing conditions. External forces continue to exploit it for their own purposes, as they have done in the past, and the present structure, to a large extent, serves their needs. The school remains a passive instrument in the hands of those seeking to instill in students ideas, beliefs, habits, and behaviors already established, with little concern for the developmental needs of the student himself. The existing structure of the school is not geared to meet individual needs, and what happens in the school is determined by its structure. Therein is the source of the logic of the school.

The Logics of Instruction

These logics differ from the logic of the school in that they are not subject to any institutional structure, even though it is the institutional structure that determines the nature of instruction on the operative

---

*In this connection, compare the opinion of the anthropologist, Jules Henry: "Meanwhile, in the drive to improve the teaching of science and mathematics we observe a present paradox, for while fear impels us to revolutionize science teaching the danger arises — as witness Mrs. Franklin — that we go backwards in other areas. Even the fear of communism, however, is not the force behind the effort to improve the teaching of science and mathematics. Basically the force is all of business — textiles, oil, supermarkets, rockets and so on, who need the scientist and the mathematician to automate and analyze, to invent and compute along with the computers; for business is so vulnerable to competition, to obsolescence, to the stock market, to imports, to a labour movement and to depression that it needs our children's brains as protection. We must not, however, let everything else in our schools remain dead and embalmed while science and mathematics spring to a new and ambiguous life" (*Essays on Education*, Penguin Education Specials [Harmondsworth, Eng.: Penguin Books, 1971], p. 18).

level. This is why there is little resemblance between what should happen in the school according to theories of instruction and what actually does happen. Theories of instruction are the result of efforts to understand teaching situations by observing them, examining and testing teachers' experience, investigating pupils' behavior and changes in it, applying the relevant findings of research, and so forth. In practice, however, instruction is limited at the outset to possibilities provided by the school, which behaves according to its own logic, while theories of instruction are formulated, abandoned, and formulated again according to different logics. Because the school is rigid, changes in theories of instruction have had little effect on its structure. Educational thought, on the other hand, is relatively flexible, and assumptions underlying theories of instruction have changed several times over the generations. They can be roughly classified under three headings: the monistic logic of imitation, the monistic logic of molding, and the pluralistic logic of growth. Each represents an archetype of logic in thinking about teaching.

The Monistic Logic of Imitation

This is the oldest of the patterns of logic in instruction. It reflects the direct experience of transmitting knowledge and skills from one man to another. In order for a man to learn something, the shortest way seems to be to tell it to him; in order for him to learn how to do something, the shortest way seems to be to show him how to do it and have him repeat what he has been shown. If he refuses to assimilate what he has been told or to repeat what he has been shown, the shortest way to bring him to the desired state seems to be by means of rewards and punishments. These procedures stem from the belief, or the underlying assumption, that there are certain things a man must know, and certain things he must know how to do. The monistic basis of this logic stems from the idea that there are certain contents which the individual is obliged to know and for which there is no substitute. Knowledge of these contents is interpreted here as the ability to reconstruct what has been learned accurately, that is, to *imitate* behavior presented by a teacher or a textbook.

Theories of instruction based on this logic reflect the practice of instruction in so-called "old" schools, and these theories continue to affect the practice of instruction in the schools of today. The pattern had various names in educational research, and, in most cases, evaluation is implicit in the name. Piaget called it the "receptive method" or the "method of transmission by the teacher."[11] For Piaget, who developed the idea of activity as a means of learning and provided it with a scientific basis, there was no more negative method of teaching than that based on "reception" or "transmission." P. Freire, one of the most radical educational thinkers of our times, calls this pattern of instruction the "act of depositing" derived from the "banking concept of education." Knowledge is deposited in the mind of the child as money is deposited in banks.[12] The criticism implied by the terms is twofold. First, knowledge is considered to be an inanimate object, and, second, the learner is considered to be a passive storehouse. Two other critics of education in our day, Postman and Weingartner, have this kind of teaching in mind when they speak of the "vaccination theory of education,"[13] a theory resting on the assumption that, once you have been injected with any aspect of knowledge, the process is over and you will never need the serum again. Sartre calls this concept of instruction the "digestion concept" or the "nutrition concept" according to which people are "fed" what is considered to be good for them, and "filled" with knowledge.[14] Nathaniel Cantor[15] has accurately and comprehensively described nine characteristic assumptions of this kind of instruction:

1. *"It is assumed that the teacher's responsibility is to set out what is to be learned and that the student's job is to learn it"* (page 59). This division of roles has several implications. In the first place it implies an idea discussed above: that certain contents of knowledge have no substitute. The teacher decides what the pupil is to learn, or at least it seems so to the pupil. Actually, the teacher has very little say in determining what his pupils will learn, for the contents of the curriculum are decided at a higher level. The mistaken assumption that it is the teacher who decides what to teach plays an important part in this method of instruction, for, in addition to learning subject matter, the pupil must also learn the principle of authority: someone above him decides what he is to learn, just as someone decides what is wrong and what is right, which interpretation of the facts is correct and which is incorrect, what is true and what is untrue. In school the teacher represents the whole authoritarian structure of society, and, although the representatives will change in the course of the pupil's future life, the principle will remain. The pupil has no authority to decide for himself what he will learn, and his only responsibility is to learn

material presented to him by the teacher, and he has obligations toward the school and his teachers. He is expected to be willing, earnest, and hard working. Learning is not a game, and the learner is not expected to enjoy it.

2. *"It is assumed that knowledge taken on authority is educative in itself"* (page 59). The importance of knowledge acquired in the school lies in the fact that, by means of it, the pupil becomes a respectable citizen. To be educated means, in terms of this logic of instruction, to be like the best adults in the existing society. The pupil becomes like them by learning the same material which they learned, thereby forming their personalities. Knowledge includes both educational and noneducational material, and the subject matter depends on what the adult models assume to be educational. There is general agreement that the younger generation must also learn the same material, as if it constituted absolute, uncontestable truth.

3. *"It is assumed that education can be obtained through disconnected subjects"* (page 61). This concept of education is not based on the pupil as a developing being; it is based, instead, on the social roles he will have to perform in the future. Preparation for such roles is inevitably connected with specific knowledge, and the knowledge is organized into such subjects as mathematics, literature, history, physics, philosophy, and biology. Most of these subjects must be taught to most of the pupils in the school since the knowledge is required in order to perform various social roles (professional, civic, family). Each subject plays a part in preparing the pupil for his role in society, and the presence or absence of any connection between them is not considered a matter of any pedagogic importance. What is important is their value as training material for the future—the extent to which the pupil will require them in his professional work, in his behavior as a loyal citizen, in his attachment to the symbols and values of his society.

4. *"It is assumed that the subject matter is the same to the learner as to the teacher"* (page 64). The teacher's authority in the classroom, according to this concept of instruction, stems not from himself but from the knowledge he represents. Having submitted himself to the authority of knowledge, it becomes his right and his duty to subject his pupils to the same yoke; to this end he exercises his personal authority over them. The knowledge which the teacher already has and which it is up to the pupils to acquire is one and the same, and there is not

much room to manipulate knowledge for pedagogic purposes. In this pattern of instruction, even the textbooks used in the school are the same professional source books used by the teacher and other educated adults.

5. *"It is assumed that education prepares the sudent for later life rather than that it is a living experience"* (page 65). This is one of the basic assumptions underlying the structure of the school, and it has been preserved intact in the logic of this pattern of instruction. So long as the learner learns what he is supposed to learn, very little importance is attached to his experiences while doing so. The goals of instruction are in the future, not the present. Unless a pupil can be made to increase his efforts by these means, it does not matter if he enjoys or takes an interest in what he learns. Just as the subject matter is chosen with a view to the supposed needs of the pupil in the future, so, too, is the method of instruction designed to ensure that he will acquire knowledge, the value of which will become apparent only at some future stage. The pupil is incapable of evaluating his studies correctly, so there is no need to consider his attitude toward them.

6. *"It is assumed that the teacher is responsible for the pupils' acquiring of knowledge"* (page 67). If knowledge is regarded as an object and the pupil is regarded as its passive recipient, then the teacher must see that the object reaches its destination, and the success of the operation depends on the qualities and efforts of the transmitter. The teacher, who is judged by his success or failure in transmitting knowledge to his pupils, soon adopts methods that efficiently and economically achieve this purpose. The most efficient and economical way to meet the demands of this type of instruction is for the teacher to lecture. The pupils listen and repeat what they hear. The lecture enables the teacher to "cover ground" and "get through" his material. Little time is wasted, and repetition assures that the material has been successfully "transmitted" and that the object has reached its destination safely. By these means the teacher fulfills his responsibilities as they are understood in this pattern of instruction.

7. *"It is assumed that pupils must be coerced into working on some tasks"* (page 68). This principle connects all the others and follows from them. If you have decided that there are some things which the pupil must know, although he will acknowledge their importance only when he grows up and cannot derive any satisfaction from them in the present, and if you have further decided that the most efficient way of

teaching him these things is by constant repetition, then it follows that you must coerce him into taking part in this activity. Young people are not enthusiastic about mechanical repetition, at least not until the school succeeds in distorting their personalities. One implicit goal of this method of instruction is to distort the personality of the child until, by means of coercion, fear of punishment, desire for the teacher's esteem, or some similar source of satisfaction, he actually prefers to learn by mechanical repetition and avoids an active, critical, experimental confrontation with knowledge. This goal serves two interests. One is the short-term interest of the school, for learning by mechanical repetition requires strictness, discipline, and punishment. The second is the long-term interest of the status quo. The society that maintains schools employing these methods of instruction is a society that wants its members to be submissive and dependent on external authority. If a child is prevented from experimenting with knowledge on his own from the outset, and required, instead, to repeat what he has heard from his teachers and read in his textbooks, there is a good chance that society will get the kind of members it wants.

8. *"It is assumed that knowledge is more important than learning"* (page 70). Learning is a process; knowledge is a product (at least this is so in the imitative pattern of instruction). When teaching is guided by the laws of learning, that is, when it begins with the internal laws of the process, then knowledge is subject to learning. In this case the choice of materials to be learned, the order in which they are learned, the aspects to be presented, and those to be ignored — all are determined in light of the requirements of the process of learning. The opposite is true when methods of instruction are determined by the nature of the subject matter to be learned. Anything the pupil does not understand he must learn by rote, and anything he does not want to learn must be learned to avoid punishment. Learning takes second place to what is to be learned.

9. *"It is assumed that education is primarily an intellectual process"* (page 71). Learning involves the whole personality, not just the mind. Character, will, imagination, and emotion also influence the learning of an individual to no less a degree. Instruction that seeks to allow for nonintellectual factors involved in the learning process must face the possibility that these factors will divert the process from its declared and immediate ends. A child's imagination may lead him away from the path laid out by the teacher that leads to mastery of a

specific subject, but lack of imagination leads him nowhere. Owing to their preference for product over process, teachers follow the logic of instruction that sets out to neutralize nonintellectual factors in the learning process. Learning is seen as taking place only in the intellectual sphere, and all other factors are seen as interfering with teaching since they can divert the learner from the set path.

These nine assumptions cover the essential features of the most persistent of all the different logics governing instruction. A logic born in the distant past continues to govern instructional practices in many schools to this day, and the majority of our schools are structured on its principles. It owes its persistence neither to theoretical advantages (for it has none) nor to practical advantages (most of the failures of the school are due to this pattern of instruction). The overwhelming support this logic enjoys stems from the unchanging structure of the school and the fact that the patterns of activity permitted by the structure mainly correspond to the premises of this logic of instruction. All teaching that takes place in the framework of the prevailing school structure, whatever its premises, will sooner or later come to conform to the monistic logic of imitation.

The Monistic Logic of Molding

Side by side with the logic of imitation, a second logic, that of molding, evolved. Again, it originated many generations ago. The monistic principle common to both these systems indicates a belief in the existence of certain subjects and behaviors that are not only worth teaching, but also necessary and indispensable for the education of the learner. The subjects themselves differ in each system, owing to the different status each assigns to knowledge. According to the logic of imitation, the child must know certain things and know how to do certain things because he will need them in the future as weapons in the struggle for existence, or as a means to improve his conditions of life. If, however, it should transpire that the accepted means no longer serve the desired ends, or if more efficient means to the same ends should be discovered, then there is no reason, in this system, for objecting on principle (though there may certainly be psychological objections) to changing subjects once considered "indispensable" for others now considered equally indispensable. This is not true of the logic of molding, which assigns a different status to knowledge. According to this system, the subject matter of instruction is not intended to train people for life in a given society, but, instead, to mold their personalities on the model of the "good man" existing in a given culture. This system divides possible teaching subjects into two categories: those that come under the heading of culture, and those that come under the heading of utility.[16] A study of subjects in the first category, it is believed, assists the individual in coming to realize the human potential existing in embryonic form in his soul, while the business of the second is to prepare him for the struggle for existence and train him for his role in society. The first makes him a better person; the second helps him to better himself. Education and instruction, according to this system, should not concern themselves overmuch with the material benefits that education may be expected to produce. Their concern, once again, is with the idea of the "good man."

Another difference between the logic of imitation and that of molding lies in the fact that the first endeavors to impart ready-made behaviors to the individual, while the second seeks to implant characteristics to control and supervise his behavior. Molding is intended to cultivate qualities considered good in the individual pupil, not to train him in behavior considered good. These qualities derive their validity from values, beliefs, and opinions implicit in specific cultures. In Jewish culture, as in the culture of Western Europe, intellect and character are regarded as the main qualities of the good man, and these are the qualities, according to the logic of molding, which the school should cultivate. It is the subject matter that is regarded as having a positive influence on the development of the intellect, and the attitude toward subject matter becomes ritualistic in that it may be added to but not subtracted from. Also, character is viewed as being indispensable to instruction.

The development of the intellect and the molding of character cannot be achieved by means of imitation. Intellect here means the mental activity of the individual which is subject to the laws of reasoning and the values of the culture, especially the value of truth. The individual cannot be taught to reason systematically and respond to cultural values solely by means of practice and training (copying demonstrated behaviors in similar situations). Disciplined, systematic thought subject to laws and values is demonstrated only when new problems are encountered in new situations. Any other kind of problem is solved not by thinking but by remembering previous solutions. The same is true of character, which is taken to mean the organization of the personality in such a way that it ensures behavior subject to laws and rules, especially the laws and rules of morality. This cannot be taught by imitation, either. It is not enough for a man to know what is good in situations where the right choice has already been made for him by others. It is certainly desirable that the individual be willing and able to behave in accord with such examples, but it is more important for him to know what is good in situations where he has had no previous experience at all. These goals demand methods different from those employed in the logic of imitation. Instead of practice and training, this system depends on the identification of pupil with teacher and with cultural values embodied in the teacher's personality. By means of this identification, the pupil is expected to internalize qualities and values considered specifically human in light of the image of the good man existing in a given culture.

The pattern of molding is, therefore, two dimensional, whereas the pattern of imitation was one dimensional. Molding recognizes the claims both of knowledge with a ritualistic status and of the individual learner in the process of instruction and must respect both—knowledge because it represents the values that justify human existence, and the individual because he cannot be molded if his nature is not taken into account. Imitation shows little interest in the human nature of the individual learner; it is product, not process, oriented, and the product it aims at is defined by the social roles that are its models.

The earliest formulation of the conception of instruction as molding is found in the philosophy of ancient Greece,[17] and it has dominated the philosophy of education and instruction ever since. Most philosophical discussions of the nature of instruction are conducted in the spirit of this conception.[18] A famous attempt to assess the place of this conception and its suitability to the needs of modern society was carried out by a group of professors at Harvard University, and the results were published under the title *General Education in a Free Society*.[19] The two-dimensional nature of this concept of instruction becomes clearly apparent with one chapter in the book entitled "Traits of Mind," and another, "Areas of Knowledge." It is the tension between knowledge and the traits of mind of the learner that distinguishes this system of thought about instruction, and the characteristics that this system seeks to cultivate in the pupil include "aims so important as to prescribe how general education should be carried out and which abilities should be sought above all others in every part of it. These abilities in our opinion are: to think effectively, to communicate thoughts, to make relevant judgments, to discriminate among values."[20]

Effective thinking here means logical thinking, or "the ability to draw sound conclusions from premises."[21] This kind of thinking finds its greatest expression in the study of mathematics. Mathematics is not, therefore, considered to be a necessary weapon in the struggle for existence or even an instrument to be used by future scientists, as it is viewed in the logic of imitation; it is considered to be a vital element in the education of man. An educated man must be able to think logically not only within his chosen profession, but also "in choosing a career, in deciding whom to vote for, or what to buy, or even in choosing a wife."[22] Logical thinking is an indispensable part of individual education. The aim of teaching mathematics is not to find solutions to mathematical problems. It is, instead, to cultivate in the individual the ability to think logically and systematically and the readiness to use this ability in many different life situations. This ability, which cannot be taught directly, is the end result of a long process of confrontation with mathematical problems through which the pupil eventually internalizes the principles of mathematics. Once the principles are firmly established, argue the adherents of this system, they extend beyond the limits of mathematics and dominate the mind of the pupil. In this way, an area of knowledge (mathematics) molds traits of mind (logical thinking).

Communication, the second goal of instruction, is understood to be "the ability to express oneself so as to be understood by others."[23] Communication in exactly the same sense is also a goal of instruction in the logic of imitation. The ability of the individual to express himself so as to be understood by others is required for effective social communication, and it is, therefore, one of the basic goals of socialization. The difference between the two systems lies in the fact that, while the logic of imitation regards communication as a set of skills, the logic of molding regards it as an ability dependent on other abilities. In the first place, the ability to communicate seems to be dependent on the ability to think effectively. If someone has nothing to say, how he says it is of little consequence. The ability to communicate also depends on character. Even someone who has something to say often needs either the courage to say it or the judgment not to say it. Effective communication, thus, "depends on the possession not only of skills such as clear thinking and cogent expression but of moral qualities as well such as candor."[24] Molding the personality according to the values of Western civilization, therefore, includes the cultivation of an ability to communicate that is dependent on the moral and intellectual characteristics as well as the technical skills of speaking, listening, writing, and reading.

The third goal of instruction—making relevant judgments—"involves the ability of the student to bring to bear the whole range of ideas upon the area of experience. It is not a question of apprehending more relationships within ideas but of applying these to actual facts."[25] This goal rests on the assumptions that education can make men into rational creatures and that rational behavior requires an ability to relate ideas to experience, that is, to act with premeditation. Despite the intellectual terms in which the goal is formulated, what is really involved is the relationship between intellect and character. "Making relevant judgments" means possessing the ability to decide how to act by means of rational thought. Here, too, it is the function of knowledge to mold character.

The ability to discriminate among values, the last goal of instruction, "covers not only awareness of different kinds of value but of their relations including a sense of relative importance of the mutual dependence of means and ends."[26] The ability to discriminate among values depends on the powers of judgment possessed by the individual, and the growth of such powers depends on instruction. It is not the function of instruction, based on this view, to provide expert teachers on various subjects; rather, it is to assist the pupil in realizing his potential human characteristics and the power of judgment in the most specifically human of all human characteristics.

In its many forms this view of teaching has been called by many names—free education, general education, humanist education, and educative instruction, among others. Despite deep roots in the history of education, however, the pattern of molding has not succeeded in usurping the place of the dominant imitative mode of instruction. This is because the structure of the school does not support the principles of the logic of molding as it does those of the logic of imitation. In its struggle to overcome the institutional pressure of the school, this pattern of instruction stresses the role of the teacher. Teachers are expected to serve as exemplary figures with whom their pupils identify and whose values they eventually internalize. Teachers are also expected to create experimental situations in the classroom so that pupils' emotions will eventually support their learning. These demands on the teacher are expected to counteract the institutional weight of the school, which pulls all teaching in the direction of imitation and drilling. As long as the logic of molding continues to exist side by side with the logic of imitation in an unchanged school structure, however, there will be tension in the school; the intentions of teachers seeking to mold the personalities of their pupils in the light of cultural ideals conflict with the imitative pattern supported by the institutional framework of the school. Unfortunately, the school has proved able to withstand all efforts to limit its power. Instances in which teaching as molding has succeeded in practice have been few and infrequent.

The school is not the only factor preventing this theory of instruction from being put into practice. Another obstacle lies in the very nature of the program the theory supports. It seems that the difference between education seen as imitation and education seen as molding is largely one of principle. Despite the fact that teaching by means of imitation differs profoundly from teaching that seeks to mold the character and intellect of the individual pupil, both systems do rely on external models to determine their goals. The monistic logic of imitation relies for this purpose on the role behavior current in a given society, while the monistic logic of molding relies on the model of the human personality preferred in a given culture. In both patterns of instruction, therefore, the teacher acts in accord with a known, predetermined model that is the desired end product of the process of education. This similarity on the operative level is more significant for teaching than the theoretical differences that polarize the two systems from a philosophic point of view. The fact that teachers working within the terms of reference of both systems require an external image of their desired product leads them to adopt similar procedures and techniques. It is the general type, not the specific content, of the end goal that determines the method of instruction, and the goals of both of the systems described above belong to the same type, that is, they depend on external models of the desired product. This is why teaching that sets out to mold character and intellect often conforms, ultimately, to the dominant pattern of imitation supported by the existing school structure.

The Logic of Developmental Pluralism

Differing in both theory and practice from the types of instruction discussed earlier is a type suggested by the logic of developmental pluralism. Based on this logic, the assumption of pluralism holds for both knowledge and learner. No aspect of knowledge is seen as "indispensable" in the process of instruction, and no two pupils are seen as being alike. The status of knowledge is instrumental in that the purpose of instruction is not to impart knowledge but to use it in order to support the individual development of the pupil, each according to his needs. Both experience and research have shown that different types of knowledge are likely to support (or undermine) the development of different pupils. This pattern of instruction concludes, therefore, that subject matter must be adapted to the needs of the pupil, rather than trying to adapt the pupil (as patterns of imitation and molding are apt to do) to the subject matter chosen for instruction. There is no such thing as knowledge that has intrinsic value. The value of knowledge in teaching is measured by the support it gives to the development of those involved in it.

Development differs from molding, even though the goals of molding and those of developmental pluralism may appear to be identical. Both, for example, seek to develop various abilities and characteristics in the pupil (as opposed to imitation, which merely seeks to impart behavior). In terms of content, too, the desired characteristics are often similar in both. The intellectual abilities and moral characteristics which the logic of molding sees as the goals of instruction are sought as well by the logic of developmental pluralism. Despite apparent similarity, however, the two systems differ materially. The essential difference between development and molding (and, for that matter, imitation) lies in the fact that the logic underlying the pattern of development has no need of final personality models in determining its goals. The role played by external models in the previous two patterns is played by development as a value in itself. The goals of instruction are determined neither by the model of a man functioning properly in his society (as in the pattern of imitation), nor by the model of a "good man" accepted in a given culture (as in the pattern of molding), but, rather, by the unique needs of the developing individual.

The idea of development has been variously interpreted in educational literature. In the monistic logic of imitation, development is seen as a process in which the individual child gradually acquires patterns of behavior similar to those current in adult society. A child is seen to be developing properly to the extent that he grows to resemble the adults living and operating in his environment. In the monistic logic of molding, development is seen as a process in which the child gradually internalizes the norms and values of his culture. During the process his mind and conscience are formed, and he becomes capable of making fine distinctions and choosing appropriate behaviors through the use of reason, value judgments, and moral sensitivity. In both of these approaches the criteria for measuring the content and direction of development are external: in the logic of imitation the criteria derive from the social roles available in a given society; in the logic of molding, from the personality image preferred in a given culture.

In developmental pluralism, on the other hand, criteria for measuring the content and direction of development are intrinsic. According to this interpretation of development the individual does not become human by virtue of the fact that he has learned to function according to models of social roles or internalized cultural norms and values. His humanity is innate.[27] The function of teaching and education is not to teach him to be human, but to enable what is human in him to be realized. Humanity is not standard; every individual is human in his own way. The realization of what is human in the individual is the realization of what is unique and different in him. To develop means to advance along the road leading to this differentiation. Uniqueness cannot be predicted or planned. Educating the individual toward self-actualization means educating him without any ready-made models that he must try to emulate.

Instruction based on the logic of developmental pluralism differs from all other forms of instruction, first, in that its starting point is the actual pupil and his needs. It is not the pupil in the abstract (one of two starting points of the logic of molding, knowledge being the second), but that pupil whom the teacher meets face to face. Where instruction in the spirit of imitation was based on the needs of society and instruction in the spirit of molding was based on the claims of culture, instruction in the spirit of developmental pluralism is based on the developing needs of the real pupil.

Development takes place when the individual interacts with his environment as a result of his need to be active, his curiosity, his social needs—in short, as a result of his primary motivations. Teaching for development is designed primarily to create conditions for bringing the student into as many and as varied interactions with his environment as possible. This concept was first formulated by Rousseau, and, despite the fact that *Emil* is required reading in teacher-training institutions, attempts to put his theories into practice have been rare until recently.

The so-called "progressive" schools which came into being during the first half of the present century adopted some of Rousseau's ideas, but most of these schools do not operate according to the concept of developmental pluralism.[28] This concept began to be realized later in a few experimental schools, the first, or at any rate the most famous, of which was Summerhill, an educational institution founded by A.S. Neill.[29] In the past decade experimental schools based on a radical concept of education have multiplied, and these schools are trying to organize instruction along the lines suggested by developmental pluralism.[30] A few countries have even started reforming national school systems, especially primary school systems, along these lines. The most comprehensive reform carried out in this spirit took place in England, and, to a somewhat lesser extent, a similar reform was carried out in Sweden.[31]

The nine principles underlying the method of instruction now in the process of being crystallized in these schools have been described by R. S. Barth,[32] principles that correspond to a great extent with the premises of the logic of developmental pluralism!

1. *"Children's innate curiosity leads to exploratory behaviour that is self-perpetuating."* Exploratory behavior is the activity by which the child experiments with materials, objects, relationships, and so forth. As a result of this activity, he learns. In their infancy children explore their physical and human environments because of their innate curiosity and their need to be active. The more satisfaction they derive from this behavior, the more willing they are to experiment further. In this sense exploratory behavior is self-perpetuating. Unfortunately, however, adults (first parents and then teachers) soon decide that they should step in and determine which activities are suitable for the child, thereby removing him from activities that interest him and encouraging participation in activities that do not interest him. The child soon discovers that learning is an unrewarding chore and behaves accordingly. The apathetic behavior that results then leads

adults to conclude that it is impossible to rely on a child's curiosity for learning purposes. He must learn, whether he is interested in what he is learning or not. The more compulsion (whether crude and simple or subtle and ingenious) there is, the less curious the child becomes, which confirms, in adult minds, the assumption that learning cannot be founded on curiosity alone. Discipline, a sense of duty, punishment, and similar substitutes eventually replace the natural curiosity of the child. Teaching based on the logic of development seeks to restore curiosity to its rightful place in directing the child's behavior.

2. *"The child will display natural exploratory behaviour if he is not threatened."* Another reason to wean the child early from attempts to explore the world around him on his own initiative and for the sake of satisfying his own curiosity is to be sought in the behavior of parents and teachers who think it their right and duty to assess the child's behavior on their own scale of values. Praise and condemnation, marks and evaluations, inevitably accompany most of the child's activities. He soon becomes more interested in praise and good marks than in his own activity, even if that is what initially attracted his attention. In this way the expectation of praise from the outside, from teachers and parents, replaces the satisfaction that originally came from within. The child's interest in earning praise and good marks has another side, too: the anxiety that results from condemnation and bad marks. As soon as the child learns that his actions are being evaluated, he also learns to be careful. It is easier to do nothing, restraining the natural impulse to act, than to risk condemnation. This threat to the child's self-esteem undermines his self-confidence, and, in turn, his readiness to act, even though learning is impossible without activity. The exploratory behavior that brings about learning is very easily damaged by supervision. The child learns when he is free from the threat posed by evaluation. The threat of positive evaluation distracts him from what is significant (that is, the activity he is actually engaged in) to what is insignificant (that is, good marks), and the threat of negative evaluation damages his confidence and his readiness to take risks and engage in activities where success is not certain.

3. *"Play is not distinguished from work as the predominant mode of learning in early childhood."* Adults associate work with suffering or at least with discomfort. Children do not distinguish between work and play. Children work when they play and play when they work, and, when work and play are one, they learn. In learning, as in play,

the process, and not the product, is what matters. And yet the school has done everything in its power to grant learning the status of work as defined by adults, and to restrict play to authorized areas such as recess and physical education periods. This distinction between learning regarded as work, that is, as serious business, and play regarded as a frivolous activity stems from the attitude that prevailed when the school was founded, and it persists to this day. Because of this distinction, children gradually lose their learning abilities and feel guilty when they follow their natural instinct to play. Restoring work and play to their natural unity in the life of the school means saving the learning potential of the child from being destroyed.

4. *"Children have both the competence and the right to make their own decisions concerning their own learning."* Learning is a by-product of activities intended to gratify the immediate needs of the learner. The child does something because he wants to do it, and, in the process of doing it, he is likely to learn something. If his activities are systematically forced upon him, that is, if they are the fruit, not of his own impulses, but of external pressure, he learns something, too. He learns, at best, to be indifferent, and, at worst, to be hostile toward learning. When, on the other hand, his activities are the direct result of decisions stemming from his own impulses, he learns, first of all, to decide. If he learns to decide and is given opportunities to use his decisions in the school, there is a good chance that his capacity for learning will increase. This, in the opinion of those favoring the developmental approach to education, is why the pupil should have the right to make significant decisions concerning his learning.

5. *"When children are interested in exploring the same problem or the same materials they will often choose to collaborate in some way. Similarly, when a child learns something which is important to him he will wish to share it with others."* Curiosity is not the only innate characteristic in the child. The need for a society of his peers is also part of his makeup. Indeed, the group-learning frameworks maintained by conventional schools are usually justified on the grounds that they meet this need and support the normal social development of the child. It is characteristic of most of these schools, however, that their pupils, to the extent that they find satisfaction for their social instincts in the school, find it outside the frameworks provided by the school, that is, outside the learning context. The formation of social groups in the school also often serves to counteract the frustration aroused by

learning. The social organization of the pupils is directed against the school, to the exclusion of its contents and values. Radical schools based on the logic of development are tackling this problem in a different, seemingly paradoxical way in the hope of achieving very different results. The basic unit becomes not the class but the individual pupil. A constant striving for the maximum individualization of instruction is the only conclusion that it is possible to draw from the basic assumption concerning the uniqueness of each individual pupil. At the same time, however, it is hoped that, if individualization makes it possible for the pupil to devote himself to activities that interest him and to perform in a way and at a pace that suits his own particular needs, his social instincts will also find satisfaction within the framework of the activities of the school. If a pupil is interested in what he is doing, he will want to share his learning experiences with his friends.

6. *"Concerning intellectual development, assumptions are made that concept formation proceeds very slowly; that children learn and develop intellectually not only at their own rate, but in their own style; that children pass through similar stages of intellectual development—each in his own way, and at his own rate and in his own time; that intellectual growth and development takes place through a sequence of concrete experiences followed by abstractions; and that verbal abstractions should follow direct experience with objects and ideas, not precede them or substitute for them."* These ideas are reminiscent of Comenius, Rousseau, Pestalozzi, Decroly, and many other critics of the school. The decisive influence leading to the renewed demand in our day for putting experience before abstraction was, however, that of Piaget. His own work and that of his pupils on the cognitive development of the child provided a scientific basis for the principle of teaching. The translation of this principle into practical terms in the school makes it necessary to take individual differences between pupils into account since each pupil is active in his own way. Abstraction is the goal of instruction, but it cannot be reached by imparting abstract information. The ability to make abstractions will be acquired by the child only after prolonged, direct, and individual experience with concrete manipulations and operations of various kinds. Concepts cannot be taught; the child must create his own. The child's activity, regulated by his interests and taking place at his pace and in his style, is the condition for progress along the path of intellectual development until the final stage of abstract thinking is reached.

7. *"The preferred source of verification for a child's solution to a problem comes through the materials he is working with."* The rejection of evaluation and marks as a threat to exploratory behavior (see the second principle, above) receives additional support from another set of considerations. When an adult assesses a child's actions (or the result of his actions), he does so in the light of his own subjective criteria. When a pupil receives an evaluation, such as "good" or "insufficient," of work he has done, he is usually unable to comprehend the reasons for this evaluation. Even if the teacher adds a verbal explanation to the mark he has given, the evaluation is still not comprehensible to the pupil because, when he was doing the work, he was acting according to his own evaluation and his own criteria. The child is not always satisfied with what he has done. On the contrary, he criticizes what he has actually achieved in the light of his intentions, in the light of what he wanted to do. This, of course, holds true only when the child is working on his own initiative. The function of the school and the teacher in it is not to judge the pupil, but to help him examine his actions and their results in the light of relevant criteria, that is, criteria derived from the materials he is working with. Evaluations external to these materials, adult evaluations of the child's work, not only threaten the child; they also place him in meaningless situations. He does not understand what makes one performance good or another bad. In the end the child is reduced to gambling or passivity. He loses the ability to direct his activities to goals, either acting aimlessly or ceasing to act at all. Instead of developing control over his actions, all the child exposed to this kind of teaching develops is a submissive attitude toward authority. The book or the teacher tells the truth, whether he understands it or not. Constant verification of the results of his work by means of evidence derived from the materials (including, of course, ideas) he is working with, on the other hand, liberates the child from emotional dependence on authority and enables him to rely on his own intellectual abilities and reasoning powers in his attempts to understand the world and himself.

8. *"Errors are necessarily a part of the learning process; they are to be expected and even desired for they contain information essential for further learning."* As opposed to learning by conditioning, where the teacher does everything in his power to prevent his pupils from making mistakes so that they do not learn to do the wrong thing, the logic of teaching we are discussing here regards mistakes not only as

being inevitable in the learning process, but even as being desirable. The pupil learns no less—perhaps even more—from his failures than from his successes. But this applies only when the pupil learns to judge and evaluate his own actions, and he learns this only when his actions are self-directed, when he really cares about the results. Under such conditions, errors advance learning by enabling the learner to see aspects of a problem that he would not otherwise have discovered.

9. *"The following are further assumptions concerning evaluation: those qualities of a person's learning which can be carefully measured are not necessarily the most important; objective measures of performance may have a negative effect upon learning; if an individual is involved in and having fun with an activity, learning is taking place. Evidence of this learning is best assessed intuitively, by direct observation; the best way of evaluating the effect of the school experience on the child is to observe him over a long period of time; the best measure of a child's work is his work."* Evaluation is not simply a means of checking teachers' actions or pupils' achievements. Evaluation is not a neutral factor in the process of instruction. It affects the pupil. What is expected of him by those evaluating him soon becomes the criterion by which he evaluates himself. But not everything can be measured. Because evaluating instruments available to us can measure only certain things, evaluation encourages the pupil to expect only certain things of himself. Unfortunately, the qualities that can be carefully measured and are thus reinforced by evaluation are of secondary importance, even from the point of view of socialization, and, from the point of view of personality and developmental needs, they are mostly negative. Any kind of evaluation distracts the learner from the object of his learning and directs his attention toward the anticipated gratification he hopes to gain from an outside source—the person doing the evaluating. The "objective" tests that have invaded our schools recently have not only failed to live up to their claims by doing away with the imperfections of old methods of evaluation; they have also made evaluation even more damaging than it was before. The "objective" test is destructive of good teaching because it deliberately encourages teachers to ignore the individual nature of learning. The achievements measured by "objective" tests are behaviors that are completely standardized. In teaching that sets out to achieve such results, the process is inevitably subordinated to the product, and the product itself is evaluated by group standards as if the only differences between people

were differences of quantity, not of quality. The interest of the pupil in his work, his attitude toward learning, his honesty in approaching problems, as well as other qualities entirely escape systems of evaluating learning current in the school today.

Schools today often lack most of the conditions necessary for implementing methods of instruction suggested by the logic of developmental pluralism. The organization of the school into classes, the authoritarianism of its structure and relationships, the obligatory curricula, the dependence on secondary motivations (sense of duty, desire for social approbation, competitiveness), the built-in system of evaluation — all these and more militate against the possibility of teaching in a way that takes the immediate needs of the individual pupil as its starting point and sets out to support his development. It is thus no accident that the rare attempts made in the past and the increasing number being made today to introduce methods of instruction based on the concept of developmental pluralism always go hand in hand with attempts to establish a new type of school. There appears to be no hope, based on the experience of past years, that the conventional school can be effectively altered. The force of gravity of its structure soon restores old procedures and rejects new ones. The logic of developmental pluralism presently serves only as a basis of comparison by which the school's activities can be critically examined. It usually gains no foothold within the school itself.

Against the single institutional logic of the school stand three different, contradictory logics of instruction. One of them, that of imitation, corresponds in many respects to the logic embedded in the structure of the school. Another, that of molding, has been struggling for generations, without great success, to influence the school as constituted. The last, that of development, requires a completely different type of school. Under prevailing conditions only instruction based on the logic of imitation is, in fact, possible. Because the other two types of instruction generally fail in the school as we know it, instruction by imitation gains additional support, not only from the structure of the school but also from people who cannot imagine that any other system has a chance of succeeding. It enjoys the support of those teachers and parents who regard the existing school and its possibilities as a preordained fact of life that men have no power to change. The fact that instruction by imitation dominates the school and is relatively successful in doing so implies neither that the concept is practical nor that it is theoretically superior; it simply proves that this method of instruction is best suited to conditions that prevail in the school. Nor is the structure of the school neutral from the point of view of the teaching that takes place in it, for not all types of teaching can survive in it.

The rigid structure of the school is not the only factor that has petrified teaching for generations. Theories of teaching that have been unable to free themselves from this structure must also share the blame. Most such theories of instruction accept the school as a given institution in which certain procedures may be changed or certain procedures introduced, but in which radical reform is impossible. This is why teaching is influenced more by the institutional pressures of the school than by theories of instruction stemming from the needs of the pupil and his development. Teaching in our time needs a theory that enables the school structure, among other things, to provide for learning through development.

TWO   The Nature of Instruction

The development and crystallization of teaching as a specific activity correspond to the process of formalization of education. When the direct participation of children in the activities of their parents or of other adults was no longer sufficient to prepare them for life, society accordingly assigned special individuals the task of looking after its younger members. In time these individuals became teachers, and their activities gradually became institutionalized and took on the form of schools.[1] As a result of this gradual and protracted process, the teacher and the school became powerful factors in education, influencing the development of human personality to a degree equaled only by the family. What the family is to the infant, the school is to the growing child and the youth, although the later influence does not, of course, supersede the earlier.

The Concept

During the course of this process, the concept of instruction came to have two meanings: one is neutral, wherein teaching is an activity by which someone teaches someone else something; the other is normative, wherein teaching is an activity that strives to promote individual development in the light of certain value criteria. According to the first meaning, teaching is not limited to any specific contents, for example, contents with a high prestige value in any given culture; nor is it restricted to the aim of promoting individual development. Teaching takes place when one person learns something new through the mediation of another, whether it be mathematics or driving, history or swimming, whether it improves the learner's thinking and refines his emotions or dulls his mind and toughens his heart.

These two meanings of the concept of instruction, both of which came into being a very long time ago, are now used in two separate realms of discourse. The neutral-descriptive meaning is the one used in ordinary daily discourse, as well as in psychology, sociology, and the other behavioral sciences. The normative meaning is the one used in education. The meaning of instruction in the neutral-descriptive sense is exhausted in the definition, and no further explanation is required. The very neutrality of the definition, which makes it universally valid, at the same time makes it too narrow to include the many different and conflicting connotations of the word. Because the normative definition, on the other hand, is broad enough to include all of these connotations, it permits more than one explanation of instruction. In time new meanings superimposed on old ones gave the concept of instruction many different connotations.

The basic normative meaning of the concept was crystallized in the ancient world, and it remained essentially unchanged until the beginning of the modern period. According to this primary meaning, instruction was an activity by which the instructor transmitted contents of value to the pupil, contents capable of changing his entire being. The essence of teaching, according to this view, was not informative but *formative*. In this volume the concept of instruction is related to two other concepts that interpret it. The first, discipline, is characterized primarily by the evaluation that the contents of a said discipline are most valuable and, therefore, indispensable. The second, general or liberal education, does not involve mastery of any specific subject but is concerned with the molding of human character or, more precisely, the molding of the intellect and the moral traits of the individual who then uses reason to liberate himself from his passions, his ignorance, and the limitations of his existence.

This primary meaning of the concept of instruction was responsible for two traits—selectivity and ritualism—that characterized the early school, and continue to affect it today. Instruction designed to mold the individual spirit with the aid of traditional disciplines implied that not every individual was capable of self-improvement leading toward intellectual and moral perfection. This selectivity of the school in accepting pupils was further reinforced by the second primary characteristic, that of ritualism. The school developed ways of processing and presenting teaching contents and ways of evaluating pupils' achievements that soon attained sacred, unalterable status. Pupils were required to adapt themselves to these goals, and those unable to do so left school. Ritualism became a sorting mechanism. Anyone whose motivations, interests, or abilities did not correspond to what was expected by the school was not qualified to be a pupil in it. As long as the meaning ascribed to the concept of instruction remained the same, these traits did not change.

Then came the demand that the school provide universal education. Since that time, changes taking place in society have altered the meaning ascribed to the concept of instruction, and, subsequently, the function and structure of formal education. Modern attempts to elucidate the nature of instruction and to understand its laws are part of this struggle to replace traditional, selective schooling with universal education. The demand that the school open its doors to all children required a theoretical basis that would convince people that all children benefit from schooling, and this had to be established before any organizational or financial plans could win acceptance. Experiments conducted in England by Andrew Bell and Joseph Lancaster (monitorial instruction) and Robert Owen (the combination of schooling with industrial work) and in Switzerland by Pestalozzi (the combination of schooling with agricultural work) were attempts to prove that a system whereby all members of society could be educated was feasible and to propose organizational and budgetary alternatives at a time when governments had not yet accepted the financial responsibility for education.

A basic concern was common to all experiments conducted before there were compulsory education laws and to many experiments conducted after such laws had been passed—that of establishing a method. Instruction was seen as a method of presenting and practicing teaching contents in a way that would ensure that the said contents would be learned. It was assumed that certain laws governed instruction and that, by acting in accord with them, learning could be affected. It was further assumed that this activity could be measured by the level of its efficiency. The meaning attributed to the concept of instruction had changed. It was no longer characterized by specific contents alone, but also by the method used to present the contents. Success was no longer measured solely in terms of the adaptation of the pupil to the demands of the school, either. The efficiency of the teacher was another consideration. One of the earliest advocates of change in the meaning ascribed to instruction was Comenius. The lengthy title of his *Didactica Magna* announced to the world the new meaning of the concept of instruction:[2]

The Great Didactic
Setting Forth
the Whole Art of Teaching
All Things to All Men,
or

a certain inducement to found such schools in all parishes, towns and villages of every Christian kingdom that the entire youth of both sexes, none being excepted, shall quickly, pleasantly and thoroughly become learned in the sciences, pure in morals, trained to piety and, in this manner, instructed in all things necessary for present and for future life in which with respect to everything that is suggested its fundamental principles are set forth from the essential nature of the matter, its truth is proved by examples from the several mechanical arts, its order is clearly set forth in years, months, days, and hours and, finally, an easy and sure method is shown by which it can be pleasantly brought into existence.

Primary Approaches—Method

The utopianism of the *Great Didactic* is characteristic of the approach to educational thought that persisted throughout the long period during which effective instruction was identified with method. The belief that there actually is a set of principles that will enable anyone who follows them to teach "all things to all men" still underlies the thinking of many educationists. Even the search for a didactic "philosopher's stone," begun when Comenius sought "Fundamental Principles" for a universal didactic in the "essential nature of the matter," has been continued by thinkers of later generations who seek the "essential nature" of the process of instruction in the findings of psychology. Such searches were initiated even before there were any psychological findings to speak of. Pestalozzi, for example, in *Wie Gertrud Ihre Kinder lehrt* (published in 1801, seventy-eight years before Wundt set up the first psychological laboratory), wrote: "Experience has made me realize that popular instruction can be based on psychological foundations . . . the power of education lies in *adapting* its influence and activity to the essential activity of nature. Educational activity and natural activity are one and the same thing."[3] Pestalozzi did everything in his power to prove that it was possible to teach everyone (albeit not everything) if only the right method were adopted. Herbart's formal stages and the new didactic methods (project, Dalton, and others) are no more than a continuation of the approach that identifies effective instruction with method. Later exponents of this approach differ from their predecessors, however, in that they have abandoned the belief in a single method which, if only they could find it, would be right for everyone. Recent methods show a marked tendency to acknowledge the existence of individual differences between pupils, which necessitate different methods of instruction, among them methods where the main purpose is to make the differentiation of instructional means according to individual needs possible.

What is surprising is the tenacity with which many educationists clung to the belief in a final, saving method and continued to seek the magic formula, even though the failure of each successive attempt indicated the futility of the goal itself. They did not allow for the fact that no two teachers, even when teaching according to the same method, behave in the same way. This fact in itself removes from the concept of method the meaning that educationists attempted to attribute to it—that it is a set of principles intended to direct the teacher's behavior. The methods propounded were based on the assumption, no doubt correct in itself, that what happens to the pupil in the classroom is the result of the teacher's behavior. Because none of the suggested methods were successful in altering the teacher's behavior, it became apparent that other factors were more powerful in conditioning the behavior of teachers.

Intermediary Factors—The Teacher and the Learning Process

The concept of instruction entered a new phase as attention turned toward identifying intermediary factors that existed between teachers and the method they adopted. The first consideration was the *personality of the teacher*. Research included the study (speculative) and the investigation (empiric) of personality traits that condition teacher behavior, on the assumption that certain traits assist instruction by helping to bring about desired changes in the pupil while other traits prevent instruction from taking place even when the teacher uses a given method. Researchers have investigated the relationship between effective instruction and personality structure as well as relationships between effective instruction and such specific personality traits as attitudes, values, interests, activities outside school hours, modes of adaptation, needs, and cogitive contents. Since its inception fifty years ago, the study of teacher personality, both speculative and empirical, has resulted in a vast body of literature.[4]

Those who hold this view see instruction as a specific manifestation of interpersonal relations. The teacher does not teach by virtue of the values inherent in the teaching contents (as implied by the original concept of instruction); nor does he teach by virtue of his mastery of a method (as implied by the conception that crystallized at the beginning of the struggle for universal education). He teaches, instead, by virtue of his personality. There are personality types that are likely to make good teachers, just as there are personality types that are likely to succeed in the sphere of the creative arts. Some of the techniques of instruction can be acquired by everyone, but the quality of the instruction does not depend on mastery of technique alone. The deciding factor appears to be the basic personality traits of the teacher. This makes instruction a kind of art, open only to those who possess certain innate gifts. It is unfortunate that, just as instruction does not rely solely on method, neither is it simply a function of personality. Getzels and Jackson, in a critical review of the literature on teacher personality and characteristics, state: "Despite the critical importance of the problem and a half-century of prodigious research effort, very little is known for certain about the nature and measurement of teacher personality, or about the relation between teacher personality and teaching effectiveness."[5]

The research in question was not based on any theory capable of relating personality concepts to concepts describing instruction. It is impossible to investigate the relationship between personality traits and any given occupational skill, even the simplest (for example, driving), as long as we do not possess criteria for defining the "professional behavior" in question and for analyzing its components. Research on teacher personality can provide data relevant to teaching only if it is conducted within a framework of clear definitions as to what constitutes effective instruction, that is, if it rests on a theory capable of providing investigators with hypotheses regarding traits likely to produce or prevent good teaching. This is where such research fails. Research into teacher personality aims at explaining instruction as a process that depends on the characteristics of those who implement it. Without a theory of what constitutes effective instruction, it is impossible to put forward hypotheses and test them, including the hypothesis that instruction depends on the characteristics of those who implement it.

The first disappointment—the failure of attempts to explain instruction as a method—led to the emergence of research into teacher personality and, simultaneously, of research into learning as the starting point for instruction, which also proved to be a disappointment. Once it became clear that instruction could not be viewed simply in terms of a set of "dos and don'ts," nor in terms of the personality and characteristics of the teacher, research began to focus on changes that take place in the pupil as a result of instruction. It was assumed, instruction being the other side of learning, that knowledge about the learning process would also guide the process of instruction. This research yielded a prodigious harvest, too, even greater than previous investigations.[6] Until quite recently this was the dominant direction for instructional research, and it is still one of the main fields of research feeding pedagogic thinking in such specific areas as the teaching of different categories and units of knowledge and the teaching of children from different ethnic backgrounds. Even moving in this direction, researchers failed to arrive at a comprehensive theory of instruction, and there is a growing feeling among educationists that a theory of learning cannot substitute for a theory of instruction.[7]

One reason why a reduction of this kind is impossible is that the objects of the two theories are different. The object of a theory of instruction is the teacher's behavior, which gives rise to learning in the pupil. This means that learning theory is one of the main sources for a theory of instruction, but not its other face. Learning theory is essentially descriptive, explaining or attempting to explain the relationships between certain facts that are revealed in the changed behavior of the individual. The theory of instruction, on the other hand, is essentially prescriptive, forcing a choice between alternative possibilities of action according to anticipated results. In the absence of a theory of instruction, theories of learning have filled the gap, despite the fact that the two types of theory are not interchangeable.

Another reason why learning theory cannot be substituted for a theory of instruction stems from the difference between a goal-directed activity like instruction and the empirical research on which learning theory is based. The final test of learning, as conceived by learning theory, is the measurable "change" in individual behavior that is called "achievement" by schools as well as by psychologists. The final test of instruction, on the other hand, depends on the underlying theory involved. Success of instruction in typing or in driving can be measured in a way that is similar to accepted procedures in learning research: by measuring change in a specific behavior isolated from all other behaviors. When the subject of inquiry is the process of instruction as a whole, however, the way in which one kind of learning influences others must be taken into account. It is quite possible that achievement in one specific area may damage achievement in other areas that, from a comprehensive educational point of view, are more important. Although such comprehensive views of education are many and varied and in opposition on most issues, one common denominator distinguishes them from learning theory: the criterion for evaluating success is not the isolated achievement but the significance of this achievement for the general development of the individual. The question at issue between the various schools of education is: What is satisfactory development? Desired achievements are selected according to their respective answers to this question. The mere fact that an achievement has been attained is meaningless until the function of the achievement has a place in the total process of development. Learning theories, even though they have provided and are continuing to provide much information about the process of instruction, cannot explain instruction. In other words, they are not a substitute for a theory of instruction (just as biology cannot substitute for agronomics; physics or chemistry, for engineering; anatomy or physiology, for medicine).

From the two main directions along which instructional research developed—the search for the relationship between teacher personality and instruction on the one hand, and pupil learning and instruction on the other—a number of secondary directions of a more specific nature emerged, apparently as a result of disappointing attempts to explain instruction. One direction was research into the behavior of the teacher as a leader. While this line of research belongs, according to its subject matter, under the general heading of research into teacher personality, it differs in the theoretical assumption that only certain personality traits are relevant to instruction and consequently concentrates on the investigation of these traits to the exclusion of all others. This assumption justifies the separate treatment of this body of research in a general review of changes in the meaning of the concept of instruction.

The assumption underlying research into leadership is that pupil learning is a function of the atmosphere prevailing in the classroom, or, in the language of these studies, it is a function of the social climate. Since the behavior of the teacher as leader determines the nature of this climate, instruction can be considered a function of the style of behavior of the teacher. Social climates are generally described in dichotomous terms: a dominative climate as opposed to an integrative climate (Anderson);[8] an authoritarian social climate as opposed to a democratic social climate or laissez faire (Lippit and White);[9] a supportive climate as opposed to a defensive climate (Gibb);[10] direct influence as opposed to indirect influence (Flanders).[11]

In these studies, as in the studies of personality and learning, the guiding theory is a psychological one except that these studies simply do not apply the findings of psychological research. They attempt to derive relevant theory from psychological research and to use this theory in investigating instruction as a specific process. Such studies have made a considerable contribution toward understanding a number of central phenomena in instruction. Like their predecessors and for the same reasons, however, these studies have not been able to provide the basis for a comprehensive theory of instruction. Leadership style is a factor without which it is impossible to understand instruction, but it cannot explain the phenomenon called instruction. Isolated from other factors, such as contents, method, pupils, and goals, leadership has little significance.

Further development along this line of research led, in a certain sense, to retreat. After the initial success of research into the behavior of the teacher as leader, the field of inquiry was broadened to include teacher behavior in general, but, whereas studies on leadership rested on certain theoretical assumptions, studies of comprehensive teacher behavior resembled blind groping. Many studies of comprehensive teacher behavior attempted to classify different types of behavior in order to compare teacher behavior with pupil achievements and thus discover which behaviors characterize the "good teacher." The conclusion reached by Hughes[12] illustrates this line of research: the "good" teacher is one whose behavior can be broken down (for example, by percentages) as follows: controlling situations, 20 to 40 percent; imposition situations, 8 to 20 percent; positive affectivity, 10 to 20 percent; negative affectivity situations, 3 to 10 percent.

The most comprehensive study in this field was made by Openshaw,[13] who attempted to develop a taxonomy for the classification of teacher behavior. The needs of empirical research may encourage this type of study in the hope that it will provide investigators with instruments for observation and measurement, despite the fact that it lacks a guiding theory (a lack shared with previous research), and it is restricted to the classification of manifest behaviors without making any attempt to relate these behaviors to their underlying motivations. Whether motivation or manifest behavior patterns have more influence on instruction is still an open question. (For example, does "strictness" stemming from concern for the pupil have the same effect on teaching as "strictness" stemming from the teacher's drive to dominate?)

Theories of Instruction: A New Stage

All of the studies along all of the lines described above have made varying contributions to instruction, but there are no grounds to hope that they will ever provide a comprehensive theory that will enable the process of instruction to be carried out on a rational basis. After traveling this long and disappointing road, instructional research has reached a new stage: inquiry (mainly speculative) into the nature of instruction as a distinct phenomenon, that is, logical and phenomenological investigation of the phenomenon called instruction. This investigation is in part concerned with an analysis of verbal classroom behavior in the hope of discovering the logical distinctness of the educational encounter, which is mainly verbal.[14] It is also an attempt to describe the specificity of instruction by comparing it with, and distinguishing it from, other activities where learning is involved, such as training and indoctrination.[15]

All of these studies constitute a stage in the establishment of a theory of instruction derived from the laws according to which it operates as a unique phenomenon. The final test of a theory is the extent to which it explains the phenomenon it sets out to explain, and the test of the explanation lies in its ability to predict. Whether this

line of inquiry will produce results capable of passing these tests, time
alone will tell. At present, attempts to describe instruction as a
phenomenon with distinct logical and phenomenological traits seem a
necessary condition for the eventual discovery of the road to empirical
research based on a relevant theory. A theory is no more than a storehouse of hypotheses in need of empirical verification. If the logical
and phenomenological tendency in instructional research does indeed
prove capable of providing categories for describing instruction as a
distinct behavior, the way will be open to clarifying the relationship
between the teacher's actions and the method he adopts, between his
actions and his personality, between his.actions and the learning of his
pupils, or, in other words, between all aspects hitherto reductively
presented as if each alone was capable of comprehending the whole
process of instruction.

And this is where the present attempt to explain instruction begins.
The essential difference between it and previous attempts lies in the
basic assumption. In previous attempts it was assumed that a certain
combination of activities definable as *instruction "as it ought to be"*
existed. The function of a theory of instruction, accordingly, was to
present the characteristics of this instruction and the conditions for its
realization. The underlying assumption of this work, however, is that
the purpose of a theory of instruction is to show what instruction can
be and what forms it may take, either according to the opinions and
beliefs of men or according to the characteristics of the different situations in which it takes place.

Instruction cannot be defined except as a combination of the contradictory logics it contains. Existing theories of instruction are, in the
last analysis, choices between alternatives, and, in this sense, show a
preference for one combination of actions over other combinations of
actions. The preferred combination is defined as instruction. This
study attempts to describe all alternatives or patterns of activities that
can be classed as instruction. An awareness of the connection between
these different patterns of activities and their anticipated products is
the starting point for choosing between them. The choice is the concern not of the theory but of those who stand in need of it.

Patterns of Instruction

All contents taught at schools can be taught in one of three ways,
each derived from a different logic of instruction. Whether the subject

to be taught is reading or algebra, it can be taught by imitation, that is, by repetition and rote learning, accompanied by praise for those who make progress in the desired direction and by criticism, sometimes accompanied by coercion and punishment, for those who fail to do so. Teaching can also be done according to the logic of molding, which means setting out to discover underlying laws and principles and relating them to the values by which people learn what is considered worth learning. Another means, that of developmental instruction, brings pupils to a stage at which they will be interested in the contents taught and wish to devote themselves to acquiring them. Organizing the environment in such a way as to arouse the curiosity of the pupils and equipping it with everything necessary to satisfy their curiosity ensure that most pupils will learn to read and some will also learn algebra.

Developmental instruction resembles the other two types of instruction in that only some of the pupils who learn according to this system will almost certainly acquire a knowledge of algebra or other contents. It is different in that this fact is accepted at the outset, which allows justification of a basic assumption that pupils are not equal and similar and that, therefore, their interests and achievements cannot be equal and similar. It is an essential characteristic of instruction that most contents can be taught by any of the types of instruction. It is the products of instruction that differ.

What did the pupil who learned reading or algebra by imitation learn? In addition to reading and algebra he learned that all important things are arbitrary. Neither his wishes, his interests, his tastes, nor his understanding play any part in determining what he is to learn. He learns that important things can be acquired only by dint of effort and that lack of effort is punished both in the present (his experience at school) or in the future (he is frequently warned). He learns that "knowing" means, first of all, remembering and that thinking is usually dangerous because it is liable to distort the accuracy of the reconstruction that is expected of him. He learns, too, that he has no authority to decide what is right or wrong and that he must submit to external authorities. He learns to fear change, and the effort and the fear of failure that accompany his learning create additional anxiety. He learns to esteem himself according to the opinion of others because each day his teachers judge whether he is good or bad, clever or stupid, industrious or lazy.

If the process is successful, he also knows how to read fluently and how to solve algebraic equations. True, he may never need to know how to read fluently or be capable of enjoying his reading, just as he may have no interest whatever in mathematics or ever try his hand at solving problems other than those he learned to solve at school. But in both subjects, if the need arises, he will be able to demonstrate considerable mastery—sometimes for many years after he leaves school.

What has the pupil who studies reading or algebra according to the logic of molding learned? He has learned to honor knowledge, books, and scholars, and he has internalized a feeling of reverence for various cultural and spiritual phenomena. He has learned to aspire to moral perfection according to an ideal he has identified with by means of the teacher's personality and his values. He has learned to accept a yoke of principles in his thinking and actions and to act in unfamiliar situations according to those principles. He has also learned, to the extent that the process of instruction has succeeded, to read and to solve mathematical problems just as well as the pupil who learned these things according to the pattern of imitation. His knowledge is, however, different.

He knows how to solve not only those algebraic problems that he learned to solve at school. Algebra becomes part of his system of thinking. He has not only learned to read, but he becomes a person who reads, and reading becomes a primary need. What he has learned has not been added to his personality; it *is* his personality. It is possible, however, that the personality that has been molded by these means will be a rigid, authoritarian one, too inflexible to adapt to changes that may take place in the areas of knowledge learned. The product of the process of molding has learned to assess contents by principles and criteria, but he has almost certainly not learned to assess the principles and criteria that have been internalized and used in making the assessments.

What has the pupil learned when he learns reading and algebra by developmental instruction? In the first place he has learned that learning is its own reward; it gives him satisfaction because it provides him with answers to questions that bother him. He has learned to decide for himself what to learn based on which particular questions are bothering him. He has learned to know himself—motivation, application, interest—through his learning. He has also learned to assess what he learns according to criteria that he understands, without having to pretend that he understands what he does not. He has learned to express his opinions without depending on, or deferring to, the opinions of others. He has not learned to praise things that bore him or are not comprehensible to him simply because others do. True, his achievements in reading and algebra, if measured by standard tests, may not be as great as those of pupils who learned these subjects according to the two previous types of instruction. Here and there he may have skipped something that failed to rouse his interest; here and there he may not have exercised something sufficiently because he felt that he had already grasped the point of the exercise.

These are the possible products of three different types of learning. Not only is the development of pupil characteristics variously influenced by different patterns of instruction; knowledge acquired is no less influenced. Algebra and reading mastered by an authoritarian, narrow-minded man who is closed to new influences are not the same as algebra and reading mastered by an autonomous, broad-minded man who is open to new influences and willing to experiment.

The word "instruction" is vague, with a meaning so general as to render it almost meaningless. As long as it is not described in terms of the logic that guides it, we know little of its nature. Instruction by imitation, instruction by molding, and instruction that promotes development are three processes with such a vast common denominator (instruction) that they are distinguished from each other only by the characteristics that give them meaning. They cannot be compared on the basis of efficiency, for it is impossible to determine which of the three styles is more efficient. Is readiness to think more efficient than reliance on the thinking of others, adherence to learned principles more efficient than the drive to discover new principles, or satisfaction derived from the pursuit of knowledge more efficient than compulsive accuracy in reconstructing learned contents?

The fact that these three different phenomena are all termed instruction does not make for clarity in discourse regarding them; they are, however, three separate phenomena, each with distinguishing characteristics. People disagree in their evaluation of these phenomena, as they disagree in their evaluation of anything else, but it is the description and implicit evaluation of the separate styles of instruction that constitute the essence of the theories of instruction.

Those writings, different in structure and language, that deal with the classroom behavior of the teacher are termed theories of instruction here. Very few writings on the subject of instruction can be classed as theoretical in the scientific sense. By structure and method such texts resemble ideological or literary compositions, or sometimes even commercial publications, more than they resemble scientific texts. By the function that they fulfill or are expected to fulfill they resemble theoretical texts in that they explain instruction in order to make it possible to direct it.* This is a function expected of a theory, although the expectation is not always realized. Theories do not always succeed in explaining what they set out to explain, and the explanation of a phenomenon may be said to have failed when it cannot be acted upon, when developments based on the theory cannot be predicted, or, upon occasion, when what has happened after the event cannot even by explained.

Proof of the failure of theories of instruction may be seen in the fact that teachers do not usually rely on them,[16] and that, in cases where teachers do make use of them, they are not necessarily successful.[17] Most teachers prefer to use "common sense," the traditional procedures of the school, passing fashions in popular views of education, or some other basis for their actions.

Approaches to Instruction

Writings dealing with instruction may be divided into two groups according to the stance adopted toward the multiple alternatives existing in instruction. One group adopts a harmonizing attitude whereby all existing styles of instruction, each in its own time and place, are valid, and the teacher is entitled to use most or all of them, depending upon, among other considerations, the subject or the kind of pupils being taught. Those whose writings fall into this group usually recom-

---

*Compositions concerning instruction may be divided into the following groups: (1) Descriptive—reports of projects accompanied, for the most part, by attempts at objectivization of individual teaching styles or by support for the theory according to which the teacher acted. (See Herbert Kohl, 36 Children [New York: Norton, 1962]; Sylvia Ashton-Warner, Teacher [New York: Simon and Schuster, 1963].) (2) Prescriptive—mainly attempts at deduction from philosophical systems that essentially describe instruction "as it ought to be." (See Th. F. Green, The Activities of Teaching [New York: McGraw-Hill, 1971]; M. Belth, The New World of Education [Boston: Allyn and Bacon, 1970].) (3) Implicative—implications of scientific theories for instruction. (See B. F. Skinner, "The Science of Learning and the Art of Teaching," Harvard Educational Review, XXIV [Spring, 1954]; C. R. Rogers, Freedom to Learn [Columbus, Ohio: C. E. Merrill, 1969].) (4) Research on instruction. (See Ronald T. Hyman [ed.], Teaching [Philadelphia: Lippincott, 1968]; Arno Bellack et al., The Language of the Classroom [New York: Teachers College Press, 1966].)

mend the teaching of writing by imitation, of literary discrimination by molding, and of written expression by developmental techniques. Of the teaching of writing it is said that drilling and repetition are needed to acquire this particular skill; of the teaching of literature, that the pupil must identify with the characters and internalize the values of any given work of literature before it can be said to have been properly taught; of the teaching of written expression, that the necessary conditions for creativity must be provided or the pupil will not be able to express himself in an honest and interesting way. The most characteristic feature of this approach is its ingenuous desire to enjoy the best of all worlds. The desire is ingenuous because it is impossible for a teacher to use the three styles at once, or even to use them alternately. Imitative techniques can destroy all hope of learning by molding or development, and molding and developmental procedures can damage the ability to learn by imitation. The first product of instruction is the way in which the pupil learns. Before he learns writing or literature, free expression or algebra, he learns to learn. You cannot teach a pupil that learning is drill that will enable him to reconstruct the "right" answers accurately and, at the same time, teach him that learning depends on the active desire of the learner to discover problems in whatever subject he is learning. Similarly, it is impossible to teach a pupil to try to remember all the information made available to him about a given unit of instruction and, at the same time, teach him that the essence of learning lies in the discovery of the problems and principles implied by that unit of instruction.

The fact that there have always been pupils whose achievements have contradicted the prediction implied by these statements does not invalidate the statements. Individual characteristics such as intelligence or imagination have always overcome the influence exerted by instruction. The fact that a pupil who has been exposed, during the entire course of his schooling, to the influence of instruction by imitation, grows up, despite this, to be a creative, innovative man, capable of daring thought and thirsty for knowledge, does not mean that imitative methods support the development of such people. It can mean, instead, that instruction by these methods does not always overcome and suppress the characteristics of individual pupils. The harmonizing approach wants all possible achievements, but ignores the fact that activities directed toward achievements of one kind make it unlikely that activities directed toward achievements of another kind will succeed.[18]

The second group of theories of instruction is governed by a reductive approach.[19] The scales are weighted from the outset in favor of one pattern of instruction, whether it is imitation, molding, or development. The authors in this group adhere to one type of instruction. They are aware that the alternative possibilities are mutually contradictory and that they must make a choice. Their preference, however, is based on a set of considerations that is partial and limited, and they limit (reduce) their point of view to certain aspects of instruction, ignoring other aspects. When the preferred aspect of instruction is social, instruction is conceived as a technique intended to train young people for social roles. In this case, the preferred style of instruction is usually imitation of models of behavior existing in a given society. But instruction is not *only* a technique intended to train people for social roles. It is also an activity intended to transmit culture and to support the optimal development of the individual as an individual. The reductive approach is characterized by a decision in favor of one of the functions assigned to instruction and a search for teaching methods suited to the implementation of this function. Other functions assigned to instruction and the methods suitable for their implementation are ignored. From the point of view of reliability in describing instruction, reductive approaches are preferable to the harmonizing one. The contradiction between the various styles of instruction — imitation, molding, development — presented by these theories is, however, resolved by ignoring part of the functions assigned to instruction. Even though the approach contributes more to explaining the process of instruction, it contributes no more to the possibility of directing it.

It must be concluded that both of these approaches are inadequate as guides for the professional behavior of teachers. The harmonizing approach blurs the contradictions existing in the process of instruction, and the reductive approach resolves the contradictions by limiting the view of instruction.

Contradictions in the Patterns

The three patterns discernible in instruction are not the product of human arbitrariness, human inventiveness, or an innovative spirit seeking gratification. Each reflects, on the one hand, the different ways in which people learn and develop as a result of their learning and, on the other hand, the different needs that led society to establish schools and orderly teaching procedures. Individuals learn in three different ways, each way leading in a different direction. Instruction has functions to perform: training the young for social roles, initiating them into a culture, supporting their self-actualization. Not all of the ways of instructing facilitate the performance of all of these functions equally, however, and it is impossible to teach in several ways simultaneously. The three patterns of instruction also bear witness to contradictions inherent in the process of instruction, contradictions that stem from facts and not merely from interpretation of facts.

A teacher can present a chapter of history or a unit in biology in such a way that his pupils are able to reconstruct with great accuracy what they have heard from him or what they have read according to his instructions. This shows that the individual can be conditioned, that it is possible to acquire certain ways of behaving by means of training techniques. The use of these techniques shows, in addition, that these behaviors are required or desired in certain situations. Pupils can be taught certain facts about the past by learning history or certain facts about anatomy by learning biology. The reasons why the pupil is required to remember the dates on which his country was victorious in war against other countries or why the medical student is required to know the names of all the bones and muscles in the human body (both of which are usually taught by conditioning) are related to the image of a good citizen or of a good doctor, respectively. Both images are social facts, stemming from the histories and structures of societies that enforce methods of instruction suited to their needs.

It is also possible to teach history and biology in such a way that the pupil will internalize their principles until he is capable of using them to assess both what he has learned, and also what he has not yet learned but is likely to encounter. This shows that the individual learns not only by conditioning but also by identification. Although in this case he also learns by imitation, the imitation is not of manifest behaviors. He does not learn to answer questions according to a model of "correct" answers. Learning by identification leads to the internalization of characteristics, of approaches, of strategies of thinking. The fact that instruction of this type exists shows not only that the individual is capable of learning by these means but also that certain social needs require that cultural values be transmitted from generation to generation, not as remembered information but as internalized individual characteristics. In this case it is not enough to teach the pupil facts about the history of his country; he must be led to identify himself with the symbols and values of his people. It is not enough to teach him facts about human anatomy; he must be induced to subject himself to the principles of science according to which the secrets of nature are discovered.

Preference for this way of teaching history or biology (or any other subject, for that matter), although it may sometimes appear to be simply the product of a conscious decision on the part of those who have grasped its advantages, is in fact an indication of the changes that have taken place in society. There are social roles in modern society that people cannot be trained to perform simply by means of imitation, just as there are social circumstances that demand instruction founded on the ability of the pupil to identify with any given set of values or principles.

This is the case, too, for the type of instruction that sets out to activate the creative powers of the pupil and prepares him to innovate rather than just to reconstruct knowledge. The existence of such a type of instruction indicates both the individual's ability to learn by exploration and discovery and society's need for people who are creative and able to innovate.

The fact that changes taking place in society influence methods of instruction, activating forces other than those previously exploited in the learning process, does not do away entirely with the need for previous methods. Because different methods have been assigned to different objectives, at present three distinct styles of instruction compete both in the school and in the theories of instruction. Each style seeks to foster different achievements, each has different objectives, and each activates different learning abilities in the pupil. At the same time it must be recognized that instruction that seeks to foster the ability of the pupil to reconstruct "correct" answers to standard questions inhibits the curiosity needed to answer different questions, not to mention the desire to discover new questions. Instruction that seeks to instill in the pupil the principles on which the various subjects he learns are based is likely to lessen the accuracy of his answers to questions of information; it is certain to lessen his readiness to test the principles learned in order to change them. Instruction that seeks to foster creativity and intellectual daring is likely to impair both the pupil's willingness to keep a large amount of information stored in his memory and his adherence to those principles on which the various disciplines are based.

The teacher who wishes to instill in his pupils a strict adherence to fact, a constant concern with accuracy, and an awareness of the need to test and retest items of information for their validity must bear in mind the possibility that their imaginations will suffer; that their readiness to dare to think in situations where all the necessary information is not available will shrink; that their ability to innovate, to the extent that it ever existed, will vanish. On the other hand, the teacher who wishes to make his pupils intellectually daring and to cultivate their imaginations and their ability to innovate must bear in mind the possibility that he may endanger their sense of responsibility toward facts and their adherence to the principles by which such facts are tested.

Many teachers imagine that instruction is a passive instrument by which they gain their ends if they try hard enough and if their pupils cooperate. This is why so much stress is placed on motivation in teaching. If the pupil wants to learn and the teacher knows how to teach, it seems that there is nothing that cannot be taught. But instruction is not a passive instrument in the hands of the teacher. It is an action governed by laws that the teacher must respect in order to be able to gain ends by this means.

A Theory of Instruction

Instruction, it is true, is what the teacher does, but what the teacher does may be a kind of aimless, purposeless groping in the dark, a series of Sisyphian endeavors in which one act damages the next and negates its influence. Or, instruction may be an activity that supports the development of pupils according to one of the concepts of development: that on which imitation in instruction is based, that on which molding in instruction is based, or that on which development in instruction is based. In order for teaching to become a purposeful activity it must be guided by a theory that describes and explains the process of instruction and its independent laws. Let us assume that the following constitute basic characteristics of the process:

It is not possible to teach according to all the logics of instruction simultaneously; nor is it possible to teach according to all these logics alternatively. Each of the three logics of instruction — imitation, molding and development — creates a specific style of instruction. Teaching acts governed by one style negate, or at least diminish, the possible influence of acts governed by a different style. You cannot, for example, teach a pupil to solve a problem in mathematics by giving him a formula that is treated like an axiom and, at the same time, expect him to discover the formula for himself. If, moreover, you have taught him that problems are solved by means of formulas that can or must be memorized, it is doubtful if you will ever be able, at any stage, to get him to work out a formula for himself. Each style of instruction also involves a special kind of relationship between teacher and pupil and a special kind of psychological climate in the learning group. Imitation requires an authoritarian climate. Pupils cannot be made to accept the repetition, drill, and practice required by this method of instruction unless the teacher holds a position of authority in the class. The nature of the authority is autocratic. The teacher is the sole ruler of the class, and he must be obeyed implicitly.

The logic of molding may also require an authoritarian climate, but it is a different kind. It is not the will of the teacher that dictates what the pupils are to do. Instead, certain principles apply to the teacher as well as the pupils, and these principles dictate the duties of both. The teacher is subject to a superior authority, derived from the values of the culture, and this authority acts as a criterion for evaluating his own actions in exactly the same way as it serves him as a criterion for evaluating the actions of his pupils.

The logic of development is antiauthoritarian. Accordingly, the atmosphere that is appropriate for learning and supports the development of pupils is one of freedom. The same teacher cannot, at one and the same time, be an authoritarian autocrat, an authoritarian representative of given values, and an antiauthoritarian seeking to create an atmosphere of freedom in his class. What is learned in the classroom is not a function of the contents that are presented for learning, but of the style in which they are taught. The psychological climate prevailing in the classroom is a decisive factor in all the styles of instruction, as well as in the type of product that each style is likely to produce. What is quite impossible is to maintain simultaneously three

conflicting psychological climates in the classroom. In instruction, unfortunately, you cannot have it all ways.*

*Every decision in favor of one style of instruction involves the risk of
losing the possible advantages of the other styles.* Since the teacher
cannot teach in three ways simultaneously, he must decide among
them (based on reasoned choice, habit, adaptation to the atmosphere
prevailing in the school, or another criterion) and behave according to
the style of his choice. Whatever his choice, in preferring one style to
the others he effectively renounces possible achievements by the other
styles. It is not simply a choice of the good; it is, at the same time, a
renunciation of another good. This is not merely a physical contradiction stemming from the fact that within the limitations of a given time
and a given learning capacity it is impossible to learn everything. The
choice is also affected by the different things that may possibly be
learned. The contradiction stems from the essential nature of instruction. A teacher wishing to develop critical thinking in a pupil will not
have much chance of succeeding if the teacher habitually teaches the
pupil to submit to authority—unless, of course, the pupil reacts
against the manner in which he is taught and develops a critical attitude toward his other problems. But this kind of approach— suppression in order to arouse the desire to be free, the demand for obedience in order to awaken critical thought—is both irrational and
dangerous, and the results are likely to be quite different from those
intended. This is not to say that rational acts are necessarily those in
which there is a logical connection between means and ends. The connection need not be logical, but it must be relevant. Perhaps there is a
logical connection between the means of placing a child in frightening
circumstances and the end of educating him to be a brave man. But
experience and theory both show that brave men are usually those who
experience a great measure of security in their environments as
children. Anyone seeking to support the development of a child into a
brave man will thus try to provide him with a large measure of secur-

---

*A similar opinion, although in another context, was expressed by Piaget: "limiting ourselves
to the matter of goals, the various finalities desired may be more or less mutually compatible or
contradictory; it is not proved, for example, that we can expect individuals we train to be con-
structors and innovators in certain spheres of social activity, where such qualities are needed, and
at the same time rigorous conformists in other branches of knowledge and activity." (Jean Piaget,
Science of Education and the Psychology of the Child [New York: Viking Press, 1971], pp.
18-19.)

rather than exposing him to frightening experiences. He will have to bear in mind, however, that this method of education might prevent the child from developing alertness to actual dangers. He will perhaps grow up to be brave, but he may also grow up to be unrealistic. In any case, choice is unavoidable: it is impossible both to provide a child with security and to expose him to frightening experiences, both to cultivate a sense of responsibility and to expect an adventurous character to emerge, both to demand politeness and good manners from a child and to hope that he will be honest and sincere with himself and others.

The decision in favor of one of the styles of instruction is not a final decision. Various contradictory ways of acting open to the teacher oblige him, if he wishes to direct the process of instruction in a rational manner, to choose among them. His considerations when making this choice should embrace both means and ends. He must choose one possible goal and the means that will enable him to reach it. According to existing theories of instruction, the teacher's problem is to suit his means to fixed or given goals, taking into account, while making his decision regarding these means, the needs and characteristics of his pupils. The assumptions underlying this approach are that it is possible to reach one goal in several ways and that, while the goals of instruction are fixed, the art of instruction lies in choosing the means leading to the goals that suit the individual pupil. On the face of it, these seem to be reasonable assumptions: any point on the globe can be reached from several directions; the same house can be built of different materials; the child who has not succeeded in learning the multiplication tables by concrete manipulations may be taught by prolonged mechanical drill. It follows, therefore, that the city reached from north or south is the same city; the house built of brick, stone, wood, or reinforced concrete serves the same purpose. The multiplication table learned by many concrete manipulations with pencils, matchsticks, blocks, and counters, is *not,* however, the same as the multiplication table learned by prolonged mechanical drill. It performs a different function in the child's thinking and influences his development in a different way. The assumption that the same goal can be reached by different methods of instruction is generally mistaken. The means, that is, different styles of instruction, influence its products. Instruction is not a neutral technique. The style determines the quality of the achievement, and not all goals can be reached

by means of all the styles of instruction. Hence, considerations that adjust the means to the needs of the individual pupil always alter the
goals. When means change, goals also change.

A teacher may encounter a child whose progress and development
are satisfactory in every respect except for a failure to master spelling.
If the teacher forces the pupil to spend a certain amount of time every
day practicing spelling, he has decided not only the means but also the
ends, and there is a possibility that the price of the pupil's mastery of
spelling may be a loss of self-confidence in other areas of learning. In
order to ensure that the pupil spend an hour a day practicing spelling,
undoubtedly a source of frustration, the teacher must emphasize the
gravity of the situation and make the pupil feel that, if he does not
learn to spell properly, his status as a pupil is not secure. If the pupil
does succeed in learning to spell by mechanical drill, there is also the
danger that he may lose faith in other ways of learning. Victory in an
area that has caused him so much difficulty may lead him to stick to
the method that proved so efficient when he needed to learn other
things. Considering all of these factors, the teacher might still decide
to force the child to practice spelling if learning to spell is considered
so vital that it outweighs any possible harm caused the child in the process of instruction. Whatever the final decision, it must be made while
the process of instruction is being implemented, and it must be based
on data that emerge during the process. Neither the means nor the
ends of instruction can be decided on an a priori, final basis. If a goal
is unattainable by certain techniques, perhaps it should be set aside
since the application of other, apparently efficient techniques can
change the goal and even damage future achievements. Insignificant
achievements gained at the risk of losing more worthwhile ones is not,
unfortunately, a rare phenomenon in teaching. Instruction is essentially a continuous process of making such decisions: choosing new
goals, choosing goals appropriate to the immediate needs of the pupil,
choosing means relevant to obtaining the goals.

The pupil is not a passive factor concerning which one assigns arbitrary goals and makes use of means that seem most likely to attain
them. The state of the pupil—social stratum, age group, stage of development, class group, passing moods that influence learning—
should influence both the means and the ends of instruction throughout the process. Not all of these data influence the learning and development of the pupil equally, but all do influence his learning and de-

velopment. Any decision regarding the aims of instruction, customary
in most theories of education, that ignores the "state of the pupil" is,
in fact, a reification of the pupil. In other words, he is reduced to the
status of a thing. No pupil is a passive object. His state at every moment and his changing needs are as important as goals originating
from the needs of society and the demands of culture. For this reason,
decisions regarding desirable procedures in instruction cannot be a
priori ones; they are an integral part of the process and accompany it
from beginning to end.

*Supporting the learning of pupils involves both activities intended
to structure and activities intended to disrupt the structure of what is
learned.* The dialectic nature of the process of instruction is most fully
apparent in the dual activities of which it is composed. One type of activity, universally known, manifest, and proclaimed, is intended to
lead the pupil to what are called "achievements" in the language of
the school and of the psychology of learning. Achievements are the
results of a process aiming at the structuralization of the pupil's behavior in any given area. Some of the activities of instruction are
aimed at structuring the pupil's behavior in the realm of thinking;
others, in the realm of skills; others, in the realm of attitudes. In all
the areas in which the teacher wishes to obtain achievements or structure his pupil's behavior, however, he finds behavior already structured, albeit different from that he and the school would support.
When the teacher wishes, for example, to establish abstract thinking
in his pupil, he usually finds an active structure of concrete thinking
already in operation. When he wishes to establish a certain strategy for
thinking about social problems, considering the place of the earth in
space, or evaluating a work of literature, he encounters existing strategies that the pupil applies even in situations where the teacher seeks
to promote alternate ones. Most theories of instruction interpret this
fact in one of two ways. According to one interpretation, instruction is
a cumulative process. The teacher builds new layers on top of the
things already known to the pupil. According to the second interpretation, instruction is a spiral process. The same subjects are treated
again and again, enabling the pupil to deepen and refine his treatment of them. The flaw in both interpretations is twofold: since
neither describes the process of instruction reliably, there are no conclusions by which the process can be directed. Instruction is composed
of activities intended to structure new behavior and activities intended

to disrupt the structure of existing behaviors as a prior condition for establishing new structures. Instruction is neither a simple, cumulative activity nor a spiraling one. It is an activity accompanied by contradictory activities: the disrupting of existing behaviors and the structuring of new ones.

The behavior learned is a function of the interaction between the learner and any given factor in his environment. By interacting with these environmental factors, the learner adopts behaviors (in the widest sense of the word) conforming, on the one hand, to the nature of the factors themselves and, on the other, to his own needs. This balance between the learner and his environment leaves no room for any further learning. If, for example, he has learned that two and two make four, he needs to learn nothing further about the matter. In any situation where he needs to add these two numbers, his knowledge will prove adequate. In order for him to learn something new in this area (for example, algebra) the structure of his relations with his environment (in his area) will have to be disrupted to allow for a new drive to reach a more comprehensive understanding. The disruption of existing structures (or, in other words, the disruption of existing achievements) is, thus, the second aim of instruction. Because teachers are generally unaware of the existence of this second goal, they fail to acknowledge it even when they are working to accomplish it. The justification for the goal of disrupting structures achieved in the past may be derived from a homeostatic theory (the upsetting of equilibrium in order to create the impulse to reinstate it), or from a theory claiming that the drive to exploratory behavior is an innate instinct in man.[20] In either case, instruction is seen as taking place between two poles: activity intended to mold relatively stable behaviors, on the one side, and activity intended to disrupt these behaviors in order to allow for the appearance of new ones, more effective and refined than previous ones, on the other side.

This means that there is no stage in the process of instruction in which the teacher is relieved of the necessity for making decisions. After deciding in favor of any one of the styles of instruction, he must then decide whether to structure or disrupt activities in order to implement it.

Because of these characteristics of instruction, harmonizing and reductive theories, both misleading as descriptions of the process of instruction, are not capable of providing it with rational piloting.

Theories of instruction can now be compared with a dialectic description of instruction, and piloting the process of instruction means deciding between alternative courses of action. The various theories of instruction differ as to the nature of these decisions.

The harmonizing approach exempts the teacher from deciding between goals. According to this approach, all goals are good, or, to be more precise, all good goals should be served by instruction. The decision-making process begins with the choice of appropriate means, and, in the harmonizing approach, no means (or only rare and extreme ones such as corporal punishment on the one hand or absolute freedom on the other) are disqualified. The choice of means is interpreted as finding the most "efficient" means to various goals. Goals and means are both determined before instruction commences. While instruction is actually being carried out, the only decisions the teacher has to make are those needed to conduct and continue the process.

The reductive approach, on the other hand, calls for prior choice of goals. According to this concept, only certain goals are worth attaining, and choice of goals implies choice of means. Only those means that suit the chosen goal can be used in the process of instruction. All the different styles of instruction can be justified in terms of this approach, each directing the process toward different goals and using different means to this end.

The dialectic approach to describing instruction differs from both previous approaches in that the focus of decision is shifted to the stage of implementation. The stage prior to implementing the process of instruction is mainly one of identifying various goals and means and the relation between them. The essence of this stage is an attempt to identify the sources of the various goals, that is, the considerations supporting the pattern of imitation, the pattern of molding, and the pattern of development, and also the means leading to the goals aimed at by each of these patterns. In contrast to the harmonizing approach, the dialectic approach attempts to describe the contradictions between the goals of the respective patterns and to distinguish between the means on the basis of their relationship to the various goals. In contrast to the reductive approach, the dialectic approach does not make an a priori choice in favor of any one of the different styles of instruction, either in terms of goals or means. The stage for making decisions comes with implementation. Appropriate activities are chosen in accord with data derived from the changing state of the learner as well as a previous knowledge of available goals and means. Decisions, once made, are frequently changed, which may lead to means and, consequently, goals being changed, or even to certain goals when relevant considerations justify this. An important part of the decision-making process involves changing activities intended to structure behavior for activities intended to disrupt existing structures.

The three approaches to describing instruction are those that are *available* in theories of instruction and, therefore, teachers are aware of them when they are faced with the necessity of choosing a course of action. The fact ignored by most studies of instruction is that the professional component of teaching lies in the stage at which the teacher decides what he ought to do. What the teacher actually does is no different from what other people do in occupations based on interpersonal relations. He speaks (asks, answers, lectures, explains), exhibits things (pictures, films, models), evaluates (praises, condemns), advises his pupils (or tells them what to do). Any of these actions could be performed equally well by grocers, artisans, army officers, housewives, social workers, or doctors. The teacher's behaviors are not specific to his profession. What is specific to the profession of teaching is the nature of the considerations that lead to the teacher's actions. Whether to explain a poem or leave the pupils to their own impressions, whether to develop a mathematical formula or teach its use mechanically, whether to tell pupils to read a chapter in a history textbook or send them to look for source material about the period—all are professional considerations, and such considerations constitute the sole professional component in instruction. Any person sufficiently acquainted with literature, mathematics, or history can explain a poem, develop a mathematical formula, or tell pupils which chapter to read in a history book. The teacher has to decide when and how to do these things. The essence of teaching lies in the way decisions are made about what ought to be done. True, the teacher might make the right decision about what to do in a given situation and then not act in accord with his decision for many and varied reasons, beginning with physical fatigue or neuroticism and ending with lack of courage or laziness. In this case the teacher is just like any other professional who, for whatever reason, is unable to function properly in his profession despite the fact that he is well trained. The opposite case—a teacher whose decisions are inappropriate, but who nevertheless acts in accord with the demands of the situation—is unlikely.

Not everything the teacher does in class is instruction. Some actions only resemble instruction because they take place in a classroom and follow the outlines of what is generally accepted as instruction. Only actions promoted by considerations relevant to teaching situations can be classed as acts of instruction. These considerations, whatever the theory behind them, are concerned with two factors: the pupil and any goal that can be classed as a goal of instruction. When the teacher tells pupils to read because the teacher feels that this reading meets the requirements of a given teaching situation, his action is instructional. When the teacher tells pupils to read in order to take a rest, the action does not constitute instruction. When the teacher tells a story, the action is instructional insofar as the story is intended to fulfill a function in whatever the pupils are learning and insofar as the teacher believes that presentation in the form of a story is the best way to present information to the pupils. If, however, the teacher tells a story in order to "pass the time," or because he does not quite know what to do next, this is not an instructional act, even if the story is exactly the same one told in the previous instance. Noninstructional acts incorporated into instruction are not necessarily wrong; each case must be judged on its merits. If all, or even a majority, of the teacher's acts come under the heading of noninstructional acts, the instruction provided will be meager. To be sure, the pupils may learn something, but the learning will be accidental. Accidental learning is not always a bad thing. Many important things have actually been learned in this way, but amorphous activity based on the pious hope that pupils will learn something cannot be termed instruction. Instruction is aimed at certain goals and proceeds according to considerations concerning the appropriate means for attaining those goals in any given situation. Not all instructional activities lead to achievement. In other words, not all instruction produces learning in pupils. Instruction cannot be defined as acts that cause learning to take place because many factors that cannot be controlled by the teacher interfere with this process. Teaching is still teaching, even if some or all of the pupils fail to learn what is being taught. Teaching occurs when activity is directed toward producing learning in pupils.[21] The professional expression of this aim or intention is the process of reasoning by which the teacher decides what must be done in order to make pupils learn, or, in other words, the professional considerations leading to such decisions.

The teacher's reasoning, or the considerations that define acts as

professional, may be appropriate or inappropriate, may take decisive
factors into account or overlook them, may be logical and based on
valid inferences or illogical and based on invalid inferences. In short,
the fact that the teacher considers what to do does not ensure that
what is done will succeed. Unconsidered behavior on the part of the
teacher is unprofessional behavior, but whether considered behavior
succeeds or not depends largely on the kind of considerations involved.
If the teacher's considerations are guided by the harmonizing approach to instruction ("anything goes"), he is likely to decide in favor
of actions where the results do not support but weaken each other. In
this case the results produced by his activities, however carefully considered, are likely to be meager. If, on the other hand, the teacher's
considerations are guided by the reductive approach to instruction
("either, or"), those goals which do not fit the particular concept that
is favored must be ignored. Since goals determine means and since
certain pupils respond only to certain means, some pupils will inevitably remain uninfluenced by this type of instruction.

The dialectical description of the process of instruction implies, first
of all, that teaching is not a linear activity leading directly to desired
goals; it is an activity that moves constantly between poles of contradictory alternatives. Since it is impossible to teach by all styles of instruction simultaneously, it is necessary to choose from among them,
even though there is the risk of losing the possible advantages of the rejected styles. Because the choice is specific and applies only to transitory situations in teaching, however, it must be reconsidered with
every change that takes place in the teaching situation. And, finally,
whatever the style of instruction, the teacher is continuously faced
with choosing between activities intended to structure behavior and
those intended to disrupt existing structures.

*The three approaches to describing instruction are also three strate-
gies for decision making in the implementation of instruction.* Which
of the three approaches is to be preferred? The answer to this question
is clear: the approach that leads to the most reliable description of the
process of instruction. What is the criterion for assessing this reliability? The answer to this question, too, seems clear: success in piloting
instruction according to a given theory proves the reliability of the
description of the process of instruction in that theory.

Unfortunately, however, this criterion cannot be used in practice.
The different factors influencing the success or failure of the process of

instruction cannot be isolated. It is extremely difficult to determine whether achievements obtained by the school stem from the actions of the teacher or the characteristics of the pupils. It is also impossible to determine whether achievements credited to the teacher are due to the professional considerations upon which he acted, or to certain characteristics of his personality, or to some accidental factors that occur during the process of instruction.

The only way to choose the desired approach from among existing ones that describe instruction is to compare their estimated contribution toward refining the teacher's ability to understand the processes of instruction in order to enable him to act according to relevant considerations. The harmonizing approach conceives of instruction as a combination of different activities that are only tenuously connected to each other. The consequences of this approach for the teacher's decision making are: he has to decide, for example, how to teach spelling, how to teach literature, and how to teach written expression. The idea that the teaching of spelling may harm the teaching of literature and that the teaching of both of these subjects may harm the teaching of written expression is generally not given any consideration. The teacher who must teach different subjects by the most "efficient" means available focuses on the identification of these means. Any consideration of the connection between the various subjects being taught is generally confined to the material aspect of instruction — the contents of the different lessons. A teacher using this approach considers details of instruction, but takes no comprehensive view of the whole field. In this molecular approach to instruction — how to start a lesson, how to illustrate a certain problem, how to make children do their homework — the connection between these items, not to mention their function within the whole system of instruction, is not considered, or at least it is not considered at a time when decisions are being made.

Reductive theories of instruction do not allow the teacher to make decisions. Each theory is a prior decision in favor of an alternative possibility in instruction. The teacher's area of choice is limited to the sphere of the one preferred alternative. The attitude of teachers operating according to one of the reductive theories resembles that of "true believers": they perceive educational reality through the filter of their belief. If considerations are predetermined, the right act is the one that fits the principles of the method. There is no need to enlarge on the reasons why such theories do not enable the teacher to view the

process of instruction comprehensively or to choose a course of action
based on rational considerations. If the harmonizing approach gives
rise to molecular didactics, the reductive approach gives rise to
scholastic didactics where the solution is known at the outset and all
that remains is to find the proof.

The dialectic approach to instruction sees the process as one created
from decisions between the contradictions inherent in the process itself. These decisions, since they must be made during the implementation of the process, are always made by the teacher. According to this
approach, the necessity for constant decision and choice between
alternatives stems from the very nature of the activity of teaching. It is
implied that, without a teacher who understands the dynamics of the
process of instruction, instruction is, in fact, impossible. It is possible
to put an untrained person into a classroom and tell him what to do,
but what is done amounts to baby-sitting. Even if children learn something from the activities of an untrained person, it would not be instruction. Just as sitting next to the patient's bed does not make the sit-
ter into a doctor, so standing in a classroom full of children does not
make the stander into a teacher. Only a person capable of understanding what is happening in the classroom is able to bring relevant considerations to bear on a situation arising in the classroom and to
choose the activities best calculated to produce the learning that supports development in his pupils. Such a person is a teacher, and his
acts constitute instruction.

Acts of different types—from the point of view of contents,
methods, and goals—are definable as instruction. Neither contents,
methods, nor even goals define instruction. *Instruction may be
defined as actions resulting from choices between contradictory goals
and contradictory means, which are made in accordance with the data
of the situation in which the instruction takes place.* Whether a given
action is definable as instruction or not depends on the nature of the
situation in which it takes place. Conditioning is instruction when, for
reasons inherent in the learner, there is no other way of preparing him
for life. This is not instruction, but indoctrination or taming, if the
learner is capable of being taught in a way that will enable him to
choose appropriate behaviors for himself. Certain activities among
culturally disadvantaged or maladjusted children are definable as instruction despite the fact that they differ in all respects from activities
definable as instruction among well-adjusted children who enjoy

cultural advantages. Furthermore, the same activities with the same children may be definable as instruction today and not definable as instruction tomorrow. The first characteristic of instruction is that it takes the actual state of the pupils to be instructed into account. Any change in their state obliges a corresponding change in the actions of the teacher.

The dialectic approach to the description of instruction is not an alternative to prevailing theories of instruction. It is a strategy for choosing between theories in a way that can guide instruction in changing situations. The picture of instruction reflected in most of the theories of instruction is a partial one only. The refining and improving of the teacher's reasoning about his actions requires practice in choosing between the various theories of instruction. The decisions reached never represent a final, a priori acceptance of a certain doctrine or article of faith. Rather, they are part of a process that is constantly being renewed according to the changing needs of day-to-day teaching situations.

Now there is a need to reconstruct the process of instruction according to the different theories in which it is described. Since these theories describe instruction from different points of view, their simultaneous presentation will reveal contradictions existing in instruction and present situations that require the teacher to decide, in each case, what is instruction and what is not.

THREE   Conceptual Dimensions of Theories of Instruction

Each theory of instruction may be classified, either wholly or in part, under one of the logics governing the process of instruction. Some theories are entirely or mostly governed by the logic of imitation,* others are entirely or mostly governed by the logic of molding,† and still others are entirely or mostly governed by the logic of development.‡ There are also eclectic theories composed of fragments of

*Modern didactic literature offers few compositions written in the spirit of the pattern of imitation, despite the fact that many of the activities that actually take place in the schools are derived from this pattern. Certain compositions published in the Soviet Union and some of the people's democracies constitute an exception to this general rule. See Jean Piaget, *Science of Education and the Psychology of the Child* (New York: Viking Press, 1971), pp. 66 – 67.

†The conception of instruction as a process of molding is common to many compositions belonging to different schools of philosophy, different educational traditions, and so forth. The diversity of the pattern of molding is illustrated by the following: Edward Spranger, *Kultur und Erziehung* (Leipzig: 1925); Georg Kerschensteiner, *Theorie der Bildung* (Leipzig-Berlin: Teubner,1926); Alain (Emil Chartier), *Propos sur l'éducation* (Paris: Presses universitaires de France, 1957); Giovanni Gentile, *The Reform of Education*, tr. D. Bigongian (New York: Harcourt, Brace, 1922); Friedrich W. Foerster, *Schule und Charakter* (Zurich: Schulhess, 1920); Jacques Maritain, *Education at the Crossroads* (New Haven, Conn.: Yale University Press, 1943); T. S. Eliot, *Notes towards the Definition of Culture* (London: Faber and Faber, 1948); R. S. Peters, *Concept of Education* (New York: Humanities Press, 1968); R. M: Hutchins, *The Conflict in Education in a Democratic Society* (New York: Harper and Row, 1953). Despite the differing, sometimes conflicting, assumptions of the authors of these works, the patterns of instruction derived from them possess basic common characteristics.

‡The first composition written in the spirit of the pattern of development was undoubtedly

these logics in varying combinations. Each theory or combination of theories indicates roads that lead to learning—different roads leading to different types of learning. Each reveals some of the goals of instruction and ignores others, but it is the simultaneous presentation of the theories that creates the framework in which the dialectic approach, which is a strategy for choosing among various possible ways of instruction, can operate.

The contradictory nature of instruction is reflected in the conflicting interpretations of the fundamental concepts underlying the various theories of instruction. The goals of instruction are interpreted one way in theories of imitation and another in theories of molding. Achievement is one thing in a theory of development and something else in a theory of imitation. Both the status of the pupil and all key concepts are interpreted differently in each theory of instruction. The fact that key concepts are interpreted in many ways has given rise to many attempts to examine these meanings analytically in order to decide among them, but the approach here will be different. The interpretation of key concepts in various ways indicates that instruction is not a monolithic process. Instead, it contains within it conflicting and contradictory trends and activities. Every concept, with the different meanings ascribed to it, represents the contradictions inherent in the process of instruction. The concept of motivation, for example, may be interpreted as a means (the teacher must motivate the child to learn), as a goal (the teacher must make the pupil sensitive to new motivations), and as an opportunity (it is possible to teach a pupil only by means of the motives activating him at any given moment). The teacher can indeed act according to each of these interpretations of

Rousseau's *Emile* (1762). The influence of this seminal work on the school, however, was confined for many generations to its interpreters, who were usually far too moderate to be ready to effect the radical changes implied by the ideas of Rousseau himself. It is only in recent generations that a number of experiments in the Rousseauistic spirit have been conducted and that a great many books have been written that continue the tradition of educational radicalism. See A. S. Neill, *Freedom—Not License!* (New York: Hart, 1966); Bertrand Russell, *Education and the Good Life* (New York: Liveright, 1970); G. Dennison, *The Lives of Children* (New York: Random House, 1970); Paul Goodman, *Compulsory Mis-education* (New York: Random House, 1962); John Holt, *How Children Fail* (New York: Pitman, 1964); Herbert Kohl, *36 Children* (New York: Norton, 1968); George Leonard, *Education and Ecstasy,* Delta Book (New York: Dell, 1969); Neil Postman and Charles Weingartner, *Teaching as a Subversive Activity* (New York: Delacorte Press, 1970); Jules Henry, *Essays on Education,* Vintage Book (New York: Random House, 1971); Paulo Freire, *Pedagogy of the Oppressed* (New York: Herder and Herder, 1970); Ivan Illich, *Celebration of Awareness* (New York: Doubleday, 1971).

the concept of motivation. He can try to motivate the pupil to learn what he, the teacher, wants him to learn. He can try to awaken new interests in the pupil that will motivate him to learn things that have not previously aroused his interest. And, he can act according to the pupil's own motivations as they are expressed at any given moment. Each of these interpretations is, however, a component in a different type of instruction. Instruction in which motivation functions as a means is very different from instruction based on the self-motivation of the pupil, and both of these differ from instruction that sets out to create new motivations in the pupil. The teacher who decided in favor of one of the meanings of motivation in accord with a certain logic might also choose one of the meanings for the concept of learning, leadership, knowledge, or some other concept according to the same logic since relevant concepts in instruction can all be interpreted in several ways. A logical connection exists between deciding in favor of the interpretation of motivation as opportunity (the pupil learns when he is interested) and deciding in favor of the interpretation of achievement as the ability of the pupil to discover laws and principles by himself. In a similar way, a logical connection exists between conceiving of motivation as a means (the interest of the pupil must be aroused so that he will learn) and deciding in favor of the interpretation of knowledge as the sum total of all the conventions the pupil will be required to know in order to perform his social functions and the interpretation of achievement as the ability to reconstruct demonstrated behaviors. A consistent combination of decisions in favor of certain meanings of the basic concepts of instruction is termed a *pattern*. According to the logic of imitation, a pattern of imitation is created in instruction; according to the logic of molding, a pattern of molding is created in instruction; according to the logic of development, a pattern of development is created in instruction. Each pattern can be presented according to the meanings it ascribes to the basic concepts of instruction, which are:

Direction
Aims in teaching
Desired achievements
Social interpretation of instruction

Process
    Status of the learner
    Status of the contents
    Status of the teacher
Means
    Motivation
    Learners' activities
    Leadership

DIRECTION

First Dimension:
Aims in Teaching

The aims of instruction are derived from two sources. The first source is the accepted norms and behaviors of society, or the patterns and values typical of the predominant culture. The second source is the image prevailing among men of individual capacities and characteristics. Although the image of individual characteristics is derived from cultural patterns and social norms, and in this sense is a part of them, there is, nevertheless, reason for distinguishing between aims derived from the needs of society and the demands of culture and those derived from the image of individual capacities. For instruction controlled by extrinsic aims — by the needs and demands of society and culture — is essentially different from instruction controlled by intrinsic aims — by an image of individual powers, capacities, and talents. The teaching of reading, writing, arithmetic, and history may be dictated by the fact that in most present-day societies communication is accomplished largely through the written and the printed word, by the fact that in most occupations people need some knowledge of arithmetic, and by the fact that states require the support of their citizens for their policies, and this support is founded on certain attitudes that are inculcated by means of learning history. Instruction that prepares individuals to use the accustomed modes of communication, to assume occupational roles, and to support the policies of governments is controlled by extrinsic aims. On the other hand, instruction that develops the pupil's thinking, cultivates his feelings, and encourages his curiosity and imagination is controlled by intrinsic aims. Reading and writing, arithmetic, and history are, of course, taught in both types of instruction.

Theories of instruction are not neutral with regard to aims (as are, for example, theories of learning). A theory of instruction unrelated to aims would be meaningless; the aim gives meaning to the activities demanded by these theories. To demonstrate or to allow the pupil to discover something for himself, to activate or to keep him passive by discipline, to accept an unconventional answer or to demand the standard one are all actions performed by the teacher in accordance with certain theories of instruction. The justification of some acts and the rejection of others are derived from the implicit or explicit aims of these theories. Thus, theories of instruction are distinguished from one another by their adherence to different aims and, therefore, can be classified into three groups:

1.1. The aims of instruction are extrinsic.

1.2. Extrinsic aims control intrinsic ones in instruction.

1.3. Intrinsic aims control extrinsic ones in instruction.

The distinction between intrinsic and extrinsic aims is equivalent to the distinction between developing capacities and training in role performance as goals of education. *Capacities*—the ability to think, to feel, to imagine—are different ways of relating to the world. *Roles,* on the other hand, are molded according to models of behavior that are specific to different societies and cultures. Concepts such as citizen, worker, teacher, son, father, and neighbor describe roles in which the individual behaves (thinks, feels, acts) according to what is expected within a given culture or society.

When instruction aims at molding the behavior of the individual according to models of predetermined roles, the goals controlling it are extrinsic. Instruction is a technique intended to bring about changes in the individual as a result of which his personality will be molded to fit the roles he will one day play in his society.

When, on the other hand, instruction aims at developing the individual's personality by encouraging his capacities, the aims controlling it are intrinsic. A distinction must be made between developing capacities when this development is controlled by models of roles in which the capacities are one day to operate and developing capacities according to an image of their specific nature or internal laws (for example, between thinking related to the performance of a given task and thinking for its own sake). It is impossible to describe a human capacity (such as intelligence, feeling, or imagination) in a state of final and perfect development in the same way that it is possible to describe a perfect social role. Encouraging the development of capacities means supporting differences between them as well as integration between them and between their various components. This support is not directed by some image of the capacity in an ideal state. It is always a developmental process whose final product, even if it can be envisaged in its general outlines, can never be exactly described. Roles, however, not only can be described in their perfect state if instruction and education are to be guided by them; they must be so described. We can have only a vague idea of what we mean by fully developed intelligence or perfect feeling, but we can describe a "good citizen," an "excellent worker," or a "devoted father." We may, therefore, call intrinsic aims *process goals* and extrinsic aims *product goals.*[1]

Process goals are derived from the assumption that development itself is an educational aim and that it always contains within itself a chance that cannot be defined or even described at the outset. Product goals, on the other hand, are based on the assumption that the lines of individual development are predetermined by culture and society; structures of social roles can, therefore, serve as models according to which individual aptitudes should be molded.

Orienting instruction by process goals is always a gamble because of the unknown element inherent in individual development. The essence of instruction oriented by product goals is guided in a predetermined direction by social norms and cultural values. The activities derived from these two types of goals are, therefore, essentially different, although both are called teaching. Supporting development and directing development are essentially different activities.

Instruction may be directed by either fostering development or directing development. Most systems of instruction in our day are, in fact, guided by both. Though many educationists claim that the two goals are complementary, they are not really compatible. Activities intended to encourage the development of individual capacities may prevent their adaptation to defined social roles, and activities intended to adapt individual capacities to social roles may prevent their development. For this reason most theories of instruction that seek to promote both aims imply some principle according to which one type of aim may be preferred to the other.

The other aspect of aims in instruction is that of their level. We cannot determine whether the development of character is an extrinsic or an intrinsic aim until we know what the teacher does (or, at least, what he intends to do) in order to realize this aim. One teacher may seek to mold the character of his pupils by having them identify with fictional figures. He is, of course, aiming at a different goal from that of the teacher who tries to cultivate his pupils' self-awareness by the teaching of literature. This means that we must give our attention to both the ultimate aims of instruction (the development of character, the molding of intellect, the cultivation of critical thinking, and so on) and to the subsidiary or partial aims derived from them. An aim such as molding the intellect leads to the elevation of hundreds of subsidiary aims and to a like number of activities intended to realize them. Specific aims, such as training pupils to put a full stop at the end of a sentence, are derived from and justified by more comprehensive aims, such as training them to communicate and to express themselves in writing. But these aims, too, do not derive validity from themselves. Their validity is ultimately derived from aims implying that an educated man must be able to communicate effectively and aesthetically in writing. Ultimate aims or ends are, therefore, the most comprehensive aims in instruction. From them are derived intermediary aims, or goals, whose various combinations are a more concrete expression of the ultimate aims, although they are not yet specific enough to direct the teacher's activities. The *objectives* derived from these goals are the most specific aims in instruction; they direct the teacher's activities on the operative level.* Many different objectives can be derived (through the intermediary goals) from each of the ultimate aims of instruction. It is only by examining the connection between any given objective and any given aim that the nature of the aim becomes clear. Thus, for example, the aim of "developing historical understanding" may be realized by the objective of "getting to know the opinions of historians on the period" or by means of the ob-

---

*For the purposes of this discussion, a discrimination between aims at three levels seems sufficient, although further distinctions are of course possible. The requisite level of discrimination must, in each case, be determined by the needs of the discussion concerned. A discussion of the didactics of a specific subject would, for example, demand finer distinctions than are required by the discussion we are conducting here.

jective of "enabling the pupils to express their own opinions about the period." Both of these objectives can be related to the aim of "developing historical understanding," although the concept of understanding will be interpreted differently in each case. In the same way, we cannot know the nature of any given objective until we know the aim from which it is derived. Though the objective of "getting to know the opinions of historians on the period" may be derived from the aim of "developing historical understanding," it may also be derived from the aim of "knowing different schools of thought in the interpretation of historical events," a different aim necessitating different activities for its implementation. Aims requiring different objectives are different aims. Objectives that lead to different aims, even when they are formulated in the same way, are different objectives.*

1.1 Extrinsic Aims

The preference for extrinsic aims in instruction is based on the philosophic assumption that the individual is not simply a member of the society in which he lives but that his personality is a product of social existence.[2] If the individual is only, or mainly, the product of his membership in society, then his instruction must train him in the behaviors acceptable in that society. Thus, every society expects its members to know certain things, to admire certain things and despise others, and to do certain things and avoid others. Every society regards certain interpersonal relationships as good and others as bad, certain ways of doing things as efficient and others as inefficient, certain modes of thinking as reliable and others as unreliable. When the aims of instruction are extrinsic, the function of instruction is to teach the young person how to behave toward his fellows, that is, how to work, how to think, how to speak, in what and in whom to believe, and whom to admire, all in accord with the patterns of behavior preferred in his society. These behaviors are organized into roles, which instruction must assign to members of the younger generation.

*It is here that the educationists advocating a system of objectives make their mistake. This system relies mainly on Bloom's taxonomy of educational objectives (Benjamin S. Bloom, *Taxonomy of Educational Objectives* [New York: David McKay, 1956]). Its application is illustrated in R. F. Mager, *Preparing Instructional Objectives* (Belmont, Calif.: Fearon, 1962). The most comprehensive attempt to date to formulate instructional objectives was made by Westinghouse Learning Corporation, PLAN*, Master Objectives (Palo Alto: the Corporation, 1971).

The role in present-day societies that everyone has to acquire is that of citizenship. Training for citizenship entails the imparting of behaviors in many human capacities. First are the intellectual capacities to know and understand one's rights and obligations as a citizen, to know and understand the collective goals of society and the state and their ideologies. Second are emotional capacities, which are responses to the symbols representing the ideals and goals of society and the state and to the leaders of society who express these ideals. Third are the individual's character and will as reflected by his readiness to act persistently on behalf of the ideals and goals he reveres.

None of the other social roles are as general as that of citizenship. Division of labor on the one hand and biological characteristics (sex, age, intelligence) on the other determine that different people perform different roles. In complex societies the number of these roles and their possible combinations are great. Instruction prepares the individual for these roles, the combination of which determines his place in society. Characteristic of instruction guided by extrinsic aims is the fact that social roles (both general and specific) act as the criteria for determining curricula, teaching methods, and organizational patterns in the schools, while individual characteristics are regarded as data providing the basis for role selection. Instruction will prepare certain pupils for complex roles and others for simple roles. After pupils have been divided according to their suitability for different roles, their individual characteristics are regarded only as factors that assist or interfere with the aims of instruction; they are never factors that determine or should influence them.

Underlying the extrinsic conception of aims in instruction are the basic assumptions that the individual is a cluster of roles and that the nature of these roles depends in each case on the distinctive structure of the particular society. Such characteristics as responsibility, accuracy, industriousness, loyalty, and submission to authority differ in their concrete manifestations from society to society and from role to role. No role can be precisely defined without knowing the society and the period in which it exists.

In its intermediate goals, instruction relates to the specific characteristics of social roles. Because these goals unite both the direction and the contents of teaching activities, their formulation tends to vacillate between concepts indicating direction and concepts indicating contents. In goals derived from extrinsic aims the formulation "to teach pupils the history and literature of their people" has the same meaning as the formulation "to foster the loyalty of the pupil to his people." The first formulation defines in terms of content what the second defines in terms of direction.

History and literature can, however, also be taught in order to develop critical thinking or aesthetic sensibility. For generations the humanistic tradition of education demanded that they be taught in order to expand the pupil's horizons beyond the experience of his own particular nation and to acquaint him with additional manifestations of the human spirit, which is not exhausted by the history and literature of one nation alone. But such goals are not, of course, derived from extrinsic aims.

As has been said, instruction directed by extrinsic aims is intended to develop capacities according to models of social roles. Thus, history and literature should develop the pupil's capacity for performing the roles of citizen and member of the national collective. Mathematics and the sciences should train him to perform roles of a professional or occupational nature. Physical education should prepare him for work or military service (according to the circumstances). The arts should help him to enjoy his leisure (which has become a need in modern affluent societies) or to enter occupations for which such training is required.

The goals of instruction are further particularized into the objectives that guide the teacher in his specific activities in the classroom. These goals determine the contents of what he will teach in any subject. The contents of the objectives may be classified into four groups: *information, comprehension, skills,* and *attitudes.*

In instruction directed by extrinsic aims only the information, comprehension, skills, and attitudes considered socially useful will be included. Social efficiency, in this context, has more than one meaning. There is information that has no practical usefulness, but serves as a "status symbol" and thus is socially useful since it fixes the place of the individual in the social structure. There is also information that is socially useful because it fosters the individual's sense of solidarity with the members of his group.

Manifest behavior is the principle determining the relation between the different objectives and the relative importance of each kind of objective in instruction governed by extrinsic aims. The more any item of instruction tends to support the establishment of this type of behavior, the more importance is granted it. Information and skills are therefore preferred to attitudes, and attitudes to comprehension, except in those cases where training in roles in which attitudes or comprehension resemble manifest behavior. Classic examples of instruction governed by extrinsic aims are found in vocational or military education and in general educational systems ruled by political institutions, that is, in totalitarian countries. All systems of general education, however, include some activities directed by extrinsic aims. These are the activities that are closely related to what is called socialization in the narrowest meaning of the term.*

From these facts it follows that each society sets up a certain ideal of man, of what he should be, as much from the intellectual point of view as the physical and moral; that this ideal is, to a degree, the same for all citizens; that beyond a certain point it becomes differentiated according to the particular milieux that every society contains in its structure.† It is this ideal, at the same time one and various, that is the focus of education. Its function, then, is to arouse in the child: (1) a certain number of physical and mental states that the society to which he belongs considers should not be lacking in any of its members; (2) certain physical and mental states that the particular social group (caste, class, family, profession) considers, equally, ought to be found among all those who make it up. Thus, it is society as a whole and each particular social milieu that determine the ideal that education realizes. Society can survive only if there exists among its members a sufficient degree of homogeneity; education perpetuates and reinforces this homogeneity by fixing in the child, from the beginning, the essential similarities that collective life demands. But on the other hand, without a certain diversity all co-operation would be impossible; education assures the persistence of this necessary diversity by being itself diversified and specialized. If the society has reached a degree of development such that the old divisions

---

*The conception of instructional aims in the spirit of the pattern of imitation is represented both in sociological literature and in the didactic literature influenced by it. In addition to the book by Durkheim, an extract from which is quoted below to illustrate this approach, compare Herbert Spencer, *Education: Intellectual, Moral and Physical* (New York: Appleton, 1860); Karl Mannheim and W. A. C. Stewart, *An Introduction to the Sociology of Education* (New York: Humanities Press, 1970). This conception of the aims of education governs most of the experiments in the field of programmed instruction. See Mager, *Preparing Instructional Objectives.*

†Reprinted with the permission of Macmillan Publishing Co., Inc. from *Education and Sociology*, pp. 70 – 71, by E. Durkheim. Copyright 1956 by The Free Press, a Corporation.

into castes and classes can no longer be maintained, it will prescribe an education more uniform at its base. If at the same time there is more division of labor, it will arouse among children, on the underlying basic set of common ideas and sentiments, a richer diversity of occupational aptitudes. If it lives in a state of war with the surrounding societies, it tries to shape people according to a strongly nationalistic model; if international competition takes a more peaceful form, the type that it tries to realize is more general and more humanistic. Education is, then, only the means by which society prepares, within the children, the essential conditions of its very existence. We shall see later how the individual himself has an interest in submitting to these requirements.

We come, then, to the following formula: Education is the influence exercised by adult generations on those that are not yet ready for social life. Its object is to arouse and to develop in the child a certain number of physical, intellectual and moral states which are demanded of him by both the political society as a whole and the special milieu for which he is specifically destined.

1.2 Extrinsic Aims Control Intrinsic Aims

Intrinsic aims in instructional and educational thought involve a rejection of the identification of individual with social existence. The individual is not simply a product of the social circumstances in which he was born and grew up but is also a being with unique characteristics that demand to be realized. It is true that the individual operates with his powers of thought and feeling and with his character and his will in all his social functioning, and that social roles influence his characteristics. Social roles do not, however, create his characteristics and are not the only factors that actively mold them. Thought, emotion, and character develop in the individual according to their own inherent laws, and their development is a necessary condition for his well being.[3] Social roles not only mold human characteristics; they sometimes impair and distort them. For this reason individual characteristics must be fostered for their own sake, before they are activated in social roles, and as distinct from them. This assumption gives rise to the intrinsic aims of instruction.

The above assumption leads to a distinction between training and education. The former trains people for given roles; the latter fosters people's capacities to perform roles, to evaluate roles, and to change them.

Sometimes these two aims are compatible. A certain way of teaching language, for example, may combine the development of the capacity and the training for a role. More frequently, however, aims of the one type contradict aims of the other. The development of intellect necessitates the development of critical thinking while the imparting of behavior is usually accompanied by an authoritarian attitude that prevents criticism. In this case, the intrinsic aim (the development of intellectual capacities) contradicts the extrinsic aim (the imparting of behaviors).

Those who acknowledge the validity of both types of aims often must decide which of the two takes priority in any given situation. In order to be able to make this decision, however, they will have to acknowledge the existence of the contradiction, and the acknowledgment of mutually contradictory beliefs does not come easily to most people. Indeed, the attempts to harmonize contradictory aims are far more frequent in theories of instruction than the acknowledgment of the contradiction. The most prevalent way of harmonizing the disparate elements is to identify intrinsic with extrinsic aims. Thus, the development of thinking, feeling, character, and other similar capacities is regarded as identical with the development of preferred behaviors in the family, the state, society, and work.

But harmony between concepts does not eliminate contradictions between phenomena. It is impossible to develop critical thinking and at the same time to suppress it by developing conditioned behavior in evaluation and judgment. The teacher must make a critical decision. Either he develops critical thinking (in which case he acts according to an intrinsic aim) or he makes his pupils responsive to authority, which will predetermine the direction of his evaluations and judgments (in which case he acts according to an extrinsic aim). In the second case, his intention shows that, although he may believe in intrinsic aims, they are controlled in his mind and his deeds by extrinsic ones and that, in cases of conflict between the two, he will act in accordance with extrinsic aims.

At the level of ultimate aims, intrinsic and extrinsic aims are merged in the concepts of ideas or ideals that bridge them: truth, goodness, beauty, justice, and equality on one side and the good man, the hero, and the gentleman on the other. In this context the meaning ascribed to these concepts is archetypal. The aims of instruction are to mold the personality of the pupil in accordance with one or more of these ideals or ideas, whose meaning in each case is explicit; there is general agreement on what constitutes truth, goodness, the good man, and the gentleman. Thus, the molding of the personality in the spirit of ideas or ideals is interpreted both as the development of capacities and as the initiation of the individual into culture and society.

The goals of instruction derived from these aims are of two types. One is defined in terms of characteristics, such as the development of intellect, the refining of emotions, and the strengthening of the will. The second is defined in terms of content, such as mathematics, literature, and history. The concepts defining characteristics serve to direct the teaching of contents. Thus the teaching of mathematics is intended to develop the individual's intellect, the teaching of literature to refine his emotions, and the teaching of history to direct his will. There is a basic difference between goals of this type and the goals of instruction governed solely by extrinsic aims. In the latter the teaching of the various subjects is not regarded as stemming from the needs of the developing personality, but from the need to place this personality in the social system, and it is this need that determines the direction of instruction. In the former, on the other hand, the teaching of these subjects is regarded as a necessary condition for the molding of personality. Mathematics, literature, and history are not simply instruments to be used in preparing young people to take their place in society, but they are ends derived from the needs of the developing personality itself. The source of the formative powers attributed to the subjects of instruction lies in the nature of the subjects themselves. Mathematics is held to possess characteristics necessary to the development of intellect, literature to possess characteristics necessary to the refinement of the emotions, and history to possess characteristics necessary for the development of the will.

Without these disciplines, it is held, there can be no development of the human capacities. Thus, where the ultimate aims of instruction are both intrinsic and extrinsic, with the latter controlling the former, the goals of instruction are conceived in such a way that they succeed in merging its contents with its direction.

The objectives derived from these goals are determined by an evaluation of the formative meaning of the various teaching contents. The information, types of comprehension, skills, and attitudes to be taught are selected according to their ability to mold individuals in the spirit of the culture and its values. The preferred objectives in developing comprehension are those that combine the information necessary to achieve this end and the objectives intended to develop desired attitudes in the pupil. The teaching of skills is regarded as complementary to other activities since, in this scheme, skills are mainly instrumental. The relative importance of the various objectives is not determined here by the principle of manifest behavior but rather by their probable influence on molding the characteristics of the learner. However, in cases where intrinsic and extrinsic intentions are not compatible and contradictions appear between the two, the principle of manifest behavior, characteristic of extrinsic aims, will determine objectives here as well.

Examples of instruction guided by the combination of intrinsic and extrinsic goals are found in the humanist educational systems founded on the concept of liberal education. Of all the alternative views of the goals of instruction, this is the most prevalent in the school systems of our day.[4]

Every man has a function as a man. * *The function of a citizen or a subject may vary from society to society, and the system of training, or adaptation, or instruction, or meeting immediate needs may vary with it. But the function of a man as man is the same in every age and in every society, since it results from his nature as a man. The aim of an educational system is the same in every age and in every society where such a system can exist: it is to improve man as man.*

If we are going to talk about improving men and societies, we have to believe that there is some difference between good and bad. This difference must not be, as the positivists think it is, merely conventional. We cannot tell this difference by any examination of the effectiveness of a given program as the pragmatists propose; the time required to estimate these effects is usually too long and the complexity of society is always too great for us to say that the consequences of a given program are altogether clear. We

*Abridged from pp. 68–72 in *The Conflict in Education in a Democratic Society* by Robert M. Hutchins. Copyright, 1953 by Harper & Row, Publishers, Inc. By permission of the publishers.

cannot discover the difference between good and bad by going to the laboratory, for men and societies are not laboratory animals. If we believe that there is no truth, there is no knowledge, and there are no values except those which are validated by laboratory experiment, we cannot talk about the improvement of men and societies, for we can have no standard of judging anything that takes place among men or in societies.

Society is to be improved, not by forcing a program of social reform down its throat, through the schools or otherwise, but by the improvement of the individuals who compose it. As Plato said, "Governments reflect human nature. States are not made out of stone or wood, but out of the characters of their citizens: these turn the scale and draw everything after them." The individual is the heart of society.

To talk about making men better we must have some idea of what men are, because if we have none, we can have no idea of what is good or bad for them. If men are brutes like other animals, then there is no reason why they should not be treated like brutes by anybody who can gain power over them. And there is no reason why they should not be trained as brutes are trained. A sound philosophy in general suggests that men are rational, moral, and spiritual beings and that the improvement of men means the fullest development of their rational, moral, and spiritual powers. All men have these powers, and all men should develop them to the fullest extent . . . .

Education deals with the development of the intellectual powers of men. Their moral and spiritual powers are the sphere of the family and the church. All three agencies must work in harmony; for, though a man has three aspects, he is still one man. But the schools cannot take over the role of the family and the church without promoting the atrophy of those institutions and failing in the task that is proper to the schools.

We cannot talk about the intellectual powers of men, though we can talk about training them, or amusing them, or adapting them, and meeting their immediate needs, unless our philosophy in general tells us that there is knowledge and that there is a difference between true and false. We must believe, too, that there are other means of obtaining knowledge than scientific experimentation. If knowledge can be sought only in the laboratory, many fields in which we thought we had knowledge will offer us nothing but opinion or superstition, and we shall be forced to conclude that we cannot know anything about the most important aspects of man and society. If we are to set about developing the intellectual powers of men through hav-

ing them acquire knowledge of the most important subjects, we have to be-gin with the proposition that experimentation and empirical data will be of only limited use to us, contrary to the convictions of many American social scientists, and that philosophy, history, literature, and art give us knowl-edge, and significant knowledge, on the most significant issues.

If the object of education is the improvement of men, then any system of education that is without values is a contradiction in terms. A system that seeks bad values is bad. A system that denies the existence of values denies the possibility of education. Relativism, scientism, skepticism, and anti-in-tellectualism, the four horsemen of the philosophical apocalypse, have pro-duced that chaos in education which will end in the disintegration of the West.

The prime object of education is to know what is good for man. It is to know the goods in their order. There is a hierarchy of values. The task of education is to help us understand it, establish it, and live by it. This Aris-totle had in mind when he said: "It is not the possessions but the desires of men that must be equalized, and this is impossible unless they have a suffi-cient education according to the nature of things."

Such an education is far removed from the triviality of that produced by the doctrines of adaptation, of immediate needs, of social reform, or of the doctrine of no doctrine at all. Such an education will not adapt the young to a bad environment, but it will encourage them to make it good. It will not overlook immediate needs, but it will place these needs in their proper rela-tionship to more distant, less tangible, and more important goods. It will be the only effective means of reforming society.

1.3   Instrinsic Aims Control Extrinsic Aims

When the predominant place in the value system orienting instruc-tion is assumed by the individual rather than by the interests of society or the claims of culture, its aims are intrinsic. But the process of in-struction cannot be directed by these aims alone because instruction must be related in some way to the contents of a culture. It is impossi-ble to develop individual capacities without reference to cultural con-tents since a capacity cannot be developed without activating it, and a capacity can be activated only by some sort of content. The contents of instruction—teaching subjects, patterns of behavior, values, and norms—always carry a social or cultural meaning. The study of mathematics or history may, of course, support the development of certain capacities, but the teaching of these subjects is not directed toward this end. Teaching is directed, in the first place, toward ensuring the emergence of behavior defined as knowledge of mathematics or history, that is, toward the molding of individual capacities in accordance with models existing in a given culture. Because contents are a necessary element in instruction, the pressures of extrinsic aims, which in many instances contradict intrinsic ones, are brought to bear on it. When there are conflicting situations and the teacher nevertheless chooses to act in accordance with the developmental needs of his pupils, intrinsic aims control extrinsic ones in his consciousness.

As in the previous conception, this conception acknowledges aims of both types, but here process goals intended to develop individual capacities take priority over product goals intended to mold them. This conception is derived from the assumption that human development is not the exclusive product of society or culture, a view supported by psychological theories arguing that the self-actualization of the individual is an essential condition for his development and well-being and, ultimately, for his satisfactory functioning in society.[5]

Individual development, which, according to this view, is merely a steady process of self-actualization, self-realization, and the emergence of a unique personality, takes place in an environment defined by social norms and cultural patterns. There is no doubt that these norms and patterns interfere with and influence individual development. But the development itself is neither dependent on them nor is it their product. It is derived from the characteristic drives of the human organism, which strives for competency and the realization of its own innate potential. From this conception of man adherents of the view derive criteria for evaluating societies and cultures. Good societies and cultures are those which enable their individual members to actualize themselves. Most societies in most periods of history, however, have prevented individuals from doing this. Some adherents of this view hold that nonrepressive cultures and societies are a real though distant possibility. Others feel that nonrepressive cultures and societies are an impossibility and that the conflict between the individual and society is one of the basic characteristics of human existence.[6] In either case, the function of education is to oppose the trend to repress individual development, which exists in every culture and society. This activity accords with the intrinsic aims of education and must control the extrinsic aims imposed on it. The social institu-

tions and cultural values of the past cannot serve as models for education since every such model limits the possibilities inherent in human
development. Human beings, both as a group and individually, are
the result of development. This development, and not its side
effects — societies and cultures — should dictate the aims of education.
Man in all his manifestations, both as an individual and as a member
of the human race, is in a constant state of becoming. Final, fixed
aims, such as those derived from images of social roles or those
presented in concepts of absolute ideas, are in fact nothing less than a
recognition that human development has come to an end. No one has
sufficient perspective to determine what the desired direction of
development for the human race is, and therefore no one has the right
or the authority to decide what the aims of education should be.

Education that conforms to the nature of man, in the spirit of this
conception, is intended to encourage processes of development and
not to mold the characteristics and capacities of the individual according to predetermined models. Education guided by intrinsic aims
is like a process that has no predetermined models or predetermined
direction. Instruction in mathematics, language, history, and biology,
however, has a clear and predetermined direction, and, since education however conceived will inevitably include these subjects, the process of instruction will always exhibit these two contradictory trends.

As far as the goals of instruction are concerned, this approach
favors intrinsic aims by stressing formal achievements and refraining
from the formulation of material achievements. Thus, intrinsic aims
are not described in terms of products but in terms of processes — not
the learning of arithmetic and algebra, but the development of
mathematical thinking; not the knowledge of facts and processes in
history, but the development of historical understanding. While here,
too, as in the goals of all types of instruction, contents are combined
with direction, this does not imply that the contents suggested for any
given purpose be regarded as indispensable. The goal is not the
knowledge of mathematics, history, or the contents of any other subject; it is their use in order to create situations in which the capacities
of the learner can be developed. If, for any reason, these contents fail
to meet the requirements of the situation, they should be replaced by
others.

The objectives of instruction guided by these aims are less subject to
preplanning than the objectives of any other kind of instruction. The

intention of serving the development of the individual pupil necessitates a constant awareness of and responsiveness to this pupil's actual, changing needs. Any detailed planning before the act of instruction is interpreted as interference with, and not support of, this development. Intellectual achievements that endanger development in other areas—emotions, interests, and motivations for example—are rejected. This means that the objectives of instruction should be determined in the classroom, while teaching is actually taking place, in accordance with the teacher's sensitivity to his pupil's reactions.

Examples of instruction combining intrinsic and extrinsic aims with the former controlling the latter are found mainly in a small number of experimental institutions advocating radical views in education. In most large school systems this conception, to the extent that it exists, is usually confined to the teaching of the arts.

Man demonstrates in his own nature *a pressure toward fuller and fuller Being, more and more perfect actualization of his humanness in exactly the same naturalistic, scientific sense that an acorn may be said to be "pressing toward" being an oak tree, or that a tiger can be observed to "push toward" being tigerish, or a horse toward being equine.* * *Man is ultimately* not *molded or shaped into humanness or taught to be human. The role of the environment is ultimately to permit him or help him to actualize* his own *potentialities, not* its *potentialities. The environment does not give him potentialities and capacities; he* has *them in inchoate or embryonic form, just exactly as he has embryonic arms and legs. And creativeness, spontaneity, selfhood, authenticity, caring for others, being able to love, yearning for truth are embryonic potentialities belonging to his species-membership just as much as are his arms and legs and brain and eyes.*

This is not in contradiction to the data already amassed which show clearly that living in a family and in a culture are absolutely necessary to actualize *these psychological potentials that define humanness. Let us avoid this confusion. A mother or a culture does not create a human being. It does not implant within him the ability to love, or to be curious, or to philosophize, or to symbolize, or to be creative. Rather, it permits or fosters or encourages or helps what exists in embryo to become real and actual. The*

---

*A. H. Maslow, "Psychological Data and Value Theory," in Maslow *et al.* (eds.) *New Knowledge in Human Values* (New York: Harper & Row, 1959), pp. 130–131.

same mother or the same culture, treating a kitten or a puppy in exactly the same way, cannot make it into a human being. The culture is sun and food and water: it is not the seed.

By education for individual development, I mean a program consciously undertaken to promote an identity based on such qualities as flexibility, creativity, openness to experience, and responsibility . . . .*

A high level of development in personality is characterized most essentially by complexity and by wholeness. There is a high degree of differentiation, a large number of different parts or features having different and specialized functions; and a high degree of integration, a state of affairs in which communication among parts is great enough so that different parts may, without losing their essential identity, become organized into larger wholes in order to serve the larger purposes of the person. In the highly developed person there is a rich and varied impulse life—feelings and emotions having become differentiated and civilized; conscience has been broadened and refined, and it is enlightened and individualized, operating in accord with the individual's best thought and judgment: the process by which the person judges events and manages actions are strong and flexible, being adaptively responsive to the multitudinous aspects of the environment, and at the same time in close enough touch with the deeper sources of emotion and will so that there is freedom of imagination and an enduring capacity to be fully alive. This highly developed structure underlies the individual's sense of direction, his freedom of thought and action, and his capacity to carry out commitments to others and to himself. But the structure is not fixed once and for all. The highly developed individual is always open to new experience and capable of further learning; his stability is fundamental in the sense that he can go on developing while remaining essentially himself.

Helping people to attain these ideals is a common aim of both psychiatry and education, though educators need more often to recognize these goals consciously or explicitly. The college years especially, the years of late adolescence, are a time when development toward these characteristics can be helped or hindered by what the college does.

Like everyone else, a student develops when confronted with challenges that require new kinds of adaptive responses and when he is freed from the

---

*N. Sanford, "Education for Individual Development," *American Journal of Orthopsychiatry,* XXXVIII (October 1958), pp. 858 – 859.

necessity of maintaining unconscious defensive devices. The fulfillment of these conditions results in the enlargement and further differentiation of the systems of the personality, and sets the stage for integration on higher levels.

Second Dimension:
Desired Achievements

In empirical research on instruction, aims and achievements are regarded as two sides of the same coin: aims that have been realized are achievements, and achievements before they have been attained are aims. These two concepts are regarded as identical in everything concerning the direct implementation of aims on the operative level — the objectives of instruction. To be able to write one thousand most frequently encountered words without mistakes, to be able to remember ten dates of events that occurred in the Middle Ages, and to be able to calculate the surface of a rectangle are at the same time both formulations of aims (objectives) and definitions of achievements.

Achievements can be assessed according to the objectives of instruction with a great measure of accuracy. What one has achieved in reading, for example, may be ascertained and assessed without any difficulty in terms of such concepts as speed, comprehension, and fluency. Even at higher levels it is not difficult to determine, albeit with less accuracy, whether our intentions in regard to reading have been realized by our pupils. We can, with some measure of accuracy, determine whether we have enabled them to be open to social communication (an extrinsic aim), molded their characters by means of the values inherent in works of literature (whereby the extrinsic aim controls the intrinsic aim), or supported the processes of self-actualization by strengthening self-awareness through reading (in which the intrinsic aim controls the extrinsic one). Aims and achievements are, therefore, not two sides of the same coin, but two distinct phenomena, at least insofar as their function in the process of instruction is concerned.

The teacher's activities bridge the gap between aims and achievements. These activities are guided by intentions, which are explicated in aims, and by an appraisal of possibilities, which are interpreted in images of achievements. When the teacher prepares to implement a given teaching unit, he considers either systematically or intuitively what he should do both in terms of what is desirable and what is possible. When these considerations are guided by aims, they are closer to the pole of the desirable; when they are guided by achievements, they are closer to the pole of the possible. The teacher's final decision is, of course, influenced by an image both of aims and of achievements.

If achievements and aims were really only different manifestations of a single phenomenon, we could classify achievements and aims according to the same criteria: extrinsic, intrinsic, and the possible combinations of the two. But these criteria do not hold for achievements. Achievements, of whatever kind, are properties added to the learner, or in other words, the new characteristics he has acquired. These characteristics may be classified according to their quantity and quality. The theories of instruction are chosen on the basis of the quality or nature of the desired achievements. These choices may be classified into three groups:

2.1. The ability to perform according to given models.

2.2. The ability to act according to given principles.

2.3. The ability to discover new principles and to test them.

Although classifying achievements requires concepts beyond those used to classify aims, the two classifications are to a large extent parallel. The ability to perform according to given models is an ability to imitate, which corresponds to the conception of instruction as an activity directed by extrinsic aims. The ability to act according to given principles corresponds to the conception of instruction as an activity directed by both extrinsic and intrinsic aims, with the former controlling the latter. And the ability to discover new principles and to test them corresponds to the conception of instruction as an activity in which intrinsic aims control extrinsic ones. This correspondence between alternative aims and alternative achievements is understandable when we realize that aims, which are influenced by all the other dimensions of instruction, influence them to the same extent.

2.1 Performing According to Given Models

In education one of the meanings ascribed to the verb "to know" is to be able to reconstruct accurately what the teacher, either directly or by means of textbooks, has presented. Though this theory is no longer as popular as it once was, it still guides the behavior of many teachers. The change in instructional theory resulted from the influence of modern trends in education, which undermined the confidence of teachers in the time-honored methods of imitation. A radical change in practice did not, however, result from the change in theory. It is true that teachers no longer praise imitation as a method of instruction, but they still employ it more than any other method. To the extent a change has taken place in practice, it consists of the fact that teachers no longer identify *all* teaching with imitation and acknowledge the existence of other methods of instruction.

Imitation teaches information and skills; the cheapest and most efficient method of imparting them is by conditioning, which is the main technique of imitation.

The anticipated achievement of imitation is behavior that accurately reconstructs a given model. Spelling effectively illustrates this type of instruction. There are few rational elements in spelling, and no one would argue that practicing spelling and learning its principles, if it indeed has any, play a role in developing the pupil's thinking or his other capacities. At least no one would contend that the amount of practice necessary to acquire the ability to spell correctly is justified by the benefits likely to accrue to the pupil in terms of his development. The product of practicing spelling is knowing how to spell, which is a highly desirable skill in contemporary society. A pupil would not be expected to reveal or increase his creativity as a result of learning to spell. Innovations in spelling are, on the contrary, inadmissible: an innovation is simply a mistake.

The only way to teach spelling is, therefore, by imitation. The teacher can sweeten the pill by using learning machines. If he does so, he can separate the mechanical drill, which is the function of the machine, from the more subtle instruction, which is left to the teacher. One may doubt if the ability to spell correctly is so important that it justifies the inevitable damage. The harmonizing approach, which is now prevalent, promises that the pupil will learn to spell without being drilled or claims that the time spent practicing spelling will have no ill effects on pupils' intellectual initiative, thinking, or attitude toward learning. This approach is misleading because all conditioned behavior exacts a price from students. Thus, imitation may determine the child's attitude in all other learning situations.

There is another danger—that which threatens the school. And, of course, whatever threatens the school inevitably threatens the pupil. When imitation is adopted in one area of instruction (as, for example, in spelling), it may come to dominate the other learning activities of the school. In the first place, it is an easy way to teach, and it can be employed in any subject area. It is, for example, easier to impart the ability to express numerical combinations (remembered by heart) in words and to solve artificial problems than to develop mathematical thinking. It is easier to have pupils learn the names of kings and places in which important events took place than to develop an understanding of the past.

In the second place, the achievements gained by these means are immediate and obvious. They reward the teacher for his efforts, and the educational administration is provided proof of the school's "productivity." "Objective" measurement of the pupils' achievements ascertains their ability to perform according to given models or to reconstruct behaviors acquired by imitation. This is generally true even of the tests that purport to measure the ability to think or to understand. The majority of these tests also measure answers that reflect memorization rather than understanding or thinking. It is not necessary to dwell on the influence that methods of evaluation exert on methods of instruction. Where methods of evaluation demand memorization, instruction inevitably addresses itself to cultivating the pupil's memory.

It is not only certain contents, such as spelling, that can be taught only by imitation; certain pupils, too, can be taught only by this method. Some contents must be taught if the socializing functions assigned to the school are not to be ignored. Most of these contents can be taught in a number of ways. Imitation, with the dangers it involves, should be the teacher's last resort, which they are for certain students. For reasons stemming either from the structure of their personalities or from the circumstances of their upbringing, these students can learn the necessary contents only by imitation. In this case the teacher must choose between evils. He may decide to forego the achievements even though they are a condition for the pupil's adjustment to the world in which he must live. He would thus avoid the dangers involved in teaching the contents by means of imitation. Or he may decide to take the risk of teaching in this way in order to ensure that the contents are learned. The risk in achievement of this type should, however, always be based on an awareness of the fact that the price of the achievement may be the loss of other achievements — achievements that tend not only to ensure the pupil's adaptation to society but to develop his individual personality.

. . . This is how teachers in training were trained to teach infants to thread needles at Nottingham University College just before the turn of the century: *

Needle drill

Apparatus. *Baby threaders and knitting cotton or very coarse cotton.*
Class. *Babies or lower division infants.*
Introduction. *Question on the needle, its parts and uses.*
  The use of needle and cotton should have been previously taught as well as the parts of the needle.
Parts in the drill. Preliminary step. *Let the children show the right and left hands alternately till they can readily distinguish them and practise them in closing in all the fingers except the thumb and forefinger of each hand.*

1. *Show the children how to take up the needle with the left thumb and forefinger. The eye of the needle upwards and straight in front.*
2. *Raise the right hand, take up the cotton near the end with the thumb and forefinger, repeat this several times.*
3. *Needle and cotton in position. Bring the cotton in front of the eye of the needle and close up.*
4. *Show children how to push cotton through the eye while the teacher counts four and tells them this is called threading a needle.*
5. *Put out three fingers of the left hand and catch the long end of the cotton to prevent it slipping.*
6. *With the right thumb and forefinger draw the cotton through the eye and show.*

---

*A. Clegg and B. Megson, *Children in Distress* (Harmondsworth, Eng.: Penguin Books, 1968), pp. 164 – 165.

Note: *In each step she demonstrates and then exercises the children till they can do it perfectly.*

Conclusion. *Let the children take the cotton out of the needle and put both on desk. The drill should be repeated till the children can thread the needle while the teacher counts six. When the children are quite proficient with the baby-threaders they should have No. 6 needles and fine cotton.*

The object of this is to teach obedience, discipline and simultaneous action.

2.2 Acting According to Given Principles

The ability to perform according to given models of behavior is based on practicing responses until they become automatic. Developing an ability to act according to given principles — to choose the appropriate behavior dictated by these principles in a given context — is based on the ability to think. Achievements obtained by imitation are by their nature final: the pupil (one hopes) knows what he has learned, but he cannot know, on the basis of this type of instruction, what he has not learned. The development of his thinking capacities, on the other hand, enables him to learn one thing from another, that is, to know more than what he has actually learned. While it is possible to impart a representative selection of human knowledge to the pupil during the years he spends in school, there can be no guarantee that this selection will include everything he will need to know in his future life. On the contrary, there is every reason to believe that even before he leaves school some part of what he has learned will be obsolete, and some of the things he "knows" will no longer be valid knowledge. This belief raises doubts regarding the value of the material aims of instruction and leads to an emphasis on formal aims instead. The training of thinking and other capacities by means of contents is derived from formal aims. Because of this training the pupil should be able to bring his knowledge up to date, to the extent that future developments make this necessary, and to fill in any contents necessary to him at various stages of his life that were missing from the contents he learned at school. The ability to fill in the gaps in his knowledge, the ability to bring this knowledge up to date, and especially the ability to behave in accordance with it lead to the same conclusion: the desired achievement will be the ability of the individual to choose appropriate behaviors with the help of principles he has learned and internalized.

Though these practical considerations are persuasive in light of the rapid transformations in knowledge, they are not the main reason for the desired achievements in this pattern of instruction. The main reason is the metaphysical assumption underlying it. According to this assumption, the human potentiality latent in the individual can be realized only by the disciplining of his mind and spirit. The essence of this discipline lies in the acceptance of the principles and the subjection to the authority of method. From the intellectual point of view this means the establishment of precise, controlled, and systematic thinking. From the ethical point of view it means the molding of a personality that will accept willingly the demands of moral imperatives.

The individual not only derives benefits from this conception of instruction; he must endure the disadvantages. Thus, the individual has little control over the principles that the educator instills in him. They control him more than he controls them. In order to ensure that they will indeed control the individual's thinking, and thereby guide his actions, the teacher must impart them in such a way as to make them impregnable to change. In this sense, these achievements are similar to those desired by imitation. There is a difference, however, in the degree of rigidity that each type of achievement imparts to the personality of the learner.

Habitual behavior is rigid behavior; it cannot usually be changed by experience or thinking. Behavior according to principles, on the other hand, because it involves a choice between possible behaviors, gives rise to situations of confrontation between decision and experience. These confrontations may undermine the principles guiding the individual's behavior, even when he has internalized them. The application of principles necessitates flexibility in the specific behaviors of the individual and enables him to liberate himself from their yoke by means of the thinking involved.

Instruction whose desired achievement is behavior according to principles differs from instruction whose desired achievement is behavior according to habit just as the process of molding the personality differs from the process of imparting skills. The imparting of habits by means of imitation does not require attention to pupils' individual differences. This is not true of the development of thinking and character; here individual differences are of great significance in the process of instruction. In order to attain the ability to act in accordance with principles, the starting point must be the pupil's characteristics and aptitudes at a given stage of development.

In the first place, the teaching of principles for the purpose of thinking, evaluating, and acting differs from the teaching of specific behaviors in that principles are, by definition, transferable. They are not learned in order to be retained by the memory or the nervous system, but to be used in new situations, different from those in which they were learned. A principle that has been learned is also a mechanism for collecting missing items of knowledge, for selecting relevant items, and for applying, analyzing, and evaluating them. The development of aptitudes is the development of the ability to use whatever principles (criteria, rules, laws) are characteristic of an aptitude, such as the principles of thinking or of aesthetic evaluation. The principles themselves, however, are fixed according to the assumptions underlying this method. When one uses the principles of proof in geometry, of explanation in history, or of evaluation in literature, he can apply his aptitudes in solving problems, describing historical events, or analyzing works of literature that he has not already learned.

Though instruction seeks to impart principles, the pupil's achievement is measured not by his knowledge of the principles but rather by his ability to act in accordance with them. In this sense, learning the principles of aesthetic evaluation or of organizing interpersonal relations molds the personality of the learner. Molding differs from imitation in that it does not provide the individual with a number of isolated habitual behaviors, but seeks to transform his personal characteristics until the totality of his behavior becomes subject to the principles that will guide it.

Because of the influence of religious and humanistic ideas, achievements of this type have long been considered the only ones of any value, and the striving toward them the main justification for the school's existence. The didactic vocabulary is filled with concepts whose meaning is derived from this view of achievements: disciplines, style, precision, responsibility.

Well, then, what sort of a thing is a method?* *First for what it is not. Despite what many folk would say, a method is not a stereotyped sequence-pattern or routine of actions, inculcatable by pure rote, like sloping arms or going through the alphabet. The parrot that can run through "Hickory Dickory Dock" has not learned how to do anything or therefore how not to do it. There is nothing that he takes care not to do.*

A method is a learnable way of doing something, where the word "way" connotes more than mere rote or routine. A way of doing something, or a modus operandi, *is something general, and general in at least two dimensions. First, the way in which you do a thing, say mount your bicycle, can be the way or a way in which some other people or perhaps most other people mount or try to mount their bicycles. Even if you happen to be the only person who yet does something in a certain way, it is possible that others should in future learn from you or find out for themselves the very same way of doing it.* Modi operandi *are, in principle, public property, though a particular action performed in this way is my action and not yours, or else it is your action and not mine. We mount our bicycles in the same way, but my bicycle-mounting is my action and not yours. You do not make my mincepies, even though we both follow the same Victorian recipe.*

The second way in which a method is something general is the obvious one, that there is no limit to the number of actions that may be done in that way. The method is, roughly, applicable anywhere and anywhen, as well as by anyone. For however many people are known by me to have mounted their bicycles in a certain way, I know that there could have been and there could be going to be any number of other bicycle-mountings performed by myself and others in the same way.

Next, methods can be helpfully, if apparently cynically, thought of as systems of avoidances or as patterns of "don'ts." The rules, say, of English grammar do not tell us positively what to say or write; they tell us negatively not to say or write such things as "A dog are . . ." *and "Those dogs* is . . . ," *and learning the art of rock-climbing or tree-climbing is, among hundreds of other things, learning never, or hardly ever, to trust one's whole weight to an untried projection or to a branch that is leafless in summer time.*

People sometimes grumble at the Ten Commandments on the score that

---

*Gilbert Ryle, "Teaching and Training," in R. S. Peters (ed.), *The Concept of Education* (Atlantic Highlands, N.J.: Humanities Press, Inc., 1967), pp. 114 – 116. Used by permission.

most of them are prohibitions, and not positive injunctions. They have not realized that the notice "Keep off the grass" licenses us to walk anywhere else we choose; where the notice "Keep to the gravel" leaves us with almost no freedom of movement. Similarly to have learned a method is to have learned to take care against certain specified kinds of risk, muddle, blind alley, waste, etc. But carefully keeping away from this cliff and from that morass leaves the rest of the countryside open for us to walk lightheartedly in. If I teach you even twenty kinds of things that would make your sonnet a bad sonnet or your argument a bad argument, I have still left you an indefinite amount of elbow-room within which you can construct your own sonnet or argument, and this sonnet or argument of yours, whether brilliant or ordinary or weak, will at least be free of faults of those twenty kinds.

There exists in some quarters the sentimental idea that the teacher who teaches his pupils how to do things is hindering them, as if his apron strings coerced their leg-movements. We should think of the inculcation of methods rather as training the pupils to avoid specified muddles, blockages, sidetracks and thin ice by training them to recognize these for what they are. Enabling them to avoid troubles, disasters, nuisances and wasted efforts is helping them to move where they want to move. Road signs are not, for the most part, impediments to the flow of traffic. They are preventives of impediments to the flow of traffic.

Of course we can easily think of silly ways of doing things which continue to be taught by grown-ups to children and adhered to by the grownups themselves. Not all methods are good methods, or all recipes good recipes. For example, the traditional ban on splitting the infinitive was a silly rule. But the gratuitous though trivial bother of conforming to this particular veto was negligible compared with the handicap that would be suffered by the child who had never been taught or picked up for himself any of the procedures for composing or construing sentences. He would have been kept back at the level of total infancy. He could not say or follow anything at all if, for example, he had not mastered conjunctions, or even verbs and mastering them involves learning how not to make hashes of them.

2.3 Testing and Discovering New Principles

The definition of desired achievements as the ability to discover and test principles of behavior means that the role assigned to instruction is that of developing creativity. Creativity as a personality trait has long been regarded as the pinnacle of human aspirations. It was not generally considered something that could be planned for in advance and achieved by means of instruction but as a divine (or satanic) gift, or, in any event, as a product of unique and unrepeatable circumstances. Only recently has creativity been presented as a desired achievement of instruction and have certain ways of teaching been acknowledged as leading to the establishment of this personality trait.

The criticism leveled against imitation by the advocates of molding is similar to that leveled against the latter by the advocates of creativity. They argue that the teaching of principles does no less harm to the development of the personality than the conditioning of behavior according to predetermined models. Both lead to changes that become fixed and therefore prevent further changes from taking place; in other words, both cause individual development to stop. Instruction whose aim is creativity differs from both these methods in that it seeks to retain and strengthen developmental potential. It does not, however, seek to exploit it in order to impose a patternized behavior on the individual, whether the source of the pattern lies in the accepted mores of a given society or the received values of a given culture.

Creativity manifests itself in new products which may be in the form of materials, ideas, events, or interpersonal relations. Creative behavior on the part of the individual is a function of his uniqueness and his drive to manifest this uniqueness in his acts. Among the conditions of the individual's self-actualization is openness, that is, his ability to ignore a given organization of reality in order to reorganize it for himself, his ability to evaluate the objects of his perception by means of an inner focus of evaluation—to liberate himself from dependence on the opinion of his fellows—and, lastly, his need to manipulate the components of the contents of his perceptions.[7] Where the desired achievement of instruction is behavior according to given principles, these qualities are damaged. Learned principles "close" the organization of reality and prevent the pupil from reorganizing it. The objects of his perception are evaluated by external focuses of evaluation—the learned principles—and his need to play with concepts, ideas, and the components of his perception is systematically suppressed by the pressure seeking to impose conceptions that are ready, complete, and comprehensible.

Creativity is supported by the psychology of the personality, according to which self-actualization is both the drive and the object of development. It is also supported by new insights into the processes of the growth of knowledge, especially of scientific knowledge. Adherence to the existing patterns of knowledge does not provide the impetus for scientific advance. On the contrary, in most cases where scientific knowledge has taken a leap forward, this advance has been accompanied by the daring to dismantle existing patterns and test things in new ways. Daring of this type is the distinguishing characteristic of the creative personality. Social research has also contributed to the growing acceptance of creativity as the desired achievement of instruction. In mass societies the individual is constantly threatened with the loss of his identity as he is drawn into the crowd and becomes part of it. When the individual loses the sense of his own uniqueness he loses the sense of his identity. Liberation of creative elements in the personality is the best defense against the processes of alienation that threaten to destroy not only individual well-being but also the fabric of social life.

There has been support for the idea of creativity in education from different quarters. As a result, a number of techniques and patterns of activity intended to encourage the creative capacities of the pupil have infiltrated the school. These innovations have not, however, brought about any changes in the fundamental structure of the school. Because of its position between the two extremes of imitation and creativity, the conception of molding may resolve the dilemma. It may impart the principles it seeks to teach by means of imitation, but it may do so by encouraging pupils to use the principles they have learned in the most fruitful, free, and daring manner possible. Creativity is thus interpreted as a mode of operating with principles, and instruction seeks to encourage creativity because without it the use of principles can be merely routine or limited mainly to the situations and problems in which pupils have learned to apply them. According to the conception of molding, the principles of the sciences, the arts, and so forth are learned in order to be used creatively, with imagination, flexibility, and daring.

Even in the above metamorphosis, however, molding differs from the conception of instruction whose desired achievement is creativity defined as the ability to discover and test new principles. The essential difference between molding, even when it fosters creativity, and instruction that develops creative capacities is that the latter does not crystallize or structure the personality; it is guided by the possibilities inherent in the process of development itself and is not blocked by attempts to mold the personality according to any given model. Molding in all its manifestations seeks to promote the submission of the individual to principles he has internalized. Creativity, on the other hand, seeks to promote the mastery of the individual over principles (including values) and to instill in him a readiness to test these principles and to discard them when they are found to be invalid and replace them with new and better ones. The totality of achievements desired by this conception may, therefore, be defined as the autonomy of the personality.

The definition of its desired achievement as autonomy indicates another difference between this conception of instruction and the other two. The objects of instruction are the contents of knowledge. Imitation requires the pupil to perform according to given models, to retrieve items of knowledge just as he learned them. Memory, either mental or motor, is its most important component. Molding seeks to have the pupil act according to given principles, to foster his ability to comprehend, evaluate, and test items of knowledge he has learned and also items of knowledge he has not learned. These achievements depend on intellectual aptitudes, emotions, and the will. Molding thus involves more dimensions of the personality than imitation. Creativity broadens the target to include the entire personality. Autonomy, even where it is revealed only in the attitudes of the individual toward the contents of knowledge, involves the whole personality. The ability of the individual to liberate himself from the influence of symbols, authorities, and habitual responses depends on the openness of his emotions, on the consciousness of his motivation, and, to some degree, on his basic security. Autonomy as the desired achievement of instruction makes the whole personality the object of instruction.

Autonomy is not to be interpreted as the abandonment of principles. The autonomous individual may behave according to principles, both in thinking and in doing, but without being enslaved by them. Characteristic of autonomy is the ability to assess principles from a certain distance (without discarding them without a valid reason). The autonomous person can recognize the fact that principles and values have an autonomous existence. Recognition of the existence of principles and values and the readiness to act in accordance with them, on the basis of independent decisions, are not identical with the adherence to principles and values characteristic of the heteronomous person, even though both may act in the same way in many instances.

The difference lies in the ability of the autonomous person to evaluate, judge, and criticize even those principles and values according to which he acts and, in certain cases, even to discard them and replace them with others.*

A further difference between creativity and imitation and molding concerns the desired achievement. In the latter two, instruction is seen as final. In imitation it is final in the most literal sense of the word: the process of instruction is intended to ensure that the learner will behave in an unvarying way according to given models. In molding the idea of finality exists in principle if not in practice: the model is ideal and instruction is intended to ensure that the learner will aspire to be as close an approximation as possible to the given ideal model, which is final. Creativity discards all predetermined personality models. It is a characteristic of a developing and changing personality, not an end product of development and change. The personality is thus in a state of constant self-actualization. Because there is no final aim in the definition of achievement, it is justifiable to define this conception as one of development. As long as the personality continues to develop and change, the desired achievement is attained.

Achievements of this type include flexibility, a critical attitude, diversity of interests, and, above all, educability.

What are the conditions within the individual which are most closely associated with a potentially constructive creative act?† I see these as possibilities.

A. Openness to experience: Extensionality. *This is the opposite of psychological defensiveness, when to protect the organization of the self, certain experiences are prevented from coming into awareness except in distorted fashion. In a person who is open to experience each stimulus is freely relayed through the nervous system, without being distorted by any process of defensiveness. Whether the stimulus originates in the environment, in the impact of form, color, or sound, on the sensory nerves, or whether it origi-*

---

*See C. Frankenstein, *The Roots of Ego and Psychodynamics of Externalization* (Baltimore: Williams and Wilkins, 1966 and 1968). In these and other studies by Frankenstein, the reader will find a clarification of the meaning of the concept of autonomy as an aim of education, as well as a description of the conditions leading to its emergence (and especially of the factors preventing its appearance.)'

†Carl R. Rogers, excerpt from "Toward a Theory of Creativity," *Etc.: A Review of General Semantics,* IX (1952), 83 – 88.

nates in the viscera, or as a memory trace in the central nervous system, it is available to awareness. This means that instead of perceiving in pre-determined categories ("trees are green," "college education is good," "modern art is silly") the individual is aware of this existential moment as it is, thus being alive to many experiences which fall outside the usual categories (this *tree is lavender;* this *college education is damaging;* this *modern sculpture has a powerful effect on me*).

This last suggests another way of describing openness to experience. It means lack of rigidity and permeability of boundaries in concepts, beliefs, perceptions, and hypotheses. It means a tolerance for ambiguity where ambiguity exists. It means the ability to receive much conflicting information without forcing closure upon the situation. It means what the general semanticist calls the "extensional orientation."

This complete openness of awareness to what exists at this moment is, I believe, an important condition of constructive creativity. In an equally intense but more narrowly limited fashion it is no doubt present in all creativity. The deeply maladjusted artist who cannot recognize or be aware of the sources of unhappiness in himself, may nevertheless be sharply and sensitively aware of form and color in his experience. The tyrant (whether on a petty or grand scale) who cannot face the weaknesses in himself may nevertheless be completely alive to and aware of the chinks in the psychological armor of those with whom he deals. Because there is the openness to one phase of experience, creativity is possible; because the openness is only to one phase of experience, the product of this creativity may be potentially destructive of social values. The more the individual has available to himself a sensitive awareness of all phases of his experience, the more sure we can be that his creativity will be personally and socially constructive.

B. An internal locus of evaluation. *Perhaps the most fundamental condition of creativity is that the source or locus of evaluative judgment is internal. The value of his product is, for the creative person, established not by the praise or criticism of others, but by himself. Have I created something satisfying to* me? *Does it express a part of me—my feeling or my thought, my pain or my ecstasy? These are the only questions which really matter to the creative person, or to any person when he is being creative.*

This does not mean that he is oblivious to, or unwilling to be aware of, the judgments of others. It is simply that the basis of evaluation lies within himself, in his own organismic reaction to and appraisal of his product. If to the person it has the "feel" of being "me in action," of being an actualization of potentialities in himself which heretofore have not existed and are now emerging into existence, then it is satisfying and creative, and no outside evaluation can change that fundamental fact.

C. The ability to toy with elements and concepts. *Though this is probably less important than A or B, it seems to be a condition of creativity. Associated with the openness and lack of rigidity described under A is the ability to play spontaneously with ideas, colors, shapes, relationships—to juggle elements into impossible juxtapositions, to shape wild hypotheses, to make the given problematic, to express the ridiculous, to translate from one form to another, to transform into improbable equivalents. It is from this spontaneous toying and exploration that there arises the hunch, the creative seeing of life in a new and significant way. It is as though out of the wasteful spawning of thousands of possibilities there emerges one or two evolutionary forms with the qualities which give them a more permanent value.*

Third Dimension:
The Social Interpretation of Instruction

The teacher's actions are directed toward the pupil as an individual. His attitude toward the pupil is determined by, among other things, his image of the role performed by instruction with regard to both the individual pupil and society as a whole. This image directs his actions to no less a degree than the images he has, whatever they may be, of the aims and the achievements of instruction.

The image of its desired achievements, as well as its social significance, is implicit in the aims of instruction. Instruction is not implemented according to the logical connections between these concepts, but, rather, according to the choices made by the teacher in deciding between alternative courses of action. In these decisions he is guided by his images. The images of the aims, of the desired achievements, and of the social significance of instruction exist independently of each other. Though they may support each other they may also contradict each other. The teacher may decide on a certain kind of aim in one way and adopt a certain image of the social significance of teaching in another. Both will influence his behavior, whether they are mutually compatible or mutually contradictory. All combinations of images of aims and images of the social significance of teaching are not, of course, theoretically possible. In practice, however, all combinations can exist in the minds of teachers. Teachers (like everyone else) possess mechanisms through which they can overcome any uneasiness caused by contradictions in their systems of beliefs. Sometimes they isolate contradictory beliefs and are thus able to ignore the contradictions between them. On one occasion the teacher may state that the aim of instruction is to instill in the pupil a skeptical attitude toward accepted truths. At another time he may say that the function of instruction is to instill in the pupil a feeling of reverence for great men. Should he be asked if the two are compatible, he may well reply, "What have skepticism and reverence to do with one another?" This is an example of the isolation of contradictory beliefs. When teachers are made aware of the contradictions in their beliefs, they sometimes feel the need to rationalize them. They may say, for example, that only persons capable of doubting accepted truths are capable of feeling reverence for true greatness, which is a verbal bridge between contradictory beliefs. At times teachers decide in favor of one of the beliefs and discard the other. They may feel that in a particular political situation it is more important for people to have respect for the leaders of society than to possess intellectual refinements. In another situation they could feel just the opposite. There are also teachers who are aware of the contradictions and are able to live with them. They may think, for example, that people must be educated to feel reverence and also to be skeptical. Though these two aims sometimes come into conflict, neither can be discarded.[8]

It is obvious that there is a logical connection between the aims of instruction and its social significance. This does not, however, negate the fact that people, including teachers, do not act only in accordance with the rules of logic. For this reason we are justified in identifying the social significance of instruction as an image that exists independently of the other images guiding the teacher's behavior.

Changes in social institutions, especially the family, have brought about alterations in expectations regarding the school. Some of the functions once performed by the family are now performed by the school. Other functions previously undertaken by the school are increasingly the responsibility of other segments of society, particularly the mass media. The image of the social role of the school will thus be related to that of the preferred distribution of roles between the school and other institutions responsible for educating the young. These different images may be classified by means of three concepts, each defining education in a different way:

3.1. Instruction as a means of socialization.
3.2. Instruction as a means of acculturation.

3.3. Instruction as a means of individuation.

Socialization, acculturation, and individuation indicate three archetypes of education. The status and function assigned to instruction differ in each. Though all regard instruction as a technique of education, each ascribes a different meaning to education.

3.1 Socialization

Sociologists use the term socialization as a synonym for education. Socialization is thus a process whereby the personalities of young people are molded until the individuals are able to perform the roles assigned to them by society. In this sense socialization entails the acquisition of characteristics, attitudes, and knowledge that are necessary in the society in which they were born and are to live. Teachers, peer groups, and mass media are agents of socialization. In this view, instruction is one of the techniques intended to further the process of socialization, a technique of adapting the individual to society by means of the contents taught and the methods employed by the school.[9]

The term socialization indicates the process by which human beings, who do not possess the characteristics necessary for taking part in social life at birth, are gradually transformed into members of society. The contents of this process, the mechanisms it activates, and the situations in which it occurs differ from society to society. In modern societies, the instruction provided by the school is an essential component of socialization. Earlier societies also had schools, but not all children could attend them. To the extent to which children attended schools or were instructed by private tutors, instruction was a component of the socialization of certain groups in society. These groups usually provided society with its leaders. In modern societies all children increasingly need the services of the school in order to function to their own and to society's advantage.

A cyclical process takes place: changes in society bring about changes in socialization, which, in turn, influence the way in which society operates. Changes in socialization are reflected in the processes of instruction from the point of view of organization (selective or universal education), methods (authoritarian or open schools), and contents (the sciences or the humanities). Despite the changes in instruction when it is regarded as a technique of socialization, its ruling principle remains the same. This principle is adaptation, which means that instruction is seen as a system of activities designed to direct the development of the individual according to the accepted models of behavior in a certain society in order to enable him to function in it.

Modern societies are complex structures of activities and interpersonal relations. The models of behavior accepted in these societies are many and varied, as are the sources of the norms and values that guide them. In the economic and technological spheres, modern societies prefer people who are capable of solving complex problems by abstract thought and who are inventive and innovative — people who are, to some extent at least, autonomous. .The political sphere, on the other hand, prefers individuals who conform, adapt, and respond to accepted symbols and slogans, and identify with the collective goals of society — in other words, a heteronomous personality. The high degree of technological development leaves people with much leisure time. Most people spend this time in the passive enjoyment of mass-produced entertainment; thus the prevalent personality type in this sphere, too, is the heteronomous one.

The principle of adaptation that guides instruction conceived as a technique of socialization thus leads to the acquisition of patterns of behavior that differ from one another. Among them are patterns of behavior that contradict the principle itself, such as the behavior required by modern economies, which demand innovation, initiative, and change. When society needs innovative people, socialization encounters contradiction. Socialization is, on the one hand, essentially a technique for adapting young people to existing social conditions. On the other hand, social conditions may demand innovative rather than conformist behavior, thus creating pressures for change within the process of socialization itself. But the school, guided by the idea of socialization, cannot at the same time promote the adaptation of its pupils to existing society and their willingness to accept or effect social change. It is true that the individual can behave in an innovative, open, and creative manner in one area (such as technology) and at the same time behave in a rigid, closed, and conformist manner in another (such as politics). The school cannot maintain a system of instruction that simultaneously promotes both creativity and conformity, both open- and closed-mindedness. Where it becomes necessary for socialization to have contradictory goals, the school will be controlled by the principle of adjustment to existing conditions. Methods of instruction that are not imitative cannot exist for any length of time in a school in which imitative techniques predominate. In competition with any other style of instruction, imitation will always win.

This is the reason why the school fails as an agent of socialization, despite the fact that in order to perform this role it neglects all others. Socialization in modern society cannot rely solely on imitation, and imitation cannot coexist with systems of instruction designed to promote innovation, initiative, and creativity.[10]

When instruction is a means of socialization, its aims are extrinsic. Its achievements are defined in terms of social roles, not of individual capacities. Many roles in modern society, however, require the development of human capacities and aptitudes. Thus, for example, people who are to perform roles in modern economic systems must be taught to think abstractly. When the role, and not the capacity, dictates the method of instruction, emphasis will be placed on the specific needs of defined social roles. It is true that thinking that has been developed in order for one to perform a given role may, by virtue of this development, overcome the limitations of the very model according to which it was developed. This is not, however, the outcome desired or intended by instruction conceived as socialization. Instruction of this type is not designed to promote social change or even changes in social roles. When such changes take place outside the school, instruction modifies itself accordingly, and attempts are made to adapt the pupils to the newly defined social roles. In the final analysis, though, instruction is seen as one mechanism by which continuity, integration, and stability in society are ensured: it is thus directed by existing social roles.[11]

In modern societies instruction conceived of as socialization is not uniform, just as the social roles that serve as its models are not uniform. The pluralism of modern societies, in which conflicting values coexist and roles are directed by conflicting aims and mutually contradictory systems of orientation, must influence instruction whose guiding idea is the adjustment of the individual to society. On the one hand, this type of instruction tends to indoctrinate students—to teach them behaviors without developing their capacity to evaluate and test these behaviors. On the other hand, it also attempts to develop critical, analytic, and innovative thinking in its pupils in order to equip them to perform the complex roles that society demands of them.

Even in this case these capacities will be regarded as characteristics or properties of the roles that are the models for instruction.

In fact, however, each society, considered at a given stage of development, has a system of education which exercises an irresistible influence on individuals.* It is idle to think that we can rear our children as we wish. There are customs to which we are bound to conform; if we flout them too severely, they take their vengeance on our children. The children, when they are adults, are unable to live with their peers, with whom they are not in accord. Whether they had been raised in accordance with ideas that were either obsolete or premature does not matter; in the one case as in the other, they are not of their time and, therefore, they are outside the conditions of normal life. There is, then, in each period, a prevailing type of education from which we cannot deviate without encountering that lively resistance which restrains the fancies of dissent.

Now, it is not we as individuals who have created the customs and ideas that determine this type. They are the product of a common life, and they express its needs. They are, moreover, in large part the work of preceding generations. The entire human past has contributed to the formation of this totality of maxims that guide education today; our entire history has left its traces in it, and even the history of the peoples who have come before. It is thus that the higher organisms carry in themselves the reflection of the whole biological evolution of which they are the end product. Historical investigation of the formation and development of systems of education reveals that they depend upon religion, political organization, the degree of development of science, the state of industry, etc. If they are considered apart from all these historic causes, they become incomprehensible. Thus, how can the individual pretend to reconstruct, through his own private reflection, what is not a work of individual thought? He is not confronted with a tabula rasa *on which he can write what he wants, but with existing realities which he cannot create, or destroy, or transform, at will. He can act on them only to the extent that he has learned to understand them, to know their nature and the conditions on which they depend; and he can understand them only if he studies them, only if he starts by observing them, as the physicist observes inanimate matter and the biologist, living bodies.*

*Durkheim, *Education and Sociology*, pp. 65 – 66.

3.2 Acculturation

The term acculturation usually indicates the process whereby individuals and groups exchange one culture for another.[12] This definition is derived from the anthropological concept of culture, which encompasses the patterns of behavior acquired and transmitted by means of symbols and manifested in artifacts (such as tools and utensils) and in ideas developed and selected in the course of history.[13] Culture is conceived of as a sociohistoric fact. All groups of people have a different culture, by means of which they solve the problems arising in their struggle for existence. Acculturation is thus the process by which one culture exchanges its patterns of behavior for patterns of another culture. This process is common among immigrant groups seeking to adapt themselves to a new environment. This meaning of "culture" in anthropology corresponds to the meaning of "society" in sociology. The term "acculturation," derived from this interpretation of the concept of culture, is analogous to a great extent to the term "socialization."

But acculturation has an additional meaning, which is derived from a different interpretation of the concept of culture. The concept of culture (from the Latin *cultus,* the past participle of the verb *colere,* which means to till or cultivate) has undergone a number of metamorphoses. According to the meaning that preceded the one used in the social sciences today and that is still current, culture is a state in which the individual or society defined as "cultured" has reached, or at least aspires to reach, human perfection. In other words, this is a view of history as a process of development moving toward a goal. Groups and individuals move from a state of preculture, in which they are primitive and barbaric, to a state of culture, in which they are civilized. Movement in the opposite direction, from civilization to barbarism, is, of course, also possible. But it is opposed to the object of human existence. Two motifs merge in this conception. One is universalist, in the sense that perfectibility is seen as a universal human characteristic. The other stresses the particularity of certain groups and sees their development as stemming from the characteristics that give each group a unique character and explain their fate. Both these motifs give rise to an approach consisting of value judgments according to which there are "cultured" and "uncultured" nations and societies and individuals possessing "superior" and "inferior" cultures.

It is from this conception of culture that the second meaning of acculturation is derived. According to this view, human beings, born as creatures totally subject to biological drives, must be liberated from their animal natures. The individual accomplishes this liberation when he subordinates himself to the yoke of human values. Acculturation is thus a key concept in the social interpretation of educational and instructional activities.

Those who see instruction as a means of socialization consider it a way by which young people are prepared to participate in social life by training them in social roles. Those who view it as a means of acculturation regard it as an avenue by which young people acquire the values and principles required by the culture. These values and principles are seen as absolute. Education and instruction are not regarded as preparation for life by training in existing social roles (as in socialization), but as processes in which the individual acquires powers of judgment and discrimination that enable him to regulate his actions. Instruction enables individuals to examine their lives in light of the system of values they have internalized.

The difference between the social significance of education conceived of as acculturation and education conceived of as socialization is equivalent to the difference between any society as it actually is and the normative ideal of what it should be. Instruction in the spirit of acculturation does not respond to the transient demands of society as it is, but seeks, rather, to instill characteristics and abilities considered good in the light of value criteria whose validity is absolute or at least stable. Norms derived from ideals and values, not models of social roles and their norms, direct instruction of this type.

Equality in education is foreign to this type of instruction. Selection is inherent in the very idea of acculturation, which sees education as a process of improvement, of climbing a stairway of human values. Everyone cannot reach the same place on the stairs. Only those who are capable of subjecting the stream of life to the rule of values are worth educating. The purpose of education is not to advance the possibilities of equality among men, but to ensure the continuity of human existence and its constant improvement. Education requires, first of all, individuals who are willing and able to accept the yoke of values and ascend the ladder of human virtues. This ascent does not promise a privileged position. Education is not concerned with rights and privileges, any more than it is concerned with individual happiness; it may lead to one or the other of these things, but may equally prevent both. Education is entrusted with the cultivation of what is human in man. Ideas of status or success in life are not relevant to it.[14]

Instruction does not serve society directly according to this conception. By its continuous efforts to impart a sensitivity to values to as many as possible of society's members, and especially to its future leaders, it ensures a certain standard of social life. The concept of "a successful man" is not identical in meaning to the concept of "a good man," and a society that functions and solves its problems is not necessarily a "good society." Values are the criteria according to which a society or an individual can be judged as good. Only individuals who perform social roles and are capable at the same time of evaluating their actions are able to establish a good society. In the distribution of roles between the school and other social institutions, the school cultivates the readiness to respond to values in the intellectual sphere (the value of truth), the moral sphere (the value of goodness), the aesthetic sphere (the value of beauty). Pupils come into contact with these values by means of knowledge. It is the function of instruction to confront the pupil with the knowledge in which these values are inherent. Instruction guided by this conception has two marked characteristics: an attachment to knowledge of the past, and an interest in creating teaching situations that encourage the pupil to identify with his teachers. History demonstrates the uniqueness of man in the animal kingdom: whereas animals are subject to the laws of nature alone, the fate of humanity is determined by its history. Thus, this type of instruction emphasizes the manifestations of the human spirit in the course of history. The child must be initiated into the historical consciousness of the human race and be made to feel a sense of personal involvement with its destiny. To accomplish this, he must identify with people who represent the values of civilization and culture that have guided humanity throughout its history. The teacher is, therefore, called upon to be an object of identification by means of which the child or youth gradually becomes a civilized human being.[15]

This interpretation of the social significance of instruction corresponds to the conception of aims in which extrinsic aims control intrinsic ones. Cultural values and the behaviors derived from them differ from training in the performance of roles, which is characteristic of instruction as socialization. The individual may use his capacities in the performance of social roles, but it is the imparting of values that is responsible for molding these capacities. Hence instruction as acculturation is concerned with intrinsic aims, which take as their point of departure the human capacities of reason, feeling, will, and aesthetic sensibility. These capacities must all be cultivated and molded according to the models of the culture and its values. Acculturation is thus concerned with extrinsic aims, with the conceptions, patterns, and values of the culture, which control the cultivation of individual capacities at every stage of instruction.

The conception of achievements that conforms to the pattern of acculturation is the ability to act in accordance with given principles. Behavior guided by given principles is the essence of molding in instruction, and molding is the aim of acculturation. The concept of truth in the intellectual sphere, of goodness in the moral sphere, of beauty in the aesthetic sphere, and similar concepts in other spheres are the principles whose internalization by the individual is the main task of molding in the spirit of acculturation. And so, according to this conception, instruction fulfills its social function when it advances the processes of molding individuals in the spirit of the values of a given culture.

*It follows from what has been said in an earlier chapter about classes and elites, that education should help to preserve the class and to select the elite. * It is right that the exceptional individual should have the opportunity to elevate himself in the social scale and attain a position in which he can exercise his talents to the greatest benefit of himself and of society. But the ideal of an educational system which would automatically sort out everyone according to his native capacities is unattainable in practice; and if we made it our chief aim, would disorganise society and debase education. It would disorganise society, by substituting for classes, elites of brains, or perhaps only of sharp wits. Any educational system aiming at a complete adjustment between education and society will tend both to restrict education to what will lead to success in the world, and to restrict success in the world to those persons who have been good pupils of the system. The prospect of a society ruled and directed only by those who have passed certain*

*From Notes toward the Definition of Culture, pp. 100-101, 104-105, Copyright, 1949, by T. S. Eliot. Reprinted by permission of Harcourt Brace Jovanovich, Inc.

examinations or satisfied tests devised by psychologists is not reassuring: while it might give scope to talents hitherto obscured, it would probably obscure others, and reduce to impotence some who should have rendered high service. Furthermore, the ideal of a uniform system such that no one capable of receiving higher education could fail to get it, leads impercep- tibly to the education of too many people, and consequently to the lowering of standards to whatever this swollen number of candidates is able to reach
. . . .

Besides the motive of giving everyone as much education as possible, be- cause education is in itself desirable, there are other motives affecting edu- cational legislation: motives which may be praiseworthy, or which simply recognise the inevitable, and which we need mention here only as a reminder of the complexity of the legislative problem. One motive, for in- stance, for raising the age-limit of compulsory schooling, is the laudable desire to protect the adolescent, and fortify him against the more degrading influences to which he is exposed on entering the ranks of industry. We should be candid about such a motive; and instead of affirming what is to be doubted, that everyone will profit by as many years of tuition as we can give him, admit that the conditions of life in modern industrial society are so deplorable, and the moral restraints so weak, that we must prolong the schooling of young people simply because we are at our wits' end to know what to do to save them. Instead of congratulating ourselves on our prog- ress, whenever the school assumes another responsibility hitherto left to parents, we might do better to admit that we have arrived at a stage of civil- isation at which the family is irresponsible, or incompetent, or helpless; at which parents cannot be expected to train their children properly; at which many parents cannot afford to feed them properly, and would not know how, even if they had the means; and that education must step in and make the best of a bad job. Mr. D. R. Hardman observed that: "The age of indus- trialism and democracy had brought to an end most of the great cultural traditions of Europe, and not least that of architecture. In the contemporary world, in which the majority were half-educated and many not even a quarter-educated, and in which large fortunes and enormous power could be obtained by exploiting ignorance and appetite, there was a vast cultural breakdown which stretched from America to Europe and from Europe to the East." This is true, though there are a few inferences which might be im- properly drawn. The exploitation of ignorance and appetite is not an activi- ty only of commercial adventurers making large fortunes: it can be pursued more thoroughly and on a larger scale by governments. The cultural break-down is not a kind of infection which began in America, spread to Europe, and from Europe has contaminated the East: (Mr. Hardman may not have meant that, but his words might be so interpreted). But what is important is to remember that "half-educated" is a modern phenomenon. In earlier ages the majority could not be said to have been "half-educated" or less: people had the education necessary for the functions they were called upon to perform. It would be incorrect to refer to a member of a primitive society, or to a skilled agricultural labourer in any age, as half-educated or quarter-educated or educated to any smaller fraction. Education in the modern sense implies a disintegrated society, in which it has come to be assumed that there must be one measure of education according to which everyone is educated simply more or less. Hence Education has become an abstraction.

3.3   Individuation

The "principle of individuation" has been defined as a process of "breaking up the general into the particular, into single beings or individuals."[16] The current meaning of this concept in psychological circles corresponds closely to that of the concept of self-actualization. Individuation is the process by which the individual actualizes his own unique personality and crystallizes his own particular identity. According to Maslow it is this drive to actualization which defines human nature.

Man demonstrates *in his own nature* a pressure toward fuller and fuller Being, more and more perfect actualization of his humanness in exactly the same naturalistic, scientific sense that an acorn may be said to be "pressing toward" being an oak tree, or that a tiger can be observed to "push toward" being tigerish, or a horse toward being equine. Man is ultimately *not* molded or shaped into humanness or taught to be human. The role of the environment is ultimately to permit him or help him to actualize *his own* potentialities, not *its* potentialities. The environment does not give him potentialities and capacities; he *has* them in inchoate and embryonic form, just exactly as he has embryonic arms and legs. And creativeness, spontaneity, selfhood, authenticity, caring for others, being able to love, yearning for truth are embryonic potentialities belonging to his species-membership just as much as are his arms and legs and brain and eyes.

This is not in contradiction to the data already amassed which show clearly that living in a family and in a culture are absolutely necessary to *actualize* these psychological potentials that define humanness. Let us avoid this confusion. A mother or a culture does not create a human being. It does not implant within him the ability to love, or to be curious, or to philosophize, or to symbolize, or to be creative . . . .[17]

The basic assumption of individuation is that people do not become human by adapting themselves to social roles or by acquiring the culture of their environment. They do so by developing their innate capacities in interaction with their environment, which includes both society and culture. Self-actualization is individuation, the process by which individuals realize their own unique personalities. Not all societies have provided the right conditions for the individuation of their members. Fromm remarked: "The social history of man started with his emerging from a state of oneness with the natural world to an awareness of himself as an entity separate from surrounding nature and men. Yet this awareness remained very dim over long periods of history. The individual continued to be closely tied to the natural and social world around him. The growing process of the emergence of the individual from his original ties, a process which we may call individuation, seems to have reached its peak in modern history in the centuries between the Reformation and the present."[18]

The social significance of individuation is rooted in this conception of it as a historical process in which individual awareness and selfhood are continuously expanded. Individuation is the crystallization of individual personalities without which men can unite in herds, but not in societies. Anything preventing individuation is harmful to both the individual and society. A society composed of individuals whose development is flawed will always be a flawed society.

The difference between this approach and acculturation, which also sees the good society as a function of the characteristics of the individuals who compose it, is the difference between a person whose character has been molded according to a specific model and one who has developed according to the unique constellation of his own individual characteristics. From the point of view of individuation, acculturation is equivalent to the systematic distortion of human nature. According to the conception of acculturation, the individual acquires the characteristics of the "good man" by identifying with exemplary figures and the values they represent. According to the conception of individuation, these figures and their values are only a mask. Behind it hides the person whose real characteristics have been repressed. A society that compels its members to live behind masks is a repressive society. Repressed characteristics and drives find an outlet in violence, fanaticism, hatred, and similar phenomena, which are the result of the repression carried out by society's ideal of the "good man." Individuation's ideal, on the other hand, is the man who "accepts himself — who acknowledges his true feelings and his weaknesses and limitations and who dares to realize his capacities and satisfy his drives. It is assumed that a society built by such people will be a healthy society, a society whose members acknowledge the existence of others and their right to be different.[19]

The relation between the individual, who possesses a sense of his own uniqueness, and society, which exerts pressure to level out individual differences and impose conformity, is complex and problematic. There are two opposing approaches to the problem. One sees the relationship between the individual and society as inherently contradictory. Freud, for example, wrote: "every individual is inherently an enemy of culture which is nevertheless ostensibly an object of universal human concern. It is remarkable that little as men are able to exist in isolation they should yet feel as a heavy burden the sacrifices that culture expects of them in order that a communal existence may be possible."[20] Herbert Read has developed this idea in a psychoanalytical spirit:

> The individual has, of course, always stood in opposition to the group — to the family group, the environmental group, the tribe, and the nation. All psychologists agree that most if not all of the individual's troubles come from maladjustment to one or more of these groups. . . .
> In one direction an extreme maladjustment leads to complete alienation and narcissism; in the opposite direction to loss of identity and participation in various forms of mass hysteria. The ideal to be achieved is not so much an uneasy balance between these two tendencies as the achievement of a separate indivisible unity or "whole" with firm foundations in education and creative activity.[21]

According to this approach, the purpose of activities that support individuation is to enable the individual to live in society and culture without losing his individuality and sense of identity. The survival of society and culture is guaranteed by the fact that people have to live in communities. Communal existence is likely to do profound harm to individual well-being. Education must, therefore, strive for individuation and arm the individual against the harmful influences of society by strengthening his selfhood.

The second approach to the possible relations between society and the individual is more optimistic. Maslow states this approach: "We can now reject, as a localism, the almost universal mistake that the interests of the individual and of society are *of necessity* mutually exclusive and antagonistic, or that civilization is primarily a mechanism for controlling and policing human instinctoid impulses. All these age-old axioms are swept away by the new possibility of defining the main function of a healthy culture and of each of its institutions as the fostering of universal self-actualization."[22]

Maslow's optimism does not stem from an analysis of society as it exists, but from the assumption that a "healthy culture" is possible. Such a culture, if it came into existence, would be recognizable by the fact that it fostered the self-actualization of its members or, in other words, their individuation.

In existing societies (and, many feel, in any society) the pressures exerted on the individual by society are hostile to development, impairing his chances to be emotionally and mentally mature. A. Neumann has described these pressures: "A large part of education will always be devoted to the formation of a persona, which will make the individual 'clean about the house' and socially presentable, and will teach him, not what is, but what may be regarded as, real; all human societies are at all times far more interested in instructing their members in the techniques of not looking, of overlooking and of looking the other way than in sharpening their observation, increasing their alertness and fostering their love of truth."[23]

Education as a process supporting individuation, in the spirit proposed by Neumann, aims at counteracting the pressures that society exerts on the individual in order to "tame" him. This support is a condition for individual self-actualization. Insofar as instruction is concerned, it means preventing rigid adherence to models and stereotypes and the automation of responses and promoting flexibility, openness, originality, and creativity.

This conception inevitably opposes education according to models of social roles (socialization) or according to models of cultural values and ideals (acculturation). For despite their differences, both of these approaches mold human characteristics; they ensure fixed responses that eventually produce the preferred personality model in a given society or culture. Individuation rejects the principle of molding and the ready-made models of behavior available in any given society. All conceptions founded on the idea of molding must have some final image of an educated person, one of whose characteristics is resistance to change. Any change in an ideal personality is of necessity a deviation from the ideal. Individuation, on the other hand, sees education as a process that has no final or ultimate aim. Individuation is not a striving for a certain product, but a principle directing a process — the process of individual self-realization. Since this process continues for as long as the individual lives, it can have no final point at which the aims of the process have been realized.

Individuation on the one hand and socialization and acculturation on the other are at opposite poles in the spectrum of ideas and theories about education. While the latter two regard the individual as no more than the product of social or cultural factors, the former insists on regarding the human personality, despite its dependence on its environment, as a unique phenomenon. In instruction, individuation emphasizes intrinsic aims and allows them to control extrinsic ones. Thus, whenever extrinsic aims (the contents of knowledge, the disciplines, conventional and accepted ways of behaving, and so on) conflict with intrinsic aims (self-actualization), the latter take priority. In this conception of instruction, the desired achievements are defined as "the ability to discover new principles and test them." This ability is not a specific aptitude; it is a general human capacity exhibited by healthy personalities.

The social significance of instruction in the spirit of individuation is thus twofold. First, it means counteracting the distorting pressures exerted by society on the individual. Second, it means liberating his unique potentialities. If instruction fulfills these two functions, then in the long run it will contribute to social life. It is not, however, the social life that exists in repressive societies. It is that of a society that satisfies the needs of its individual members without forcing them to surrender their selfhood and individual differences.

39. From this point of view, a society or a culture can be either growth-fostering or growth-inhibiting. * *The sources of growth and of humanness are essentially within the human person and are not created or invented by society, which can only help or hinder the development of humanness, just as a gardener can help or hinder the growth of a rosebush, but cannot determine that it shall be an oak tree. This is true even though we know that a culture is a* sine qua non *for the actualization of humanness itself, e.g.,*

---

* A. H. Maslow, *Toward a Psychology of Being*, pp. 211 – 213, © 1971, reprinted by permission of D. Van Nostrand Company.

language, abstract thought, ability to love; but these exist as potentialities in human germ plasm prior to culture.

This makes theoretically possible a comparative sociology, transcending and including cultural relativity. The "better" culture gratifies all basic human needs and permits self-actualization. The "poorer" cultures do not. The same is true for education. To the extent that it fosters growth toward self-actualization, it is "good" education.

As soon as we speak of "good" or "bad" cultures, and take them as means rather than as ends, the concept of "adjustment" comes into question. We must ask, "What kind of culture or subculture is the 'well adjusted' person well adjusted to?" Adjustment is, very definitely, not necessarily synonymous with psychological health.

40. The achievement of self-actualization (in the sense of autonomy) paradoxically makes more possible the transcendence of self, and of self-consciousness and of selfishness. It makes it easier for the person to be homonous, i.e., to merge himself as a part in a larger whole than himself . . . . The condition of the fullest homonomy is full autonomy, and to some extent, vice versa, one can attain to autonomy only via successful homonomous experiences (child dependence, B-love, care for others, etc.). It is necessary to speak of levels of homonomy (more and more mature), and to differentiate a "low homonomy" (of fear, weakness, and regression) from a "high homonomy" (of courage and full, self-confident autonomy), a "low Nirvana" from a "high Nirvana," union downward from union upward. . . .

41. An important existential problem is posed by the fact that self- actualizing persons (and all people in their peak-experiences) occasionally live out-of-time and out-of-the-world (atemporal and aspatial) even though mostly they must live in the outer world. Living in the inner psychic world (which is ruled by psychic laws and not by the laws of outer-reality), i.e., the world of experience, of emotion, of wishes and fears and hopes, of love, of peotry, art, and fantasy, is different from living in and adapting to the non-psychic reality which runs by laws he never made and which are not essential to his nature even though he has to live by them. (He could, after all, live in other kinds of worlds, as any science fiction fan knows.) The person who is not afraid of this inner, psychic world, can enjoy it to such an extent that it may be called Heaven by contrast with the more effortful, fatiguing, externally responsible world of "reality," of striving and coping, of right and wrong, of truth and falsehood. This is true even though the healthier person can also adapt more easily and enjoyably to the "real" world, and has better "reality testing," i.e., doesn't confuse it with his inner psychic world.

It seems clear now that confusing these inner and outer realities, or having either closed off from experience, is highly pathological. The healthy person is able to integrate them both into his life and therefore has to give up neither, being able to go back and forth voluntarily. The difference is the same as the one between the person who can visit the slums and the one who is forced to live there always. (Either world is a slum if one can't leave it.) Then, paradoxically, that which was sick and pathological and the "lowest" becomes part of the healthiest and "highest" aspect of human nature. Slipping into "craziness" is frightening only for those who are not fully confident of their sanity. Education must help the person to live in both worlds.

Fourth Dimension
Learner

The elements in the process of instruction are the learner, the teaching contents, and the teacher. The conception of the nature of instruction determines the status of each of these elements in teaching situations. In the organization of instruction, metaphysical conceptions of the three elements are translated into patterns of activity that determine their status. The status of the learner is, on the one hand, an expression of beliefs and opinions regarding the nature of man, especially of man in a state of becoming, and, on the other hand, a way of organizing situations that determine what the pupil does and how the teachers behave toward him. The most prevalent way of organizing teaching situations is the class.

For many years teaching was interpreted as the art of leading a class in which the individual learned along with other individuals. This interpretation gave rise to many methods that enabled one teacher to instruct a group of children simultaneously. Because of this approach, compulsory education laws were extended to encompass children from all strata of society and to be in effect for a steadily increasing number of years. In addition, this conception transformed the class into the basic framework of instruction, formal instruction into its basic method, and group concepts into the basic concepts of theories and teaching. Thus the status of the learner was determined in advance as a result of his membership in a certain group (the first or second grade; gifted, average, or backward; scientific or humanist; academic or vocational). The status of the learner is also determined by the image of the group as a group and by the image of the specific group of which he is a member.

The class as a peer group is likely to perform many functions in the life of the individual pupil. Some of these functions play a decisive and unique role in his development; no other institution can perform them. Learning, however, is not one of them. Learning is always an individual process (which may, of course, be either supported or interfered with by factors stemming from the learner's experience as a member of a group). Justification for the experiments carried out in generation after generation to establish methods for group learning stemmed from the limited possibilities available to the school. The manpower released by society for the purpose of instruction was too limited and the level of technological achievement was too low to enable the school to think in any terms other than those of group instruction. Since group instruction was, in fact, the only practical possibility, various attempts were made to overcome its inherent disadvantages. Tracking, grouping homogeneous classes, and other similar solutions were proposed to resolve the contradiction between the necessity of maintaining the class as the basic framework of teaching and the fact that learning is and always will be an individual process. Only recently, owing to the readiness of society to place greater resources at the disposal of the school and to technological developments that made it possible for some of the teacher's functions to be taken over by machines, have new possibilities of resolving the contradiction between the administrative needs of the school and the learning needs of the pupil been opened up. The essence of these new possibilities lies in their ability to promote the individuation of instruction, to organize it according to the needs of the individual pupil.

Possible conceptions of the status of the pupil may therefore be located on a continuum with the class determining the nature of instruction on one end and the individual on the other. The following classification represents three points on this continuum:

4.1. The pupil as a member of a homogeneous group.

4.2. The pupil as a member of a heterogeneous group.

4.3. The pupil as a unique individual.

4.1   Homogeneous Group Member

In educational literature the term "homogeneous group" indicates a
way of organizing pupils into groups on the basis of certain criteria:
age, intelligence level, and so forth. When the pupil is a member of a
homogeneous group, his way of learning is regarded as resembling the
way of learning of the other members of the group. This conception of
instruction justifies the elevation of group methods. In these methods
the teacher's behavior is directed toward all pupils and is intended to
arouse learning in each of them. Individual differences among pupils
are occasionally ignored when these methods are employed. The conception is sustained, however, by a view that, while recognizing individual differences, attempts on various grounds to deny their validity
as an influential factor in teaching. One of these grounds is that the
common denominator among pupils with similar characteristics (age
or intelligence, for example) is more significant than their individual
differences. This common denominator is the basis on which one
method of instruction can be established. According to this method
the status of the learner corresponds to that of a member of a homogeneous group when the aims and means decided upon for him are the
same as those decided upon for all the other members of the group.
Difference is taken into account by organizing the pupils into groups
on the basis of characteristics relevant to learning: gifted, average, or
backward; normal or disturbed. Once organized in this way, the
group is regarded as homogeneous. Justification exists, therefore, for
one kind of aim and one kind of means as appropriate for all its members. The status of the pupil is determined by the group into which he
has been placed. Once he has been placed in such a group, his individual characteristics have no influence on the nature of instruction.

In the above context the status of the pupil is an expression of the
attitudes directing his educators. The pupil who is conceived of as a
member of a homogeneous group need not, in practice, be a member
of such a group or, indeed, of any group at all. A pupil may, in fact,
be assigned this status even when he is being taught alone. This is true
if the teacher decides upon his course of action on the basis of his
stereotype of a pupil as part of a certain group. Programmed instruction is the classic example of teaching that conceives of the pupil as a
member of a homogeneous group where no such group exists in prac-

tice. These programs (especially linear programs) rest on the assumption that all those who will learn from them possess exactly the same ways of learning, with the exception of their rate of learning—a distinction between pupils made possible by programmed instruction.* Another example is the frontal method of instruction. By this method, teachers behave as if all their pupils were the same. Thus, they transform classes that are heterogeneous from every point of view into homogeneous classes. Instruction of this type is made possible by the teacher's neglect of pupils at both ends of the spectrum and his exclusive concentration on the ones in the middle—the average pupils in the class.

Adopting the principle of homogeneity in grouping pupils seems, superficially, to be a step in the direction of accounting for individual differences. Because it is impossible to consider all pupils' characteristics simultaneously, the students must be grouped according to their common characteristics. Thus, the method of instruction employed in such a group will be appropriate for all the pupils since they will all be the same. The problem is that pupils are not all the same, even in homogeneous classes. Despite the admirable intentions of this system and all of its achievements, there is at least one extremely negative result: teachers in such classes tend to ignore the differences among their pupils more easily than they would otherwise do.

The fact that instruction of this type may produce results in the form of pupils' achievements does not necessarily confirm the assumption that the pupil in such a group learns in the same way as his classmates do. All it confirms is that by means of these methods he learns to be a member of a homogeneous group. This is an illustration of the contention that the medium is the message, or, in other words, that the method is the content of instruction. By means of this method, and not just by means of its contents, the pupil learns to respond to extrinsic aims. He learns to adapt himself to the group norms, and that faithful repetition of behaviors produces rewards. This type of learning conforms to the conception of instruction as socialization in the

---

*In this connection, see Piaget: "these machines [teaching machines] have performed at least one great service for us, which is to demonstrate beyond all possible doubt the mechanical character of the schoolmaster's function as it is conceived by traditional teaching methods; if the ideal of that method is merely to elicit correct repetition of what has been correctly transmitted, then it goes without saying that a machine can fulfill these conditions correctly." (Jean Piaget, *Science of Education and the Psychology of the Child* [New York: Viking Press, 1971], p. 77.)

sense that socialization has been understood by the school since its inception.

Seeing the pupil in collective terms—as a member of a group who is the same as all the other members—tends to dominate every facet of teaching. Aims, means, ways of evaluating, forms of organization, preferred kinds of interests and activities, and all the other dimensions and characteristics of instruction will become uniform and standard for everyone.

. . . Starting at least at the beginning of the fifteenth century, the school population was divided into groups of equivalent capacity, but under the same master and in a single room (a transitional formula to which Italy remained faithful for a long time). Then, in the course of the fifteenth century, a particular master was allotted to each of these groups, though they were still kept within the same four walls, an arrangement which was still to be found in England in the second half of the nineteenth century. Finally, on an initiative originating in Flanders and Paris, the classes and their masters were isolated in special rooms, which resulted in the present-day structure of the class. We have here a change corresponding to a desire, new as yet, to adapt the master's teaching to the student's level. The desire to bring education within the pupil's understanding was in direct opposition not only to the medieval methods of simultaneity or repetition, but also to humanist pedagogy which made no distinction between child and man and confused schooling (a preparation for life) and culture (an acquisition from life). The separation of the classes therefore revealed a realization of the special nature of childhood or youth and of the idea that within that childhood or youth a variety of categories existed. The creation of the hierarchized college in the fourteenth century had rescued school children from the hotchpotch in which, in the outside world, the ages were mixed up. The institution of classes in the sixteenth century established subdivisions within that school population.*

What then were these categories, roughed out sometimes for reasons of expediency, which at first bore no relation to what would later be expected from them in the way of order, discipline and educational capacity? Were they age groups? Admittedly Baduel in 1538 saw in this system a means of sharing out pupils according to "their age and development." In the same period Thomas Platter, at the end of a vagabond youth, went to a Schlestadt school which was attended by one hundred discipuli *at once. He already considered it not entirely normal that his ignorance should thrust him at the age of eighteen among a lot of children: he felt the need to record the incident as an anomaly—"When I entered the school, I knew nothing, I could not even read Donat, yet I was eighteen years old. I took my place in the midst of the little children, like a hen in the midst of her chickens."*

However, we should beware of being misled by isolated anecdotes. Age and development sometimes but not always coincided, and when they did not, people were only slightly surprised, often not at all. They still paid much greater attention to development than to age. At the beginning of the seventeenth century, the class had not yet attained the demographic homogeneity which it has possessed ever since the end of the nineteenth century although it was constantly drawing nearer to that homogeneity. School classes had come into existence to separate students according to their capacities and the difficulty of the subject-matter, not to separate students according to their ages. The new penchant for analysis and division—which characterized the birth of modern consciousness in its most intellectual zone, namely pedagogics—inspired in its turn further distinctions and divisions. The desire to separate the ages was only gradually recognized, and separation asserted as a principle, when separation had already been established in practice after lengthy empirical experiments. And this leads us to make a closer study of school children's ages and their relation to the class structure.

4.2 Heterogeneous Group Member

The conception of the pupil as a member of a heterogeneous group stems from two assumptions. One asserts that he is a member of a group; the other contends that, despite his membership in the group, he differs, to some extent at least, from the other members. This conception is an attempt to bridge two trends, each of which is implicit in one of the two assumptions. The first trend responds to individual differences between pupils as factors that influence their learning. The second maintains the group as the learning framework either for reasons of principle—education by the group for life in society or for practical reasons—or for the necessity of organizing pupils in groups because of limited teaching and financial resources.

These two assumptions and the tendencies implicit in them are both apparent in the concept of instruction that they dictate: while the group continues to be the framework in which teaching is conducted, the methods of instruction provide for some degree of adaptation to the characteristics of individual pupils. Since the conception of the pupil as a member of a heterogeneous group is a factor influencing the style of instruction, this definition of the status of the pupil is not dependent on whether he is actually learning in a heterogeneous group, a homogeneous group, or no group at all. His status will be that of a member of a heterogeneous group when his individual characteristics are considered factors in the process of instruction so long as they do not interfere with aims derived from the group or with collective tendencies of instruction.

A distinction should be made between the meaning ascribed to the term "heterogeneous class" and the meaning derived from the definition of the status of the pupil as a member of a heterogeneous class. A heterogeneous class contains pupils who differ from one another in such areas as their levels of intelligence and achievement. Since the methods of instruction in schools are group methods—based on a uniform set of activities directed equally toward all the children in the class—heterogeneous grouping is regarded as an obstacle in the way of successful teaching. Thus, there is the recurrent tendency to homogenize classes. The high incidence of failure in heterogeneous classes strengthens the tendency toward homogeneous grouping. When it is determined that this system, in turn, does not accomplish the desired results, the educational administration returns once more to heterogeneous classes. No system of grouping can abolish individual differences among pupils. When the method of instruction — whatever it is — is based on a uniform set of activities directed toward all pupils in the group, it induces learning only among those few pupils whose needs the particular activities happen to suit. Homogeneous grouping attempts to solve a problem that does not stem from the individual differences among pupils, but from the illusion that there is any one set of activities capable of meeting the needs of all members of the group. When teachers recognize the heterogeneous nature of the group (and no group can actually be otherwise than heterogeneous), they approach a correct appraisal of the situation in which they must act. Thus, their chances of acting in a way that will meet the needs of their pupils are greater. The definition of the status of the pupil as a member of a heterogeneous group is, therefore, more relevant to the needs of instruction than the definition of the pupil as a member of a homogeneous group.

Considering the pupil a member of a heterogeneous group implies an intention to individualize instruction. This tendency applies, however, only to the means of instruction, not to its aims. The aims are collective: they apply equally to all members of the group. Individualization attempts to adapt its means to the needs and characteristics of individual pupils. Recognition of the necessity to adapt the means of instruction to individual needs leads to a more flexible attitude toward techniques of instruction, contents of curricula, and the organization of the school. Independent learning is the most characteristic technique used to individualize instruction. This technique enables individual pupils to learn at their own pace, level of development, and standard of previous achievements. In the field of curricula planning the tendency toward individualization is apparent in the fact that alternative programs are offered for teaching the same contents. As a result of individualization, the rigid organization of the school into classes is gradually being weakened, and there are now subdivisions within the class, interclass groupings for various projects, and other similar arrangements.

Even the advocates of this approach question the extent to which these arrangements can apply to the means of instruction without affecting its aims. The way this question is answered will determine both the extent to which the means of instruction are adapted to suit the learning requirements of the individual pupil and the nature of the adaptation. At one extreme of the range of opinion on this matter is an approach that permits manipulation of the teaching contents on condition that these contents are learned by all pupils as a result of the manipulation. At the other extreme is an approach that substitutes contents in accordance with the needs, characteristics, and interests of the individual pupil. The assumption underlying the latter approach is that it is possible to influence individual development only by means of contents that conform to the needs of individual personality structures.[24]

Generalizations derived from psychological research on personality structure sustain the conception of the learner as a member of a heterogeneous group. This approach, which stresses the differences among people, gave rise to paedocentric methods in education and instruction. At the same time, however, the approach that defines the status of the learner as a member of a heterogeneous group does not necessarily involve a paedocentric point of view. The view that places culture at the center of the educational process may adopt this approach equally well. The acquisition of culture means the internalization of values, patterns of thinking, and ways of behaving. Processes of internalization are influenced by individual characteristics; once this is recognized, the acknowledgment of individual differences among pupils and the organization of instruction must inevitably follow. Thus, the view of culture at the center of the educational process approaches paedocentrism insofar as the status of the learner in the process of instruction is concerned.[25]

The conception of the learner as a member of a heterogeneous group is characteristic of the pattern of molding in education and instruction. Molding is conceived of as a means of acculturation, a way of ensuring the internalization of cultural values and contents. This internalization necessitates a respect for individual differences among pupils. The basic assumption underlying the pattern of imitation is that pupils have more common than distinguishing characteristics. The pattern of molding begins with the assumption that pupils differ from one another; it is, therefore, the function of this process to establish common cultural characteristics in its pupils. Individual differences among pupils must be taken into account, if only at the initial stages of the educational process; this is expressed by the view that the pupil is a member of a heterogeneous group.

If the purpose of education be to impart an understanding of life, the point of orientation will necessarily be the life of the immediate vicinity.* Communities vary in language, in historical background and traditions, in industrial, economic, and climatic conditions; and these differences may warrant corresponding differences in the subject matter of the curriculum. Differences of this sort, as well as differences in the capacities and talents of the pupils, must be taken into account, but none of these differences should be made an excuse for overlooking the fact that we are, first of all, members of the human race.

In this connection, I wish to hazard the suggestion that the doctrine of individual differences has been greatly abused. There are, undoubtedly, all sorts of differences among human beings, but these differences do not justify the construction of water-tight compartments in the curriculum. In our reaction against the rigidity of the past we have been far too ready to introduce new courses for the purpose of accommodating every shade of interest. Individual differences should serve first of all to give a new meaning to the teaching of fundamental subjects. The fundamental subjects in the curriculum are fundamental because they are so intricately interwoven with the life outside of the schools. Consequently it is possible, in teaching these subjects, to make appeal to a wide variety of interests. A course in history, for example, may attract one student through its dramatic appeal, a second through curiosity about origins and causes, and a third through the love of excitement and adventure. All this is grist for the teacher's mill. The means may be various, though the end is one. However wide the range of interests that are enlisted, the result in every case may be both a taste for logical organization and a gain in insight into the meaning of present-day institutions and practices, with a corresponding gain in the power to cooperate with others in matters pertaining to the improvement of human living.

4.3 Unique Individual

Although the definition of the status of the pupil as a unique individual is only a further development of the previous definition, it nevertheless involves a different conception of the process of instruction. This conception does not regard the group as a framework that is justified in terms of the aims of instruction. (In instruction conceived

*Boyd H. Bode, *Modern Educational Theories* (New York: Vintage Books, 1927), pp. 305 – 306.

of as socialization, the group symbolizes the aim, which is society. In instruction conceived of as acculturation, the group serves to educate in the aims of culture considered as a collective.) The group is thus regarded as a means at the very most and, even then, as a means to be used only in specific situations. That instruction may require the framework of the group on specific occasions does not imply that members of the group have enough in common to learn by one method, or even to learn together. Every pupil is regarded as unique, as distinct from every other pupil. This definition of the pupil does not deny the validity of such group concepts as gifted, average, borderline, stable, and disturbed. It merely confirms that the combination of such personality traits will always be unique. As a result of this, the individual belongs to a great many groups at the same time without belonging to any one of them exclusively. It is the learner's unique combination of personality traits that influences the processes of learning, and not the isolated characteristics that exist only as abstractions created to meet the needs of psychological research. The pupil who is the object of instruction is not an abstraction; he is a concrete individual who differs in every respect from his fellow pupils.

Considering the pupil a unique individual need not necessarily involve a rejection of group situations in instruction. A number of schools structured on radical views of education stress the social life of their pupils while at the same time regarding their status in the learning process as that of unique individuals. In this case the group is the framework of the pupil's social life; the learning that stems from the social experience is expected to take place within it. But learning that stems from the interaction of the individual with other aspects of his environment, and is based on his interest, his motivation, and his thinking, is freed from the pressure of the group to which the individual belongs in order to gratify his social needs. The definition of the pupil as a unique individual is not based on a denial of his social needs, but on a rejection of the idea that these needs should motivate him to learn. It is also based on a rejection of the idea that there is any one set of activities by means of which different pupils can learn the same things, at the same time, in the same way, and in the hope of obtaining the same results.

This conception of the status of the pupil stems from an anthropological-philosophical view of human nature that was formulated by Herbert Read:

This diversity is not a biological accident. It is the dialectical basis of natural selection, of human evolution. Any attempt, therefore, whether by education or coercion, to eliminate the differences between persons would frustrate the natural dissemination and growth of the human race. It is possible and even "scientific" to hold that we should attempt to control this growth, just as we have controlled the growth of species like the horse and the sheep. But such control could only be effectively exercised if we had an agreed aim in view. We breed horses for strength or speed, sheep for a finer fleece. But it is a godlike assumption to breed the human race for any predetermined quality, and the idea has entered the minds of only totalitarian philosophers like Plato and Hegel, or been the policy of extreme fanatics who have attempted to put the ideals of such philosophers into practice.[26]

The conception of human nature presented here implies a criticism of the educational conceptions that seek to direct the individual's development. Such direction is interpreted as interference, which is antagonistic both to the nature of the individual and to the deeper interests of the human race, whose development depends on fostering the diversity of its individual members. The denial of individual differences, which are the most meaningful expressions of what is human in man, is inevitable in goal-directed education. Education of this kind means forcing human nature into predetermined molds as conceived in a given society or culture. But the true function of education is to enable new forms to emerge. When there is interference with development, a chance exists for the appearance of new forms.

The status of the pupil as conceived on the basis of this view of human nature and development justifies the subordination of all the other factors of instruction to his needs. In instruction of this kind there is no room for fixed curricula, stable techniques, or uniform organizational frameworks. All these factors must be flexible so that they can be adapted to his specific needs. The pupil is thus accorded first place among all the other elements in the process.

Fernwood was an effort by two dedicated teachers to translate concepts that were important to the author and to them (and that were basic as well to theories of self-actualization and intrinsic learning) into educational practice. Prior to beginning the venture the author talked for many hours with these teachers and then spent several weeks reading Third Force psychological literature to develop a statement of aims entitled "Beyond Curricu-

*E. M. Drews, "Fernwood," in *Radical School Reform,* ed. Beatrice and Ronald Gross (New York: Simon and Schuster, 1969), pp. 265 – 271. Used by permission of Professor Drews.

lum." (Dorris Lee, Professor of Education, Portland State College, was an inspiration to all of us in these early stages. Later she served as our consultant.) The major emphases of this statement and selected happenings at Fernwood which illustrate "Beyond Curriculum" concepts follow:

"Item 1: Each individual is different. *The range of these differences extends far beyond the reach of textbook levels and the intelligence derived from testing. Each is unique as to rate, style, tempo, and pattern of learning. Each chooses his own values and interests and develops personal tastes. By honoring these directions of growth and allowing them to flourish naturally, we found that students could master what had been difficult topics and material and do this easily. As we have seen, a nonreader began to read without the pressure of applied methods and scheduled class periods. Students who habitually failed English found they could speak fluently and well when they could talk about something of interest rather than on an assigned topic. Just as the school came to a close, a boy who had been an indifferent mathematics student did four months' work in three days and ended up six weeks ahead of his former classmates. . . .*

"Item 7: Individual differences and unrealized potential dictated self-selection and individualized learning. *The freedom in Fernwood was such that students could learn in their own ways about things they wanted to know. Most of the suggestions about things to do came from the children, although the teachers did encourage them to visit the Portland Art Museum, the airport, and the zoo. Books were always available and new ones could be obtained on the weekly trips to the library. Some became so addicted to reading that parents complained. The mother of one of the girls was a chronic complainer—a woman of easy virtue who welcomed a variety of men into her home but felt her daughter's love of books showed an inability to focus on important matters.*

"As the young people became practiced in decision making, they learned to center their interests—a boy learned much about history by studying the strategies of Napoleon and Caesar and reenacting battles in a sand pile at home—and to widen their horizons—four girls decided to go to England and read the daily papers diligently searching for jobs for fourteen-year-olds. When they could not find work, they decided to become columnists and began writing a teen-age column which they sold to the local paper. Later a publisher of a Northwest teen-age paper 'discovered' their talent and one was asked to become his editor."

Fifth Dimension:
Contents

The contents of instruction are mainly the contents of knowledge. Its other contents include specific behaviors such as manners and cleanliness, and the accepted beliefs current in a given society. Epistemology asks the question "What is knowledge?" Psychology performs the same functions for the question "How is knowledge acquired?" In theories of instruction both of these questions are asked and answered from a different angle. Spencer formulated the didactic version of the first question over a hundred years ago: "What knowledge is of most worth?"[27] The didactic formulation of the second question is "What must the school (the teacher and the pupil) do in order for the pupil to acquire knowledge?" Different people at different times have answered in different ways the question of the educational value of knowledge. According to one criterion, the most valuable knowledge is that which enables the individual to solve the problems of the struggle for existence most efficiently. Another criterion assesses the value of knowledge according to its relation to the values that define human existence. Knowledge representing these values sustains the continuity of human existence; this is the source of its importance. Yet another criterion measures the value of knowledge by its latent possibilities for helping the individual to actualize his characteristics, capacities, and talents. These three criteria determine the nature of the school curriculum. Curriculum is the area in which epistemological choices (among various epistemological theories) and psychological choices (choices among various theories of learning) meet.

The status of knowledge in instruction thus results from a combination of decisions in favor of one of the possible answers to the questions "What knowledge is of most worth?" and "What kind of activities on the part of the teacher and the pupil are best calculated to promote the acquisition of knowledge?" No matter what the decisions are, they will be reflected in the organization of the curriculum. Curricula as such do not, however, constitute a fundamental problem in education. They can be changed without altering instruction, that is, without affecting the direction and mode of influence on the development of the individual pupil.

When, on the other hand, methods of instruction are changed, even if no corresponding change takes place in the curriculum, the status of knowledge is likely to change also. It is true that the patterns of instruction adopted in the school determine the kind of curriculum that will be preferred. If for any reason, however, the curriculum remains unchanged despite changes in the aims of instruction, the image of desired achievements, and the status of contents, a change will still take place in the way these contents are employed in the process of instruction; it is this change that determines what instruction will be like in practice. The status accorded the contents in the process of instruction is what actually determines their nature. Different types of instruction accord the contents of instruction one of three statuses derived from the following three conceptions:

5.1. The contents of instruction are utilitarian.

5.2. The contents of instruction have intrinsic value.

5.3. The contents of instruction are a means of developing the learner's capacities.

5.1   Utilitarian Contents

From the beginning, this conception has guided instruction, at least in part of its activities. When the instructor teaches his pupils to read or write, to do arithmetic or understand a map, he is teaching them to use their knowledge. When contents are taught in order to be used, what is actually learned is specific behaviors. When instruction is oriented by an image of knowledge as a set of contents meant to be used, its dominant style will be that of imparting skills. In this context the meaning ascribed to the concept of use is very wide. When knowledge of certain contents serves to distinguish the members of certain strata in society from others, then this knowledge is extremely useful to its possessor. A knowledge of the classics cannot be called a skill in the sense that reading and writing are skills, but, if the classics are meant to be a status symbol, then they are taught as if they were a skill. The teaching of skills is likely to be influenced by the lessons of experience. If the teaching of writing or driving is not producing lasting and rapid results, there is every reason to substitute an alternative method of instruction that provides greater prospects of success. This is not the case when literature, mathematics, or history are taught as if they were skills. Since the criterion that directs instruction of this type is use, and since the use of these subjects is ritualistic, the lessons of experience cannot influence the methods of instruction employed to teach them. The ritual status of these contents is expressed in an unwillingness to see them change in any way, not only in their interpretation but even in their organization, form, and sequence of instruction.

Whenever the use of knowledge is ritualistic — not controlled by experience — instruction will be conducted in a style characteristic of the teaching of skills. All instruction is a process by which the teacher builds a bridge between contents and pupils. When one of these factors is more rigid than the others, instruction becomes a process by which the less rigid factor is adapted to the more rigid one. If the contents are ritualistic, instruction must adapt the learner (and the teacher) to the contents.

All instruction is, in the final analysis, intended for use. It would be difficult indeed to justify the teaching of any contents that are useless to the learner or are unlikely to influence his behavior. But the utilitarian conception of the status of knowledge, or the teaching of contents because they are useful, is not identical with the conception of instruction as a process intended to develop the ability of the learner to use the contents of knowledge. The development of this ability must always involve manipulating the contents of knowledge, adapting them to the needs, possibilities, and level of development of the individual learner. A pupil must be trained to use any given contents at the level appropriate to his development. Training of this kind means processing the contents for pedagogic ends. If the contents are ritualistic, such processing is impossible. We are thus led to a seemingly paradoxical conclusion: when the contents of instruction are utilitarian, instruction will not lead to competence in their use, or not, at least, in a use based on individual mastery of the contents learned.

A pupil can be taught to calculate his father's salary and the amounts his mother spends at the market without being taught mathematics. He can be taught to read without becoming a reader. He can be given "useful" information about history and geography without learning what these subjects are about. When the school teaches utilitarian contents—when knowledge is regarded as a collection of useful items of information—the emphasis will be placed on making the pupil skilled in these specific uses, and not on imparting knowledge as such. Though the distinction between teaching the *uses of knowledge* and teaching *knowledge in order to use it* may seem academic, it is, nevertheless, real enough. A man may be a competent bookkeeper without being a mathematician, a competent navigator without being a geographer, or a competent vegetable farmer without being a botanist. Training for such occupational roles depends, to some extent, on mathematics, geography, and botany, but it does not involve mastering the contents of these subjects. And it certainly does not involve developing the capacities required to master them. If one is taught mathematics in order to budget his income or to perform his occupational role, it is not actually mathematics that is being taught but a limited selection of operations that may be derived from it.

A pupil taught mathematics in this way will be able to derive only those operations from it that he has been specifically taught. The teaching of the uses of knowledge is not identical with the teaching of knowledge in order to use it.

Though the above implies criticism, it is not intended as an outright rejection of this method of teaching. "General education," in which mathematics, history, literature, and all other subjects are taught for their own sake, does not meet all the demands of instruction. For example, the school is also required to teach its pupils elementary rules of personal hygiene. It would certainly be desirable for the pupil to come to the relevant conclusion about his personal hygiene from his study of biology. But it would be wasteful to teach a subject like biology in order to lead the pupil to a few conclusions concerning personal hygiene. The program of study in biology is determined by broader considerations. Thus, the most economical way to obtain results is simply to teach the pupil the desired habits in the field of personal hygiene without subordinating the entire biology curriculum to this end. When we tell a child to wash his hands before eating because it is healthful to do so, we are teaching a use of knowledge without teaching the knowledge itself. The teacher must always decide whether his aim is to teach the uses of a branch of knowledge or the knowledge itself.

To the question with which we set out—What knowledge is of most worth?—the uniform reply is—Science. This is the verdict on all the counts.* For direct self-preservation, or the maintenance of life and health, the all-important knowledge is—Science. For that indirect self-preservation, which we call gaining a livelihood, the knowledge of greatest value is— Science. For the due discharge of parental functions, the proper guidance is to be found only in—Science. For that interpretation of national life, past and present, without which the citizen cannot rightly regulate his conduct, the indispensable key is—Science. Alike for the most perfect production and highest enjoyment of art in all its forms, the needful preparation is still—Science. And for purposes of discipline—intellectual, moral, religious—the most efficient study is, once more—Science. The question which at first seemed so perplexed, has become, in the course of our inquiry, comparatively simple. We have not to estimate the degrees of importance of different orders of human activity, and different studies as severally fitting us for them; since we find that the study of Science, in its most comprehensive meaning, is the best preparation for all these orders of activity. We have not to decide between the claims of knowledge of great though conventional value, and knowledge of less though intrinsic value; seeing that the knowledge which we find to be of most value in all other respects, is intrinsically most valuable; its worth is not dependent upon opinion, but is as fixed as is the relation of man to the surrounding world. Necessary and eternal as are its truths, all Science concerns all mankind for all time. Equally at present, and in the remotest future, must it be of incalculable importance for the regulation of their conduct, that men should understand the science of life, physical, mental, and social; and that they should understand all other science as a key to the science of life . . . .

*Herbert Spencer, *Education: Intellectual, Moral and Physical* (New York: Appleton, *1929*), pp. 49 – 50.

One of the first and best-known specific definitions of the school's purposes was formulated in 1918 by the Commission on the Reorganization of Secondary Education.* The commission proposed for the schools a set of Seven Cardinal Objectives:

1. *health*
2. *command of fundamental processes*
3. *worthy home membership*
4. *vocational competence*
5. *effective citizenship*
6. *worthy use of leisure time*
7. *ethical character*

5.2. Intrinsically Valuable Contents

"Knowledge for its own sake" defines this conception of the status of the contents in instruction more by the associations it evokes than by its literal meaning. It stems from the humanist conception of man as a rational being whose actions are guided by the knowledge he acquires in the exercise of his intellectual faculties. Learning thus becomes identified with individual progress toward achieving the highest human good: the exercise of these faculties. Since, in this view, the learner is not expected to receive material benefits, it has no aims outside itself. Knowledge is not a means; it is its own reward. This conception of learning is usually limited to traditional and classical humanist education. Wisdom and virtue, noble feelings and imagination, reverence, loyalty, and other similar qualities are thought to be implicit in this knowledge, which, by being transmitted from one generation to the next, perpetuates human existence.

The metaphysical foundations of this approach are sounder than its didactic applications. Instruction based on it suffers from an internal contradiction. In many cases the pupil who is supposed to learn for the sake of learning is not willing or able to do so; he is, at any rate, not willing or able to learn the contents his teachers consider worth learning in this spirit. Education that advocates learning for its own sake is, therefore, unable to proceed in the spirit of its own cardinal principle and is forced to resort to other means.

Two ways are open to advocates of learning for its own sake. One way is compulsion. Contents considered worth learning for their own sake and whose transmission is regarded as essential to the continua-

**J. C. Stone and F. W. Schneider, *Foundations of Education* (New York: Thomas Y. Crowell, 1965) pp. 27-28.*

tion of human existence must be taught. It is advantageous if pupils are willing to learn them. If they are not, however, the school is not thereby relieved of its duty to teach them. On the contrary, pupils' unwillingness to learn contents that are essential to their own well-being only proves how necessary it is to teach them. This unwillingness is precisely what provides the teacher justification for compelling the students to learn them.[28]

The second way, which does not necessarily contradict the first and in many instances complements it, is to influence the pupil's willingness to learn. This may be done by manipulating the contents to be taught until they are attractive to the pupil. Knowledge that is worth knowing is usually found in books that are not appealing to the beginner. By selecting those portions that would interest the student and by presenting them in an attractive and readable way, the teacher will impart the essential knowledge to the pupil.[29]

Another way to promote the willingness of pupils to learn contents that are regarded as essential to their education is by making the students part of a community of scholars. In this type of instruction knowledge serves as a symbol identifying a group. For example, Latin for many generations in European schools, the Talmud among the Jews, foreign languages, especially in backward countries, and ancient literature in China were not only the contents of instruction; they were, at the same time, symbols of identification with certain groups in society. The student knew that by studying these contents he was preparing himself for membership in the group. In many instances, as a matter of fact, the original reason for learning the contents—their intrinsic value—was overshadowed by the second reason—learning them in order to be accepted as a member of a prestigious social group.

Both compelling the pupil to learn and overcoming his resistance in indirect ways contradict instructional assumptions that attribute intrinsic value to contents. In neither case is there learning for its own sake. It is vain to hope that learning that is not for its own sake at the beginning will become so at the end. This approach to instruction is far more likely to lead in one of the following directions. Some pupils may conclude that there is no such thing as learning for its own sake, but that hypocrisy can bring its own rewards. Successfully compelled or seduced into learning against his will, the pupil will realize that learning itself cannot possibly compensate him for his efforts, but that he will receive compensation in other forms, such as material rewards or enhanced prestige either in the present or the future. Other pupils may become compulsive learners. In this case the pupil internalizes the commands and blandishments of his teachers and/or parents so successfully that he will continue to be a "good pupil" for the rest of his life. His motivation is not a disinterested love of learning and a thirst for knowledge but a compulsive drive over which he has no control.

Because of its internal contradiction, this conception of the status of contents wavers between two poles. In some cases its advocates approach the previous conception, which implies an authoritarian attitude toward education, despite their rejection of the principle of utilitarianism on which it is based. In other cases they approach the second pole — creativity — where knowledge activates the capacities of the learner despite the fact that this conception contradicts their basic assumptions.*

In the previous approach the uses to which knowledge is put were accorded a ritual status; in this approach the attitude toward knowledge itself is ritualistic. Thus, certain contents are indispensable to education because they are indispensable to the continuation of human existence. Though new contents may be added to the totality of human knowledge during the course of time, none may be subtracted from it. Because of this approach, pupils over the generations have come into contact with the original works of important writers and thinkers. With the general recognition that knowledge taught in schools was valuable despite the fact that it could be put to immediate use, both the school and the teachers in it began to enjoy a certain measure of independence and autonomy. In the course of time they became factors working for the isolation of the school from society and created a separate world — "the world of the school." The idea that there are contents worth teaching for their own sake supported this process of isolating and detaching the school from the events taking place in its environment.

*This contradiction is apparent in the controversy that finally ended the progressive stream in education in America. See L. A. Cremin, *The Transformation of the School* (New York: Vintage Books, 1964), ch. 9.

The liberal disciplines are not chunks of frozen fact. * *They are not facts at all. They are the powerful tools and engines by which a man discovers and handles facts. Without the scientific and scholarly disciplines he is helpless in the presence of facts. With them he can command facts and make them serve his varied purposes. With them he can even transcend facts and deal as a rational man with the great questions of meaning and value.*

The scholarly and scientific disciplines won their primacy in traditional programs of education because they represent the most effective methods men have been able to devise, through millennia of sustained effort, for liberating and then organizing the powers of the human mind. It is nonsense to say that they occupy their position in intellectual life because some clique of men have agreed to confer an arbitrary prestige upon them. The reverse is true. It is the diciplines that have conferred prestige—and more than prestige, power—upon mankind.

Consider how the disciplines of science and learning came into being. The world enters the consciousness of the individual—and it first entered the consciousness of mankind—as a great tangle of confused perceptions. Before man could deal with it at all he had to differentiate one experience from another and to discover relationships among them: similarity and diversity, cause and effect, and the like. Gradually he discovered that one kind of relationship could best be investigated in one way (by controlled experiment, it may be), and another in another way (by the critical study of written records or of fossil remains, perhaps). Thus the separate disciplines were born, not out of arbitrary invention but out of evolving experience. The process of trial and error, prolonged over centuries, has resulted in the perfecting of these tools of investigation. The methods can be systematized and taught, hence the intellectual power that mankind has been accumulating throughout its entire history can be passed on to successive generations. Thereby each generation is enabled to master the new environment and to solve the new problems that confront it. This ability to face unprecedented situations by using the accumulated intellectual power of the race is mankind's most precious possession. And to transmit this power of disciplined thinking is the primary and inescapable responsibility of an educational system.

The disciplines represent the various ways man has discovered for achieving intellectual mastery and hence practical power over the various prob-

---

*From *The Restoration of Learning*, pp. 34 – 35, by Arthur Bestor. Copyright © 1955 by Arthur Bestor. Reprinted by permission of Alfred A. Knopf, Inc.

lems that confront him. He lives in a world of quantity and relationship, and he has put four thousand years of ingenuity into creating the mathematical tools by which he handles quantity and relationship. He knows that the wisdom of mankind has been set down in a multitude of languages, and he has cultivated the linguistic disciplines so that he may unlock this storehouse, and then add to it his own ideas, expressed with precision and vigor. He realizes that his present is influenced by his past, and he has therefore devised, through unremitting effort, the historical techniques which provide the maximum of reliable knowledge concerning this aspect of his environment. He works every day with matter, and he has subdued matter to his purposes by sorting out its various characteristics in his mind and eventually creating the sciences of physics and chemistry, which have grown more useful to him in proportion as they have grown more abstract and theoretical. There is nothing arbitrary or fortuitous in any of this. The older disciplines have emerged, and newer ones are emerging, as responses to man's imperious need for that wide-ranging yet accurate comprehension which means power—power over himself and over all things else.

5.3 Contents Supportive of the Learner's Capacities

The greater the importance of contents in instruction, the lesser the importance of the pupil in influencing instruction. Thus, in order for the pupil to become more important in the process of instruction—in order for his needs to be taken into account, his personality to be respected, and his individual ways of learning to influence the methods in which he is taught—it is essential for the contents of instruction to be demoted from the top of the scale of priorities. This occurs when contents are conceived of strictly as a means of serving the developmental needs of the learner.

All views of instruction assign contents a role in the development of the pupil. What distinguishes them from each other is the meaning they attribute to the concept of development. When contents are defined as "utilitarian," development is interpreted as a gradual acquisition of the ability to use these contents. A small child knows only how to read and write. When he grows older he is able to compose a letter and understand the contents of a newspaper. When he is still older he can write a detailed report. According to this view, the increased complexity of the uses to which the individual puts knowledge indicates the stage of development he has reached.

When contents are defined as "intrinsically valuable," development is interpreted as the gradual internalization of the principles according to which the human race has accumulated knowledge. At the beginning the pupil knows how to perform four arithmetical operations. If he develops properly, he arrives at an understanding of the principles of mathematics and an ability to operate with them in the appropriate circumstances. At first he knows only a few selected facts about the past. With satisfactory progress he acquires the ability to reason about the past on the basis of his study of historical facts. Development is measured by the individual's ability to draw on the structural foundations of knowledge and the principles underlying the various disciplines and to use them in his thinking. According to this conception, the crowning achievement of education is the individual's ability and willingness to engage in learning for its own sake.

The third approach sees contents as a means of supporting individual development. According to this conception, knowledge is regarded as a means of supporting the self-actualization of the pupil as a unique human being. The status of knowledge is, therefore, instrumental, and its role is that of fostering the development of the learner's individual characteristics, especially creativity, subjectivity, and self-awareness.

Creativity is regarded as a condition for individual well-being, and this well-being is considered the aim of existence.[30] The function of creativity is not to produce creative works, although it does ensure that such works will come into being. Creativity is a style of living that prevents life from becoming meaningless. Knowledge acts as a raw material with which and by means of which the individual activates his creative drives; by so activating them, he discovers meaning in his existence. In this conception it is not the laws according to which knowledge is organized that dictate individual behavior. It is the characteristics of the creative person that determine his manipulations of knowledge.

It is not difficult to identify the background of this approach. The rapid and continuing transformations in knowledge, the ever-increasing number of theories in various fields of inquiry, and the dynamism of modern science strengthened belief in an experimental attitude, intellectual daring, and nondependence on accepted conventions and authorities. These conditions made possible the growth and crystallization of a conception that emphasized the creative spirit of the individual rather than the time-honored principles transmitted from generation to generation.

Another factor that influenced the preference of creativity to competency was the identification of accumulated knowledge with culture, which was considered a repressive mechanism.[31] This conception of culture, derived from psychoanalysis, is one of the principles on which most radical theories of education are founded. These theories see creativity as the individual's reaction against culture, which is a combination of ready-made patterns of behavior and thought. According to this view, creativity means manipulating knowledge without submitting to the repressive mechanism of culture, which operates against the individual by means of organized knowledge.

This conception of instruction also seeks to foster subjectivity, which is what gives knowledge meaning. An individual who possesses a meaningless knowledge becomes dehumanized. He is transformed into a kind of vehicle bearing a load of knowledge for which he is not responsible. It is subjectivity that gives knowledge validity; truth can only be subjective.

The choice of subjectivity (acquiring, understanding, and imparting individual meaning to knowledge) is epistemological, and it is clearly influenced by existentialism.[32] But epistemological considerations are not the only factors supporting subjectivity as a desirable characteristic to be fostered in the learner by means of knowledge. In this conception of instruction, the assumption of subjectivity relieves the teacher of the necessity to manipulate his pupils. Any other assumption increases this necessity. When knowledge is regarded as useful or intrinsically valuable the teacher must "direct," "mold," and "structure" the minds of his pupils. Unless his activities are so directed, there can be no certainty that the pupil will acquire the knowledge. The moment the teacher recognizes subjectivity as the test of the validity of knowledge, the pupil becomes the "hard" factor in the process of instruction that must be manipulated as little as possible. In this case knowledge becomes the "soft" factor that allows manipulation. Knowledge is thus relieved of its authoritarian factor. Subjectivity places the pupil, not the knowledge, at the center of learning.

Self-awareness is another characteristic that the individual is expected to acquire in his interaction with knowledge. In this view the function of knowledge is to enable the individual to understand the world and himself. Rationalism is conceived of in Western culture as a basic value and as one of the justifications of instruction; knowledge is a means of enabling the individual to be rational. It is unfortunate, however, that rationalism often ends up as rationalization, a defense mechanism employed by the individual when he finds himself in situations where it would be disagreeable for him to face the facts as they really are. In this sense rationalization prevents the individual from being rational.

There are two ways in which an emphasis on intellectual development can harm the individual. In the first, his personality is distorted until he becomes an instrument of the knowledge he has acquired. An example of this is the scientist whose own existence has become part of the scientific apparatus with which he operates. Such a diminished life may be assessed as a necessary price for mankind to pay for discovering the secrets of nature. Many doubt, however, the value of achievements whose price is the distortion of human existence. The second danger inherent in intellectual development is even greater. People whose total experience has been intellectual — people who have lost the ability to use their emotions, their imagination, their instincts — may well be unable ultimately to function in the intellectual sphere either. The nonintellectual faculties must control the activities of the intellect. The usual mode of instruction employed in the school has deprived students of a readiness to rely on imagination, emotion, and other controls necessary to the proper functioning of the intellect.

Those who advocate instruction in terms of individual development interpret self-awareness in two ways. First, they consider it a mechanism intended to ensure the mental health of the individual. Psychoanalysis is the source of this interpretation; thus, by means of self-awareness, the individual lessens his need for suppression and repression and, ultimately, his dependence on defense mechanisms, including rationalization. Second, self-awareness is the basic characteristic of individuation and, as such, not a means but the aim of education. Self-awareness means here that the individual has arrived at a state of awareness of himself as a being distinct from the rest of the world, as a unique individual. In this sense self-awareness is a process of becoming separate and crystallizing an identity, the identity of an autonomous human being. Self-awareness also means acknowledging the implications of choice in human life — choosing among alternatives and knowing that choosing one means denying others. Self-awareness involves the acceptance of the limitations of human existence and the individual responsibility for choice. By means of self-awareness the individual also accepts reality with its limitations and responsibility for his actions within that reality.

In summary, knowledge as a means of acquiring individual capacities means that the pupil's interaction with it is intended to develop in him creativity as a way of life, subjectivity as a strategy for testing the validity of knowledge, and self-awareness as a way of attaining autonomy. All of these lead to self-regulation as the ultimate definition of the status of knowledge in this conception of instruction. Self- regulation involves a rejection of secondary motivations as a means of accelerating learning, a conception of learning as a result of the learner's interest in whatever he is learning, and a nonauthoritarian atmosphere as the only one in which the desired kind of learning can take place — a learning that liberates the pupil from his affects, his need for rationalizations, and his dependence on external authority. Self-regulation transforms instruction into a situation in which the interest and needs of the individual take priority over knowledge accumulated and organized by others.

The status of knowledge in this conception of instruction is thus instrumental. Knowledge is an instrument by means of which the pupil discovers who he is: the objective of this process of self-discovery is his self-actualization as a unique individual.

There are many ways of thinking, many ways of relating one's self to situations.* What is crucial for existential knowledge of the world, however, is the priority of consciousness, of existence. ("Sum ergo cogito": I am, therefore I think.) The thinker—or the subject—does not ask what he can know, but how he can know. He does not stand apart from the world, seen as object or substance; he tries first of all to become conscious of the way the world reveals itself to him in its lived concreteness. Not all knowledge, of course, is to be grasped immediately, in terms of what is "given" in experience; but, in order not to falsify his relationship to the world, the individual knower must begin with the disquieting consciousness of himself "in the midst of life."

*Maxine Green, *Existential Encounters for Teachers* (New York: Random House, 1967), p. 66.

To deny the importance of subjectivity in the process of transforming the world and history is naive and simplistic. * *It is to admit the impossible: a world without men. This objectivistic position is as ingenuous as that of subjectivism, which postulates men without a world. World and men do not exist apart from each other, they exist in constant interaction. Marx does not espouse such a dichotomy, nor does any other critical, realistic thinker. What Marx criticized and scientifically destroyed was not subjectivity, but subjectivism and psychologism. Just as objective social reality exists not by chance, but as the product of human action, so it is not transformed by chance. If men produce social reality (which in the "inversion of the praxis" turned back upon them and conditions them), then transforming that reality is an historical task, a task for men.*

In other words, you end up with a student-centered curriculum not because it is good for motivation but because you don't, in fact, have any other choice. †

There is no such thing as "subject matter" in the abstract. Subject matter exists in the minds of perceivers. And what each one thinks it is, is what it is. We have been acting in schools as if knowledge lies outside the learner, which is why we have the kinds of curricula, syllabi and texts we have. But knowledge, as Kelley points out, is whatever we know after we have learned. It is an outcome of perception and is as unique and subjective as any other perception. Thus, if you assume you are confronted by a "meaning maker" rather than an "empty bucket," you would quite logically stop the practice of preparing and using syllabi and texts which state exactly what knowledge is to be learned. You would certainly not expect that the "same" knowledge is to be learned by every student. Indeed, you would feel that such an occurrence would be most undesirable, even if possible, which it is not. You would resent "standardized" examinations which devalue, even denigrate, the uniqueness of each learner's perceptions. You would never be able to say what your class has learned, since there is no such thing as a class, only twenty-two or thirty-four or forty-three individual perceivers. Your entire system of evaluation would have to be scrapped. How would you know whose perceptions to value most, and whose least?

---

*Paulo Freire, *Pedagogy of the Oppressed* (New York: Herder and Herder, 1970), pp. 35 – 36.

†Neil Postman and Charles Weingartner, *Teaching as a Subversive Activity* (Harmondsworth, Eng.: Penguin Books, 1971), p. 95.

Sixth Dimension:
Teacher

In addition to the learner and the contents there is a third factor without which no teaching situation would be possible — the teacher. The teacher's characteristics are usually presented as if they were more important than the totality of all the other factors in the process of instruction. There is no doubt that the personal and professional characteristics of the teacher are extremely influential in instruction and determine its outcome to a considerable degree. But these characteristics are largely the result of the status possessed by the teacher in different systems of instruction and the role he plays in those systems. They are not the result of the social status of the teacher as it is reflected in the prestige he enjoys in relation to members of other professions although this is also undoubtedly a factor that influences instruction.

The status of the teacher varies from one system of instruction to another. Every theory envisages a certain type of teacher, whose characteristics, training, and behavior reflect the assumptions implicit in the theory. From this point of view, the status of teacher, though it varies, is an inherent attribute of instruction.

The connection in instruction between the teacher's status and his personality traits is twofold. On the one hand, status determines the population groups from which candidates for teaching are drawn. Since there is a connection between personality types and their social groups, the status of the teacher in instruction will determine to a great extent which personality types become teachers. On the other hand, the status accorded the teacher in the different systems of instruction influence his personality traits. Traits considered desirable are strengthened, and traits considered undesirable are weakened. Thus, for example, educational systems in which the teacher carries out the instructions of his superiors will attract individuals belonging to social strata whose members do not generally enjoy a wide range of occupational possibilities. If such educational systems esteem the teacher who can intimidate his pupils, the position is further restricted to those individuals with personality traits compatible with this particular role. Thus, the conception of the teacher's status in instruction functions as a kind of selection mechanism that determines both the social strata from which teachers will come (according to their group characteristics) and the people belonging to these strata who will be attracted to teaching (according to their individual characteristics).

Another factor determining the personality traits of teachers is adaptation to the demands of the role as it is defined and implemented in the particular educational system. Those who fail to adapt themselves to the role drop out of the system.[33] Thus, teachers are as much the product of instruction as the pupils they teach.

Not all kinds of teaching can be implemented by all teachers. (We are not referring here, of course, to the contents. The teacher's role is not defined by the possession of expert knowledge in teaching it.) Every way of teaching requires for its implementation a teacher who possesses characteristics appropriate to the particular system in use. An individual who teaches according to the pattern of imitation will differ as a person from his colleagues who teach according to the patterns of molding and development. A person can sometimes adapt himself to different styles of teaching but this adaptation always involves divergent characteristics.

The alternative conceptions of the status of the teacher in instruction are:

6.1. The teacher as an employee.

6.2. The teacher as a cultural agent.

6.3. The teacher as a specialist.

6.1 Teacher as an Employee

It is difficult to reconstruct the beginnings of teaching as a distinct occupation, but it is almost certain that the first teachers in this sense were hired domestics. Upper-class parents engaged people belonging to the lower classes who possessed some degree of education to teach their children. The kind of relationship that existed between these parents and teachers was to a large extent preserved even after the latter were no longer hired domestics. This relationship is comparable to that bewteen a craftsman and his customer. The customer orders the work and knows what he wants done. The craftsman must satisfy the customer. He may pride himself on his expert skill, which is the source of his prestige, but his status as an expert is confined strictly to the work he is commissioned to do. According to this definition, the status of the teacher was even less independent than that of the craftsman. The fact that his customers were once involved in the process of instruction as pupils made them believe that they were entitled to interfere with the way the teacher performed his job as well as dictating its aims.

In the course of time various kinds of public bodies — local authorities, charitable institutions, larger agencies of government — assumed the responsibility for engaging teachers. The principle, however, remained unchanged: the customer always knows what he wants and often interferes in order to see that his desires are satisfied. Indeed, the history of unionism among teachers may be seen as a struggle against this type of relationship. Despite the fact that the social status of the teacher has changed considerably since the days when he was a hired domestic, the tendency to regard his relation to his employers as that of a craftsman to his customers is still with us, to a greater or lesser extent.

This definition has a number of implications. One of them determines the social status of the teacher and his place on the scale of relative professional prestige. Although there is no doubt that a connection exists between the social status of the teacher and the way in which he performs his role, especially in relation to the selection of candidates for the profession, we shall not discuss that subject here. Our concern is with the status of the teacher in the process of instruction itself. When the teacher's role is similar to that of a craftsman, his status in the process of instruction will have a number of characteristic features.

The first of these features is paradoxical. The teacher whose authority and powers vis-à-vis the outside world — parents, community, and so forth—are severely limited has the right to exercise almost unlimited power over his pupils. The source of this power may lie in the fact that the teacher performs his role in this spirit only when instruction is conceived of as compelling the learner to learn. Thus, the teacher is expected to know how to exert his authority and overcome the resistance of the pupil to learning. It is also possible that the teacher adopts such measures because he is put in the position of having to prove the value of his services to his "customers." His success in exerting his authority in the classroom determines his value in his own eyes, in the eyes of his pupils, and in the eyes of those authorized to evaluate his services.

The teacher's power in this situation begins and ends with his unlimited authority over his pupils; in all other aspects of teaching he has almost no authority. Thus, he is not expected to determine the aims of instruction. In most cases he is not even expected to support them enthusiastically. It is sufficient for him to behave in accordance with them. In the area of means his authority is also severely limited. The means of instruction are transmitted to him either by tradition or by instructions he is expected to follow. Should he try to change any of the accepted practices of the school, he will have to convince his superiors that his changes have not caused deviations from what they consider desirable.

The limited authority of the teacher's role and its character as a service are expressed concretely in the nature of those to whom the teacher must submit. The people who appoint the teacher and supervise his work (when this is not done directly by parents) are generally representatives of the public. The authority of those who supervise and evaluate the teacher derives from the fact that they pay his salary. Their evaluations and judgments are usually guided by their own past experience as pupils and by their beliefs and opinions about teaching. These people need not have superior education, and they are certainly not expected to have any expert knowledge of education and instruction. This dependence of the teacher on the public has made it virtually impossible for a teaching profession governed by relevant considerations to come into being. Teachers thus operate on the basis of accepted conventions and change these conventions only when they are rejected by people outside the profession of teaching.

It is no wonder that educational systems that defined the teacher's role in this fashion attracted only those who hoped to escape an even lower social status than what they could expect as teachers. It is also no wonder that an occupation so conceived and so defined exposed for generations those who engaged in it to scorn and ridicule. This attitude has persisted, in fact, even though the status of the teacher has changed considerably.

The above describes the least professional type of teacher to be found in educational systems. He is not expected to be a specialist in any field of knowledge, and he is certainly not expected to be a specialist in education. What is demanded of him is to know what he has to teach and to know how to impose his authority on his pupils. Any positive characteristics or advantages he may possess are likely to get him into trouble. A teacher whose role is conceived of in these terms refrains from revealing any initiative, readiness to change his methods, or even signs of independent thought in the field of knowledge that he has been hired to impart.

Teacher Evaluation*

Teacher: Socrates

A. Personal Qualifications

Rating (high to low)   Comments

	1	2	3	4	5	
1. Personal appearance	☐	☐	☐	☐	☑	Dresses in an old sheet draped about his body
2. Self-confidence	☐	☐	☐	☐	☑	Not sure of himself—always asking questions
3. Use of English	☐	☐	☐	☑	☐	Speaks with a heavy Greek accent
4. Adaptability	☐	☐	☐	☐	☑	Prone to suicide by poison when under duress

B. Class Management

	1	2	3	4	5	
1. Organization	☐	☐	☐	☐	☑	Does not keep a seating chart
2. Room appearance	☐	☐	☐	☑	☐	Does not have eye-catching bulletin boards
3. Utilization of supplies	☑	☐	☐	☐	☐	Does not use supplies

C. Teacher-Pupil Relationships

	1	2	3	4	5	
1. Tact and consideration	☐	☐	☐	☐	☑	Places student in embarrassing situation by asking questions
2. Attitude of class	☐	☑	☐	☐	☐	Class is friendly

D. Techniques of Teaching

	1	2	3	4	5	
1. Daily preparation	☐	☐	☐	☐	☑	Does not keep daily lesson plans

*Saturday Review, July 21, 1962, p. 47.

2. Attention to course of study	☐	☐	☑	☐	☐	Quite flexible—allows students to wander to different topics
3. Knowledge of subject matter	☐	☐	☐	☐	☑	Does not know material—has to question pupils to gain knowledge

E. Professional Attitude

1. Professional ethics	☐	☐	☐	☐	☑	Does not belong to professional association or PTA
2. In-service training	☐	☐	☐	☐	☑	Complete failure here—has not even bothered to attend college
3. Parent relationships	☐	☐	☐	☐	☑	Needs to improve in this area —parents are trying to get rid of him

Recommendation: Does not have a place in Education. Should not be rehired.

6.2   Teacher as a Cultural Agent

The first profound change regarding the position of the teacher occurred when he was freed from his direct and complete dependence on his employers and was granted the status of an expert whose work could be evaluated and criticized only by other experts of a higher standing than himself. This change also involved molding the personalities of the young in relation to the values of their culture. Cultural values, according to this conception, are implicit in knowledge and by means of it are transmitted from one generation to the next. Only a teacher who specializes in at least one field of knowledge is capable of performing an educational role by imparting to the young the values inherent in his field of specialization. Therefore, only individuals considered cultured were found worthy in terms of this conception to supervise and cirticize the teacher's work. With this change in the definition of his role, the teacher was freed from the direct control of his pupils' parents and from their control of the public representatives who paid his salary. Public opinion continued to influence instruction, either by means of the beliefs and ideologies current in the culture or by means of political pressure groups. As soon as the teacher's status was defined as that of the agent and representative of the culture, however, the influence of parents and pressure groups was reduced. From then on he was protected, to some extent at least, by the fact that everyone who could read and write was entitled to evaluate his work.

Because of this definition of the teacher's role, his place in the community and in society as a whole was strengthened. As a result, his status in the classroom also rose. This change in the teacher's status in relation to his pupils did not, at least in theory, involve an increase in the tyrannical behavior characteristic of the teacher as employee. This type of teacher derived his authority from his status as a specialist. As such he also became a model and object of identification for his pupils. Admiration and identification, therefore, took the place of fear and submission. This change was based on the differing conception of the desired achievements of instruction. Pupils are initiated into a culture by the process of internalizing the values of that culture. Internalization occurs when the young person encounters in his environment figures with whom he can identify. The teacher became a cultural agent for his pupils. He came to be regarded as a transmitter of the contents of the culture and as a representative of that culture in his personal characteristics, his way of life, and his behavior in general. He was, in short, expected to be an exemplary figure.

The above describes the personality people expected of this type of teacher. Their expectations were not always fulfilled. In terms of its ideal model, the role of the teacher as a cultural agent was, as a matter of fact, only rarely realized. The reason for this lies in the other characteristics of the role.

While the definition of his role as that of agent and representative of a culture freed the teacher from direct dependence on the community, it did not provide him with the amount of freedom required by a specialist operating within his own field of specialization. He was no longer required to justify his actions to parents or even to the city council but his behavior was still dictated largely by external, nonprofessional factors. This was readily apparent in curricular planning and, to a lesser extent, in methods of instruction. In both of these areas his authority remained severely limited. He was allowed to manipulate contents to a certain extent in order to adapt them to the needs of instruction. He could do so, however, only on condition that he remain within the limits of what was accepted and agreed upon in the social environment in which he was operating. Society possesses formal and informal controls to prevent teachers from deviating from the accepted norms. In terms of his dependence on factors external to his profession, the teacher of this type did not differ in principle from his predecessor, despite his lack of direct dependence on his employers and despite his superior social status. For this reason his status in the classroom was not what it was expected to be — an exemplary human being, educating the young by virtue of their identification with his personal characteristics. Because he was subject to pressure, he exerted pressure on his pupils.

The teacher operating within this definition of his role is constantly in a state of conflict. On the one hand, he considers himself responsible for teaching the young to think, to judge, to evaluate, or, in short, for initiating them into civilization. On the other hand, he is dependent on external social factors that supervise his acitivities and by virtue of this supervision contradict his self-image. This conflict is exacerbated by the fact that a teacher whose role is so defined regards himself as belonging to the elite group of society; this group is not, however, usually enthusiastic about receiving him as a member. A number of teachers partially solved the problem by isolating themselves from society and withdrawing into the world of the school—a world governed by its own laws and administered according to its own procedures. If the teacher as employee was despised by society, the teacher as cultural agent lived in isolation from it and enjoyed being an eccentric, which entitled him to special treatment.

This special treatment reflects an additional aspect of the situation. In societies that are undergoing rapid changes, the school is often called upon to moderate people's reactions to these changes. The stability of the school helps to balance the fear and resistance aroused by change. As long as education remains conservative, changes in society appear to be only transitory. The teacher who lives apart from the changing society represents tradition; thus the opponents of change expect him to preserve and maintain the values that are declining everywhere else. The image of the teacher as the representative of culture but detached from worldly affairs appears to guarantee relative stability, holding out the hope that not everything will be swept away in the accelerated tempo of change.

Whatever the definition of the teacher's role, however, one of his functions must be to bring the real world into the classroom, present it to his pupils, and help them to understand it. A teacher isolated from the world will have little chance of getting his pupils to identify with him. This is especially true of pupils growing up in a society in which the changes provide them with an abundance of stimuli and many possible objects of identification (both real and imaginary). In this situation the teacher who expects his students to emulate him will be disappointed. When this expectation is frustrated, the teacher loses his orientation. The definition of the teacher as a cultural agent must be credited with the rejection of the teacher as a disciplinarian, and with the confusion that resulted from changing this role, a confusion that gave rise to new ideas about the status of the teacher in the process of instruction and to attempts to redefine his role. In cases where the teacher as cultural agent refuses to acknowledge the failure of this definition of his role, he must resort to the methods he had initially rejected — those of the teacher as employee — in order to sustain it.

What Is a Teacher? *

The teacher is a prophet. *He lays the foundations of tomorrow.* The teacher is an artist. *He works with the precious clay of unfolding personality.* The teacher is a friend. *His heart responds to the faith and devotion of his students.* The teacher is a citizen. *He is selected and licensed for the improvement of society.* The teacher is an interpreter. *Out of his maturer and wider life he seeks to guide the young.* The teacher is a builder. *He works with the higher and finer values of civilization.* The teacher is a culture-bearer. *He leads the way toward worthier tastes, saner attitudes, more gracious manners, higher intelligence.* The teacher is a planner. *He sees the young lives before him as a part of a great system which shall grow stronger in the light of truth.* The teacher is a pioneer. *He is always attempting the impossible and winning out.* The teacher is a reformer. *He seeks to remove the handicaps that weaken and destroy life.* The teacher is a believer. *He has abiding faith in the improvability of the race.*

6.3 Teacher as a Specialist

Any occupation, however simple or complex, entails specialization. Mechanics and medicine are vastly different fields, but both require specialization. The multiplicity of definitions of the teacher's role corresponds to the multiplicity of types of specialization that people expect of him. The teacher as employee is expected to be a specialist in disciplining his pupils and in training them in specific, predetermined behaviors. The teacher as cultural agent is expected to be a specialist in a certain area of knowledge and in representing its values and principles to his pupils. These two definitions of the teacher's role have one factor in common: their specializations relate to characteristics that are not restricted to education. Leadership abilities and familiarity

---

*Joy Elmer Morgan, *NEA Journal,* XLVII (March, 1958), back cover.

with various branches of knowledge are necessary components in many occupations.

The third definition of the status of the teacher in instruction, on the other hand, is based entirely on specialization in education. By bringing professional considerations to bear on the situation, the teacher is expected to promote the development of his pupils. This definition emphasizes the professional aspect of teaching.

Teaching has not yet achieved full professional status. The image of the role of teaching exists as a demand, an orientation, and an ideal, but most of the conditions for its fulfillment have not been created. The first deficiency is a theory according to which the teacher could choose behaviors that would enable his pupils to develop on the basis of rational considerations. At present this gap is being filled by largely intuitive conjectures and by the findings of different sciences, mainly psychology. These sciences have not yet, however, reached a stage at which conclusions relevant to educational behavior can be derived from them. Even if, in the foreseeable future, they were to provide a theory according to which teaching could be conducted on a professional basis, teachers and schools would not be prepared to receive it.

The professional role of the teacher will be possible only when his administrative orientation has been separated from his professional orientation. When this occurs the teacher is not dependent on administrative bodies in the area of his professional decisions. His consultants, guides, evaluators, and judges are his fellow professionals, just as a doctor's judges are his fellow physicians, not those who pay his fees or salary. The demand for professional independence made in the last generation, even though it was not fully realized, bears witness to the change that had taken place in the conception of the teacher's role. Reasons for the change may be due to a number of factors. For example, certain types of knowledge connected with specialization in education, especially psychology, impart some of their prestige to teaching. Also, many parents (who are, in fact, society) have lost their faith in traditional education. They now expect the same sort of guidance and orientation from teachers in the field of education as they expect from doctors in the field of health and from experts in the field of their own occupational concerns. This readiness to be guided by teachers in matters pertaining to education is an indication of the confusion existing among parents in our society. It is also, however, an indication of the esteem in which they have begun to hold the teacher.

Inside the classroom, the way in which the teacher uses his authority (which has been strengthened externally) will depend on the professional considerations he brings to bear on any given situation. Authority here is not regarded as an attribute of status but as a means. In the light of professional considerations an educator may decide to exert his authority in one situation and to avoid exerting it in another.

If full professional status is ever accorded the teacher, it will be necessary to grant him powers that have been reserved previously for the leaders of society on one hand and its bureaucratic institutions on the other. When this occurs, the teacher will demand the authority to choose the aims of his activities and the means of attaining them according to his own professional considerations. Because of the nature of education, these considerations include social aspects and aims. Administrative decisions regarding the social needs that education must satisfy are not the same, however, as the professional decisions taken by the teacher. Educational administrators seek solutions to social problems by means of educational processes. Professional teachers, on the other hand, deal with individuals with whose development society and culture interfere, and not always in a supportive way. This type of teacher will not ignore society (as does the teacher as cultural agent); nor will he be subjugated by it (as is the teacher as employee). He will seek to promote the optimal development of his pupils both by exposing them to the influences of society and culture, and by protecting them from these influences. His ability to decide which of these contradictory positions to adopt in any given situation is a sign of his competence in the performance of his professional roles.

The main factor supporting the teacher's demands for professional authority stems from the present crisis in education. As long as the school functioned more or less successfully, the kind of teaching it perpetuated, by means of tradition and inertia, could be implemented by teachers who were not specialists. When the school began to show signs of disintegrating, and the results of this disintegration became apparent in its products (a high percentage of illiteracy among graduates, the spread of juvenile delinquency, the appearance of a counterculture, open revolt against the school), it was no longer possible to rely on teachers whose only resources were tradition and conventional procedures. The situation demanded a new type of teacher, one who is a specialist in his field.

In the way in which the teacher is expected to relate to his students, his role may be compared to that of the clinical psychologist or the psychotherapist.[34]

The teacher initially is responsible for creating an accepting, non-judgmental atmosphere where each individual is valued as a person. * *His presentation is a way of pointing to or denoting essential values in a theory of health and growth. He must express himself with feeling and conviction for only if he experiences with his entire being what he says can he help to create a learning experience for another or even to initiate a process by which a growth experience can occur. The teacher expresses his experience as his own, in a personal approach, not as something objectified or impersonal. He must not impose himself on the learner but, on the contrary, must encourage the learner to evolve his own values and convictions with greater clarity and to develop insights consistent with his own experience. He must regard the many questions and reactions of the learner with utter respect, listening with complete acceptance and making elaborations where this is important to the learner. He must allow the learner's point of view to emerge, be treated with respect, and valued. During the initial meetings an atmosphere of mutual acceptance, trust, and love must develop which helps free the individual participants, including the teacher. The teacher, with his whole being, actively encourages each individual to be and become more fully himself. He recognizes the individual perceptions of each person as worthy. He attempts to nurture and cultivate the learner's ideas and shows his belief in the dynamic value and social significance of the learner's experience.*

The beginning is made by the teacher, not as an authority, but as a person concerned with the becoming nature of each member in the group and with his own personal growth. He starts with his philosophy, his convictions, his attitudes, not with a definition of his function or role. Definition is just another form of authority. It means "to end off." As has been observed by Cantor, the time for definition is at the end of exploration not at the beginning . . . . And when an exploration ends, definitions are no longer important.

The teacher does not begin with hypotheses about learners for this makes belief in growth tentative, and suggests doubt. He must have firm faith in the potentiality of the learner. If he fails, it means that a true occasion for learning failed to emerge. To doubt the validity of one's belief in the person,

*From *Teaching as Learning*, by Clark E. Moustakas. Copyright © 1972 by Clark E. Moustakas. Reprinted by permission of Ballantine Books, a Division of Random House, Inc.

of one's value of the person, is not to believe or value at all. Only when the instructor is present in the full human sense, not hypothetically but truly, is he able to grow as a unified totality and thus provide an occasion for the growth of others.

With each group the teacher begins in a new way for he is a learner too, concerned with his own being and growth. Every person he encounters in his teaching constitutes a new experience and a new opportunity for development. He does not function in any predesignated or predetermined fashion. He expresses himself spontaneously, intuitively and in terms of the immediate situation as he sees it. Buber . . . has emphasized this value, as follows: "In spite of all similarities, every living situation has, like a newborn child, a new face that has never been before and will never come again. It demands of you a reaction which cannot be prepared beforehand. It demands nothing of what is past. It demands presence, responsibility; it demands you."

MEANS

Seventh Dimension:
Motivation

Not until the school was transformed from a selective to a universal institution did educationists begin to concern themselves with motivation. So long as education remained the privilege of the few, motivation was completely neglected in the educational debate. It is doubtful, in fact, if it was even recognized to exist. Motivation to learn was guaranteed by the school's selectivity: only those who were motivated to learn became pupils. In most cases the motivation to learn was secondary; people born into certain classes of society were forced to use the services of the school if they wanted to enjoy the social status of their parents or even to improve their status. The motivation to learn was primary in a few cases. There have always been individuals who are curious and have a strong desire for knowledge. In the selective school motivation functioned mainly to strengthen the students' capacity to withstand the many distractions from their studies. Neither the methods of instruction nor the contents taught aroused the interest and curiosity of the average pupil. In societies in which education determines social status and in which educational facilities are limited, being a pupil means being a member of a privileged group. It was thus unnecessary for the elitist school to be overly concerned with the motivation of its pupils to learn. The expulsion of those who were unwilling to learn was sufficient to strengthen the desire to learn in those remaining. Pupils were aware that attending school was a privilege, and they usually did what the school required in order not to lose the advantages of education.

With the almost total decline of the selective school, the situation changed radically. When education ceased to be the privilege of the minority and became a universal obligation, the previous motivations to remain within the school were destroyed. From then on it was impossible to expel a pupil on the grounds that he was not learning. The school was obligated to keep him within its walls whether he wanted to learn or not. When the school was forced to ask itself how to make its pupils want to learn, the problem of motivation was born.

The transition from selective to universal education was gradual, especially in regard to teaching by motivation. During this transitional period the school opened its doors to every child, but it long continued to behave as if all its pupils were motivated to learn, either by a desire to ensure their social status or by an intrinsic curiosity and wish for knowledge. The early period of transition was marked by failure among pupils who were attending school for the first time. We must conclude, therefore, that the social classes that had benefited by selective schools continued to benefit by the new system of universal schooling, but that those who had not attended school previously failed to benefit by the schooling that had now become available to them as a result of the compulsory education acts. The explanations for this failure (inferior intelligence, family traditions, cultural patterns, social environment) overlooked its main cause: the school did not adapt itself to the new type of pupil and his motivations, which differed from those of previous pupils.

Motivation thus emerged as a problem during the same period in which schooling lost its external justification as a status symbol. It became necessary, therefore, to find a new justification in terms of the inherent attributes of the process itself. A number of slogans — "The pupil must be interested in what he is taught at school"; "School attendance must be based on the interest of the pupils in their studies"; "The pupil must see the school as meaningful to himself" — resulted from the high rate of failure among the new school population.

The history of motivation in modern education reflects the mutual relationship between educational ideas and the organizational structure of the school. Once the problem was identified, a search for solutions began. At the beginning this search was characterized by an unwillingness to make any radical changes in the accepted structure of instruction and the school. It seemed that it was necessary only to add to existing structures something that would answer the newly discovered need to motivate pupils to learn. A striking example of this approach is found in the "Preparatory Stage," which Ziller added to Herbart's formal stages of instruction.[35] The purpose of the preparatory stage was to engage the interest of the pupils in what was to be learned. According to this interpretation, arousing the curiosity of the pupil before instruction commenced would ensure the holding of his interest to the end. This is a mechanical approach to the problem of motivation in instruction, which holds that the problem can be solved by adding something to what already exists without changing it. A few words by the teacher at the opening of a lesson would thus suffice to deal with the problem of motivation.

But motivation is not a *stage* in instruction; it is a dimension that affects all other dimensions. It affects the aims of instruction because these aims should not be determined without taking into account the types of motivation existing among pupils. It affects pupils' achievements since these achievements greatly depend on motivation. It affects pupils' status since their status in instruction is determined by whether or not motivations are taken into account. It affects the status of knowledge since the very act of considering motivation involves a willingness to manipulate the contents of knowledge. All the other dimensions of instruction are affected to some degree by motivation. For this reason the mechanical solution to teaching is usually disappointing.

Another solution to the problem of motivation was reorganization of the curriculum and the endeavor to present pupils with material "interesting" to their age group. Tremendous efforts went into composing and editing textbooks that would be attractive to pupils in content and form. Engaging the interest of pupils in their schoolwork became the foremost concern of educational planners.[36]

This approach gave the concept of motivation a broader significance for teaching than had its predecessor. Motivation was no longer seen as an addition to instruction but as one of its principles. Interest or lack of interest is not, however, an attribute of the contents of teaching. It is an attribute of learners in relation to these contents. Attempts to determine what interests children of a given age group or social background, however convincing they may appear from a statistical point of view, cannot provide a solution to the problem of motivation in teaching. There are no group solutions to this problem. Data indicating that children of a certain age are interested in literature about family life does not ensure that an actual child in an actual class will have this interest. The objects of instruction are not abstract groups of children but actual individual children. If there is no way of deciding in advance what will interest an individual pupil at any given time, then it follows that there is no way of preparing in advance "interesting" programs of instruction. A pupil may, moreover, be interested in one aspect of the material and not in others. For example, while a child may be fascinated by the contents of a certain story, it is unlikely that he will be interested in a literary analysis of it. Thus, teaching contents are, in themselves, neither interesting nor uninteresting; there are only pupils who are either interested or not interested in the contents. And, the interest that either appears or fails to appear is related to the way in which the contents are manipulated. Motivation is more closely connected to the method of instruction than to the contents.

The connection between methods of instruction and motivation is, however, also problematic. Different methods of instruction activate different types of motivation. The frontal method of instruction is closely related to the motivation of achievement and competition. Individual exploratory instruction is closely related to motivation stemming from curiosity. An authoritarian method of instruction may arouse motivations based on conscientiousness and duty. All these methods of instruction not only activate the pupil's motivations; they also reinforce them. A pupil motivated by the desire to achieve will exert himself if the method of instruction is one that gratifies his need to achieve, and this gratification will, in turn, reinforce his motivation of achievement. The same is true of all the other ways in which the pupil's motivations are used in instruction. We must, therefore, ask ourselves an ethical as well as a didactic question: do we want to reinforce these motivations in the pupil? Is teaching neutral with regard to the type of motivation it activates in the pupil, as long as he is motivated in some way to learn? Or perhaps the fact that he learns at the same time to respond to certain motivations rather than others should be taken into account in deciding which motivations to activate.

In summary, decisions regarding the preferred kind of motivation, the right ways of arousing this motivation, and the place that motivation should occupy in considerations regarding the contents and methods of instruction are all decisive factors in the process of instruction. The problem of motivation in instruction may be conceived of in one of the following ways:

7.1. Motivation is the object of specific teachers' activities.

7.2. Motivation is a means as well as an end of instruction.

7.3. Instruction should be based on self-motivation and self-regulation.

7.1 Motivation as an Object of Specific Teachers' Activities

"Now I'm going to read you an interesting story." "I wonder who'll be the first to solve the problem on the board." "Let's see who knows how to sit nicely in his place." These are some typical examples of statements made by teachers endeavoring to motivate their pupils to learn. The first is intended to arouse curiosity, the second to encourage competitiveness, and the third to exploit the child's need to win the approval and affection of his teacher. What they all have in common is that none is directly related to the subject of instruction.

The teacher's promise that the story will be interesting is not, of course, a guarantee that it will prove to be so to his pupils. The promise is not intended to activate the students' motivation with regard to the contents of this specific story, but simply to ensure that they will pay attention to the teacher's reading of it. A statement of this kind could have been used for any story at all—about family life, about war, about friendship, or about a sea voyage. The story is not the object of the motivation, but a certain kind of behavior: paying attention to the teacher while he reads.

The distance between motivation and teaching contents is even greater in the second statement. The statement is not intended to arouse motivations connected with arithmetic, but to encourage competitive instincts that will induce the pupils to solve the problem.

In the third statement the teacher lets his students know that he wants them to sit in a certain way, which he calls sitting "nicely." He is prepared to look approvingly at or call out the names of those who do so. The pupils, on the other hand, are not in the least interested in sitting "nicely," but they are concerned about the rewards they hope to receive as a result of their behavior.

Statements and activities of this type, intended to arouse pupils' motivation, are means to ends, but the means themselves are neutral. These motivations are, therefore, secondary in two senses: they are not connected to the contents being taught but to certain behaviors regarded as appropriate for learning these contents; and they do not stem from the primary needs of the pupil's personality but from needs derived from them. What, then, is the justification for defining these practices as motivation?

If the use of this concept is at all strict, then there is little justification. As has been said, activities of this type are not directed toward motivation. Sometimes they are a means to awakening associations ("Now I'm going to read you an interesting story" associates the present situation to enjoyable experiences in the past). At other times they are a way of making use of previous conditioning ("I wonder who'll be the first to solve the problem on the board" and "who knows how to sit nicely in his place" arouse competitive responses). These activities have been included in the concept of motivation for pragmatic reasons since the function expected of motivation has been attributed to them. That is, they are expected to make the pupil want to do what is required of him, which is interpreted by his teacher as learning. True motivation involves meaningful experience. The things a person does because he is motivated to do them are meaningful to him (whether in an intellectual, an emotional, or a social sense). The use of associations and conditioning to make an individual learn, however, is likely to have the opposite effect and act as a factor in emptying his activities of meaning and in making him feel that what happens at school has no point or purpose. Thus, the pupil may fulfill all his obligations toward the school without any learning taking place. He pays attention to what the teacher says, answers questions, does his homework, and sits up straight, but derives no benefit from any of these activities.

When teachers insert in the process of instruction activities intended to motivate pupils, these activities are in the nature of incentives. By means of these activities the student learns to act in response to an outside incentive. There is, however, a corresponding lack of ability to act in accordance with inner needs. This type of teaching thus impoverishes the inner motivation of the pupil and makes him uninterested in the contents of learning. Since, however, the rewards are soon discovered to be fictitious (How long can a pupil be gratified by being the first to solve the problem on the blackboard?), many pupils cease responding to this kind of incentive. Those who continue to respond show that their development has been hindered in certain aspects. If they never realize that the rewards are fictitious, their intellectual development has been impaired. If they continue to be gratified by the rewards, their emotional development has been impaired. In most cases, the impairment results from the pressure of activities intended to make them conform.

It would, nevertheless, be rash to declare unequivocally that this way of activating pupils' motivation has no place in education. Either because of the nature of the activities involved or because of the composition of the class, situations may arise in which the teacher needs to use this method of motivation. Sound professional considerations may lead the teacher to employ these methods in specific situations, but he must take into account the dangers involved. Their use may be compared to the use of a dangerous drug: as long as the teacher knows that motivating pupils by external incentives impairs their self-motivation and may lead to apathy, he may apply these methods where he considers that all the relevant data justify his doing so. As in all the other aspects of instruction, here too the teacher will have to decide among alternative courses of action. To choose wisely he will have to know what he wants to achieve by their means and what price has to be paid for each alternative.

Two days after vacation I received a note from the secretary that Mrs. X (another name I don't remember) was coming down to talk to me. * *Mrs. X was the District Language and Social Studies consultant for GW.*

Mrs. X didn't visit my classes. She met me in the teachers' room during my free period and opened the conversation by telling me that she came, as she did with all the new teachers, to offer any help or advice she could.

This Mrs. X was white, elderly, tall, stringy, wore a print dress—the very picture, I must say, of the old-lady schoolteacher. She asked me if I had any problems I cared to mention. Did I? I began to outline them—9D's apathy, 7H's conglomeration of inabilities. I raced enthusiastically into a point-by-point description of the problems of 7H for a starter; I considered myself something of an expert on the subject. I spoke as if we two were going to reform the entire system, then and there.

*From The Way It Spozed to Be, pp. 111–112, copyright © 1965, 1968, by James Herndon. Reprinted by permission of Simon and Schuster.

Before I'd gotten fairly started, she interrupted. Now, we all have our problems, she said, and sometimes we're tempted to consider our own problems as being unique. But with these children (leaving out The Word, as usual) I've found that a simpler, more direct approach works best. I feel already that you may be making it all too complicated for yourself. In my experience, the best advice I can give you beginning teachers is, hold out a carrot.

A carrot? I didn't get it.

You know, she said brightly, the carrot, or perhaps we should say a sugar cube. If you want the goat to pull the cart, but he doesn't want to, you hold a carrot out in front of him. He tries to reach the carrot because he does want it. In doing so, he pulls the cart. If, she said with a kind of wink, if you've attached the carrot to the cart.

I must have seemed a little stupid to her. Seeing that I just sat there, she tried to explain. Teaching these children is like training animals. For each task you want them to do, you must offer them a carrot.

You mean, I finally said, you try to get the goat to pull the cart without his realizing it. That is, the goat actually does what you want him to do, but all the time he thinks he's just trying to get that carrot. He doesn't realize he's pulling the cart. Not only that, but pulling the cart isn't something that any goat, any normal goat, ever wants to do, but . . . .

I think you're trying to make it complicated again, she said, frowning.

You mean, I tried again, to get the students to do the assignment because of some reward he's going to get, not because he realizes that the assignment is valuable or interesting to him. You mean, the assignment itself can't be the carrot . . . .

She felt happier. That's it, she said. Of course the reward must vary. There are individual differences as we know. A carrot for one, a sugar cube for another.

Mercifully the bell rang. Mrs. X went back to her desk in the district office, downtown. I sneaked a quick smoke, my mind filled with carrots and outrage, and arrived upstairs a bit late to greet 9D.

7.2 Motivation as a Means as Well as an End of Instruction

When motivation is treated as an integral part of instruction (and not an appendage to it, as in the previous approach), it is expressed in all the main aspects of the process—in the curriculum, in the methods of instruction, in the organization of the learning group. This integration can be achieved in two different ways. First, motivation is treated as a means of instruction. In this case, curriculum planning will take the interests of the pupil into account, methods of instruction will take his needs into account, the organization of the class will take his social motivations into account, and so on. The teacher's behavior will be directed, above all, toward stimulating the pupil's motivations. According to the logic of this method, the teacher should be attentive to the reactions of his pupils and to learn from these reactions how to motivate them to make the effort required for learning. He may use the motivation of achievement if he finds that by these means he can make his pupils increase their efforts. He may use intellectual motivation if his pupils reveal intellectual curiosity that demands to be satisfied. He may use his pupils' sense of duty or their need to win his approval and affection. He will regard any or all of these means as legitimate, as long as they induce a readiness to learn in his pupils.

The second approach regards motivation as an end of instruction and is not neutral concerning the pupil's motivations. This view sees some motivations as desirable and others as undesirable. It is the function of instruction to support the former, or to establish them if they do not already exist, and to eradicate or at least weaken the latter. According to this approach the wish to learn is not only a means of instruction; it is also, and perhaps mainly, its end. Learning is a value, and responsiveness to this value is the kind of motivation the school exists to cultivate. Motivation is a means that can be evaluated by criteria of efficiency. The teacher should avoid some motivations even if the pupil can be made to learn by means of them. There are, on the other hand, motivations that the school should implant in the pupil if they are not already present; in the course of time he will adopt them as his own. Curiosity or a sense of duty are good examples. It is the function of the school to strengthen its students' curiosity, even when they learn from a sense of duty, just as it is the function of the school to implant a sense of duty in its pupils, even when they learn because they are curious and interested in learning.

Thus, motivation can be integrated in instruction either as a means that is neutral with regard to aims or as an end in itself. This is, however, more of a logical than a psychological distinction. A teacher who uses a motivation that already exists in his pupil reinforces it. To use a motivation means to provide a specific satisfaction that corresponds to a specific need. The motivation used as a means to get the pupil to learn thus becomes the product of the learning. If the teacher, for example, recurrently uses the motivation of achievement to make his pupils learn, he is educating toward achievement-motivated behavior. There is no point in distinguishing between education and instruction because all instruction educates. The question is what it educates toward: what characteristics does it establish and strengthen in the learner?

What these two logically contradictory approaches have in common is that both mold the learner's motivation systems. One molds existing motivations; the other molds motivations selected according to certain value criteria. Even when motivation is regarded as a means it becomes a goal, whether or not this is the teacher's intention. By activating motivations to which the pupils respond, the teacher transforms them into a part of his basic personality structure (there is no more certain way of molding traits than by using them). The logical distinction between motivation as a means and motivation as an end is therefore of small educational significance. Both conceptions direct activities that result in the acquisition of stable motivational patterns, which then become traits of the learner's personality.

This shared characteristic of the two approaches to motivation stems from their common assumption that in order for the pupil to learn it is necessary to motivate him. The assumption is grounded in the common belief that the pupil does not, as a rule, want to learn; it is, therefore, up to the teacher to make him want to do so. For generations, both the individual and society have conceived of the role of the school in this way. According to this conception, the purpose of the school is to initiate the child into a world of culture, which is not innately his world. This initiation is not a process of satisfying the child's "natural" needs and desires, but of changing them. It is thus taken for granted that the pupil will resist the changes that the school wishes to effect in him. The purpose of motivation is to overcome or soften this resistance. Furthermore, this motivation is not, in most cases, based on the pupil's primary needs, but on such secondary needs as the need to compete, to be dutiful, and to be accepted by the group. Motivation of this kind is intended to overcome the unwillingness of the pupil to subject himself to the rigorous requirements of civilized behavior in the intellectual, emotional, or social sphere. Discipline is the alternative to using the pupils' motivations. In this view, what cannot be achieved with the willing cooperation of the pupil must be achieved by using authority, on which all discipline is based. Both the findings of psychological research and the values embraced by the school in our day support the preference for using motivation rather than compulsion based on discipline.

But this distinction too is one of logic rather than practicality. For much of the motivation used by schools in which this conception dominates would not, in fact, be possible without their rules of discipline. In this approach the use of motivation is not, therefore, a substitute for discipline; rather, it depends on discipline. It is no wonder that schools that seek to integrate motivation into instruction regard discipline as an instrumentally and intrinsically justified motive. The school must establish in its pupils characteristics that will lead them to subject themselves to both internal and external discipline. From then on, discipline will function as a motive. If the pupil is asked to read or write, describe or analyze, draw or construct a model, he will do so in order to satisfy the need to be disciplined, which has been inculcated in him.

Thus, although motivation is regarded as a desirable alternative to discipline, it is doubtful that it would be possible without discipline to activate the type of motivation considered superior or desirable for learning.

Interest means self-activity. * *The demand for a many-sided interest is, therefore, a demand for many-sided self-activity. But not all self-activity, only the right degree of the right kind, is desirable; else lively children might very well be left to themselves. There would be no need of educating or even of governing them. It is the purpose of instruction to give the right direction to their thoughts and impulses, to incline these toward the morally good and true. Children are thus in a measure passive. But this passivity should by no means involve suppression of self-activity. It should, on the contrary, imply a stimulation of all that is best in the child . . . .*

Attention may be broadly defined as an attitude of mind in which there is readiness to form new ideas. Such readiness is either voluntary or involuntary. If voluntary, it depends on a resolution; the teacher frequently secures this through admonitions or threats. Far more desirable and fruitful is involuntary attention. It is this attention that the art of teaching must seek to induce. Herein lies the kind of interest to be sought by the teacher . . . .

*J. F. Herbart, *Outlines of Educational Doctrine* (New York: Macmillan, 1913), pp. 60, 62, 71.

The fact should not be overlooked, however, that even the best method cannot secure an adequate degree of apperceiving attention . . . from every pupil; recourse must accordingly be had to the voluntary attention, i.e., the pupil's resolution. But for the necessary measures the teacher must depend, not merely on rewards and punishments, but chiefly on habit and custom. Instruction unites at this point with government and training. In all cases where the pupil begins his work not entirely without compulsion, it is particularly important that he should soon become aware of his own progress. The several steps must be distinctly and suitably pointed out to him; they must at the same time be easy of execution and succeed each other slowly. The instruction should be given with accuracy, even strictness, seriousness, and patience.

7.3   Instruction as Based on Self-Motivation and Self-Regulation

The third possible approach to motivation differs in principle from the two previous ones. According to this approach, motivation, like all the other facets of the human personality, is not an object of manipulation. By means of motivation the individual interacts with his environment. As a result of this interaction he develops himself. Thus, to interfere with an individual's motivation is to interfere with his development. A number of studies of the humanist school in psychology form the theoretical basis of this approach. Maslow, a primary spokesman of this school, argues that the psychologically healthy individual is one who receives sufficient gratification to fill his needs for security, belonging, love, esteem, and self-esteem, and he is motivated mainly by a drive for self-actualization.[37] Self-actualization is a continuous process by which the talents and abilities of the individual are realized; they lead him to act in accordance with inner sources that cannot be activated by others without causing damage.

Other psychologists have in other ways reached similar conclusions regarding motivation. White[38] criticizes both the psychoanalytical theory of instincts and the behaviorist theory of drive reduction, which claim to explain the motives of human behavior. He attempts to establish a theory of "competence motive," which explains individual behavior resulting from a continuous aspiration to perfect competence. Buhler speaks of a "lust to function."[39] These, as well as a number of other approaches to motivation, have in common an anthropological conception. This conception seeks the human's weakness at birth as his primary motivation for actualizing the abilities that existed in him in embryonic form.

The acceptance of this conception of motivation by educationists implies a thorough reexamination of the school system. It is impossible to rely on pupils' self-regulation while at the same time maintaining a compulsory curriculum or formal organization of instruction. This conception of motivation changes the conception of instruction. Thus, instruction can no longer be regarded as an activity taking place in an institution that, in advance, sorts its pupils into classes and formulates a program of studies in accordance with a scale of grades. Instead the school emerges as an environment in which are created a maximum number of opportunities for satisfying the needs of the pupil. He then decides upon the opportunities of which he should take advantage.

The place occupied in the first conception of motivation (specific activities of the teacher) by incentives and in the second (motivation as a means and an end) by discipline is occupied here by self-regulation. The third conception distinguishes not only among the different approaches to motivation in instruction, but also among general conceptions of education and teaching. Instruction based on the self-regulation of pupils differs in all its characteristics from every other kind of instruction. The basic assumption underlying self-regulation states that the drive to be active is an innate human characteristic. As long as the individual is free to do so, he will seek satisfaction for this drive by exploring his environment. These explorations, prompted by the drive to be active, are opportunities for learning. Any learning that takes place in conditions other than these is due to taming and distorts the personality. As has been said, it is possible to induce a pupil to learn by means of incentives associated with rewards and by a cunning use of secondary motivations (honors, grades, the approval and affection of those he respects). The result of these inducements, however, is not only the learning of the contents but the loss of interest in learning itself (and the acquisition of interest in the rewards connected with it), the loss of a sense of responsibility for what the individual does (and the acquisition of interest in the impression made on others by what he does), the loss of curiosity, or the joy of doing, and the loss of the readiness to rely on inner self-direction. The school and the home before it usually succeed in crippling the will of the child to explore his environment and to learn from these explorations. A critic of the school in our day states:

We destroy the disinterested (I do not mean uninterested) love of learning in children, which is so strong when they are small, by encouraging and compelling them to work for petty and contemptible rewards—gold stars, or papers marked 100 and tacked to the wall, or A's on report cards, or honor rolls, or dean's lists, or Phi Beta Kappa Keys—in short, for the ignoble satisfaction of feeling that they are better than someone else. We encourage them to feel that the end and aim of all they do in school is nothing more than to get a good mark on a test, or to impress someone with what they seem to know. We kill, not only their curiosity, but their feeling that it is a good and admirable thing to be curious, so that by the age of ten most of them will not ask questions, and will show a good deal of scorn for the few who do.[40]

Self-regulation, therefore, means chiefly a choice in favor of primary motivations, of activities that are based on curiosity and not on competition, of the need to belong, or of a sense of duty.

Motivation is not something that the school or the teacher can create. It is innate in the pupil (so long as his personality has not been distorted), and the school can activate it by providing an abundance of activities from which the pupil can choose. By regulating his own activities the student recorgnizes his motives and which take priority over the others. But, most important of all, he learns to act in accordance with his own inner urges and not in accordance with the expectations of others. The activities regulated by his own motives bring him into contact with objects, ideas, and people. These contacts demonstrate what is of real interest to him. Learning of this type leads to the emergence of man as a creature who learns.

Instruction based on this conception of motivation will have to reconcile itself to the fact that contents considered important by adults will not always be learned since pupils may not regard them as interesting. Advocates of this approach argue that if these contents are really important—if they are necessary to man in thinking about his problems or in trying to understand the world in which he lives—then the students will eventually learn them because of their own curiosity. If they are never learned, one may doubt whether they are, in fact, important.

. . . True learning—learning that is permanent and useful, that leads to intelligent action and further learning—can arise only out of the experience, interests, and concerns of the learner. *

*From *The Underachieving School*, pp. 13–14, by John Holt. Copyright © 1971 by Pitman Publishing Corporation. Reprinted by permission of Pitman Publishing Corporation.

Every child, without exception, has an innate and unquenchable drive to understand the world in which he lives and to gain freedom and competence in it. Whatever truly adds to his understanding, his capacity for growth and pleasure, his powers, his sense of his own freedom, dignity, and worth may be said to be true education.

Education is something a person gets for himself, not that which someone else gives or does to him.

What young people need and want to get from their education is: one, a greater understanding of the world around them; two, a greater development of themselves; three, a chance to find their work, that is, a way in which they may use their own unique tastes and talents to grapple with the real problems of the world around them and to serve the cause of humanity.

Our society asks schools to do three things for and to children: one, pass on the traditions and higher values of our own culture; two, acquaint the child with the world in which he lives; three, prepare the child for employment and, if possible, success. All of these tasks have traditionally been done by the society, the community itself. None of them is done well by schools. None of them can or ought to be done by the schools solely or exclusively. One reason the schools are in trouble is that they have been given too many functions that are not properly or exclusively theirs.

Schools should be a resource, but not the only resource, from which children, but not only children, can take what they need and want to carry on the business of their own education. Schools should be places where people go to find out the things they want to find out and develop the skills they want to develop. The child who is educating himself, and if he doesn't no one else will, should be free, like the adult, to decide when and how much and in what way he wants to make use of whatever resources the schools can offer him. There are an infinite number of roads to education; each learner should and must be free to choose, to find, to make his own.

Children want and need and deserve and should be given, as soon as they want it, a chance to be useful in society. It is an offence to humanity to deny a child, or anyone of age, who wants to do useful work the opportunity to do it. The distinction, indeed opposition, we have made between education and work is arbitrary, unreal, and unhealthy.

Unless we have faith in the child's eagerness and ability to grow and learn, we cannot help and can only harm his education.

Eighth Dimension:
Learner Activity

Learning and teaching are not two sides of the same coin. Learning is a process that takes place in a living organism; as a result of it, the behavior of the organism changes. This process is the object of psychological research. The role of teaching, on the other hand, is to organize the environment in such a way as to enable learning to take place. In order to organize the environment, we must know the conditions under which learning takes place.

The products of learning are thus changes that take place in the learner's behavior. A child who was not afraid of dogs and has become so because a dog or the owner of the dog frightened him has learned something. A child who did not know how to write and now has that ability has learned something. A child who did not realize that two phenomena are connected and who is now aware of such a connection has learned something. Though each example illustrates a different process, all are called "learning." The fear of dogs may occur as a result of a single experience. Learning to write requires a relatively long period of practice. It would be difficult to indicate the point at which one begins to think in terms of cause and effect and to estimate the time required to accomplish it.

The learning period is only one distinction among these three examples. There are types of learning that are easily acquired and easily forgotten, types that are acquired with difficulty and forgotten with ease, and types that are easily acquired and forgotten with difficulty.

It is also possible to distinguish among different kinds of learning according to the area of the personality affected. Thus learning may affect the memory, emotions, thinking, muscles, and so on.

The way the environment is organized determines the type of change that will result. In other words, different kinds of learning require different kinds of instruction. Organizing the environment for purposes of instruction entails arrangements that enable the pupil to engage in certain activities. For example, in traditional instruction the pupil listens to the words of the teacher and repeats them in one of many possible ways. In this case the environment was organized so as to make sure that the pupil paid attention to the teacher and was not distracted by incidental stimuli. Suitable mechanisms were provided to return him rapidly to a state of attention, should he have been distracted. The usual mechanism was the teacher's vigilance coupled with the authority to punish the student.

The project method, on the other hand, organized the environment to provide the pupil with opportunities for activities of a very different nature. The pupil was expected to become absorbed in his work, to plan what he wanted to do before doing it, and to assess the results in accordance with his intentions. Just as the decision in favor of passive attention and mechanical repetition was derived from a certain image of the learning process, so the decision in favor of projects planned and evaluated by the pupil was derived from a different image of the same process. The transition from the psychology of learning to the process of instruction is, therefore, a transition from the explanation of a process to the planning and implementation of conditions in which that process can take place. Since there is more than one explanation of the learning process, there is also more than one type of instruction.

The above seems to imply that every theory of teaching involves applying to it one of the existing theories of learning. Although this is correct as far as it goes, it does not begin to comprehend the relationship between theories of instruction and theories of learning. This relationship is sometimes interpreted as close and necessary. According to this interpretation, instruction is an activity dictated by theories of learning. Thus, William James argued: "And so everywhere the teaching must agree with the psychology, but not necessarily be the only kind of teaching that would so agree; for many diverse methods of teaching may equally well agree with psychological laws."[41] T. P.

Green has interpreted the relationship differently.[42] He makes teaching responsible for choosing among the possible ways of learning in accordance with the logic derived from teaching itself. Not every activity that leads to learning will be included in instruction, because, according to the criteria of instruction, not all learning is desirable. This could imply that some kinds of learning—those which have gained the approval of instruction—should be allowed to dictate its methods. One might justify this interpretation on the grounds that it undermines the previous, oversimplified, approach, which implied that instruction has no option but to bow to the dictates of learning (that is, psychology).

It is not necessary to dwell on the desirability of rejecting certain kinds of activities, even though they lead to learning, in the light of considerations derived from instruction. Thus, for example, no reasonable person would admit the threat of physical violence in instruction, even if the findings of empirical psychological research had shown it to be an effective way of bringing about learning.

We have not yet, however, answered the question of what relationship exists between the activities of instruction and the theories of learning that interpret them. One possible answer might be that instruction, according to its own logic, may reject certain learning activities (such as indoctrination or conditioning) and approve others (such as learning by discovery or learning based on understanding). Once instruction has approved certain kinds of learning, psychological research into them should dictate the activities of instruction.

Plausible as this answer seems, it is not supported by the reality of instruction. The findings of research on learning are generally derived from laboratory experiments. It is obvious that teaching cannot take place under these conditions, if only for technical reasons. Teaching always activates a great number of variables. It is impossible to isolate one of these variables and to maintain a teaching situation. (The same is true of a working situation in which one of the variables, such as the effort invested, is isolated. Though it is possible to investigate the number of calories required for a given physical effort, this effort, without a defined aim, rules of implementation, and so forth, can no longer be defined as "work.") The variables existing in teaching situations may and should be investigated. The findings of these investigations will be relevant to the considerations governing the activities that should occur in the teaching situation. Teaching is not, however, a mechanical combination of variables; it is a process created by a relatively stable combination of many variables. Learning—one of these variables—can never exist in isolation from the other factors in instruction. Combined with the other factors, learning that takes place by means of instruction is never the same as learning that takes place in the laboratory. Though concepts taken from the theories of learning may describe instruction, their use will remain essentially descriptive.

The problem concerning the theories of instruction is not only how to describe what happens, but how to ensure that what does happen is what should happen. Since all types of learning result from the pupil's activities, the main concern of instruction is to activate the pupil. Theories of instruction differ from one another in their assessment of particular activities as leading to certain kinds of learning and of other activities as preventing or sabotaging desired kinds of learning. Thus, what determines the kind of learning, if any, that occurs is the pupil's activity, which any kind of instruction can effect. The connection between the learning that actually takes place and the theory of learning directing the teacher is purely hypothetical. The connection between the activities in which the pupil engages as a result of instruction and the learning that takes place is factual.

We shall, therefore, identify the different theories of instruction according to the type of activity they prefer, not according to the theory of learning they follow. All systems of instruction expect the pupil to do something, whether it is to sit quietly and pay attention, to ask questions, to explore, or to initiate. When a teacher tells a pupil that he "asks too many questions," or when he suggests in response to a question that a pupil should "try the way that seems best to you," he is acting (often without being aware of it) in accordance with certain psychological and epistemological conceptions. It is not, however, these conceptions that direct him; it is, rather, the image he entertains of which activities are desirable for the pupil. Three images of desired activities (or, in other words, activities that are expected to make learning take place in the pupil) are the following:

8.1. Attention.

8.2. Teacher-directed activities.

8.3. Pupil-initiated activities.

8.1   Attention

According to this conception the pupil is expected to pay attention, and, by so doing, he will learn. This view is based on psychological notions that have long since been refuted. Teachers have not, however, abandoned them because, as usual in the sphere of opinions and beliefs, "common sense" seems to favor the grain of truth that they possess. It is true, of course, that the individual comes into contact with the world by means of his senses, including the sense of hearing. If I want to know what time it is and have no watch, I can ask someone and learn from his answer what I want to know. This illustrates the conception that identifies learning with hearing. The proof that I have learned lies in the fact that I now *know* what time it is because I have heard it from someone who knows. The obvious fact that a baby would not know what the time was even if he were told a hundred times does not cause advocates of this conception to ask a pertinent question: what happens to the child between the stage at which he hears what time it is but does not learn anything from what he hears and the stage at which it is enough to tell him for him to know? Learning, in the spirit of this conception, is interpreted as the absorption of information through the senses. How the sounds received by the ear and transmitted to the nervous system are transformed into something that the hearer "knows" is not regarded as a matter with which teaching need concern itself. The main business of the teacher is to be heard.

The pupil may not, however, listen or pay attention to what the teacher says. In this conception, therefore, the central problem is how to ensure that the pupil will pay attention to and concentrate on what his teacher says. Discipline is the primary means of doing this. As conceived here, discipline is a mechanism intended to keep the pupil in a state of constant alertness, with all his energy focused on absorbing the teacher's words. Whenever a student's energy is diverted into other channels, he will be regarded as deviating from the rules he is expected to obey. Generations of teachers, parents, and educationists agreed that the paralysis of spontaneous activity on the part of the pupil was the best way to ensure his readiness to learn. Of all the senses accorded a central role in learning, two were granted a special status: hearing and seeing, in that order of importance. Thus, the brain absorbed impressions by means of hearing and sight. In order that these impressions not be confused with other, incidental, impressions, it was necessary to prevent additional senses or faculties from operating during learning. But discipline, despite the fact that, in this view, its importance never waned, was constantly proved insufficient to ensure that learning took place. It was found that a class could be perfectly disciplined—that no activity took place in it except for listening to the teacher—and still not learn. The answer to this problem was to place greater stress on seeing and perhaps even to activate other senses. Objects were substituted for words and exhibits for concepts; in a word, "concretization" was the metamorphosis of this conception.

Concretization was not, however, a success. It did attack the verbalism that dominated teaching and exposed its essential weakness: absorbing words does not ensure that their meaning will be understood, let alone that they will be used correctly. But the attempt to ensure that the meaning of words would be understood by showing the learner objects from which he was expected to construct concepts suffered from the limitation imposed by the very nature of the learning process. A child does not, for example, learn what a lever is because, in addition to hearing a verbal explanation, he is shown a lever. He internalizes the concept of lever when he uses a lever (or any instrument that operates according to the same principle). Whether instruction is based on hearing alone or on hearing and seeing, its fundamental mechanism is attention. That is, instruction neutralizes any activity on the part of the pupil other than that of absorbing the impressions the teacher wants him to receive.

While attention is the essence of this method of instruction, it is not the only activity expected of the pupil. Sometimes he must speak. Speaking has two functions: to prove that the student has indeed paid attention to what the teacher had said; and to practice what he has heard in order to remember it. Attention and the reconstruction of what has been heard or seen are the activities expected to advance learning.

Despite all the criticism of this method of instruction and despite its repudiation by teachers and teacher-training institutions, it remains in effect in untold numbers of schools. Sometimes it survives side by side with other ways of teaching, but frequently it is the dominant or only pattern of instruction in the school. The primary reason for this situation lies in the structure of the school itself, which supports this type of teaching and, to a large extent, prevents other modes. Another reason lies in the functions that instruction is expected to perform: so long as the transmission of information is regarded as the main aim of instruction, making himself heard will remain the primary role of the teacher.

It makes no difference what you teach a boy so long as he doesn't like it.

8.2 Teacher-Directed Activities

Changes in conceptions of learning led to changes in the kind of activity considered desirable for pupils. Passive audiovisual attention was rejected, at least in theory, and the pupil's activity as a way of learning was recommended.

According to the new conception, it was not sufficient for the pupil to listen or to see or to listen and see simultaneously in order for learning to take place. He must not only "absorb" something, but do something. Before the pupil can do something, however, he must want to do it. It may be possible, by means of discipline, to make the pupil pay attention, but discipline is not sufficient to force him to do something he does not want to do. Thus, the need to motivate pupils received additional support from the new conception of learning. But there is a hidden contradiction here. Activity is conceived of both as a way of learning and as an innate human need that must be satisfied. If activity is a need, why is it necessary to motivate the pupil to be active? The reason for this contradiction is that this conception does not regard all types of activity as legitimate; in other words, not everything the pupil wants to do is considered desirable. Only the teacher knows what he wants the pupils to learn, and they must, therefore, receive his guidance and direction in their activities.

Once the school absorbed the principle of activity, it was adapted to the other principles existing in it, especially to those determining the status of certain contents of knowledge as irreplaceable and indispensable. It followed that the only desirable types of activity were those that would lead the pupil to acquire the knowledge that the school had decided it was necessary for him to acquire. Activity is an innate need of man and requires no encouragement or support so long as the interest of the learner regulates it. When the teacher decides what the pupil must do, the activity is no longer the same activity. In the first place, it will not lead to learning in every instance because it is not sustained by the drives of the pupil in every instance. The routine performance of imposed tasks in the home, the office, or the factory, for example, will not lead to learning (even if it could do so) because it is not prompted by the interest of the individual. If it is not the individual's own interest that directs his drive to activity, but other factors such as the expectation of rewards or the fear of reprisals, then the activity will usually lose its meaning as a learning situation.

In this way the principle of activity became devoid of meaning even before it was put into practice. According to this approach, the pupil is expected to do more than pay attention and to reconstruct what he has heard or seen. When he is studying the humanities, for example, he is supposed to discuss, analyze, translate, present, or recite. When he is working in the exact sciences he is obliged to conduct experiments, collect specimens, or observe the phenomena of nature. In the arts he is expected to draw, paint, dance, or play an instrument. In every case, however, the teacher decides which activities the pupil will engage in and when. Though activity is conceived of as a way of learning, the contents of the activities are determined by teachers in accordance with the characteristics of the knowledge the school wants its pupils to acquire.

This conception interprets the acquisition of knowledge differently than the previous one. In the previous conception the knowledge mastered by the individual was measured by his ability to recall information transmitted to him and to perform skills in which he had been drilled. Here the knowledge mastered by the individual is measured by his ability to use the principles he has internalized. The principles of knowledge are implicit in the various disciplines. Those of mathematics differ from those of history and those of literature. Specific activities—solving mathematical problems, discussing historical problems, and analyzing works of literature—make possible the internalization of these different principles. The individual cannot internalize these principles simply by listening to and repeating them. He must actively experience the operations characteristic of the different disciplines in order to internalize their respective principles.

As mentioned above, the teacher, not the pupils, decides which of these activities to engage in and when. Only rarely do the directives of the teacher correspond with the interests of the pupils. Though the activities will often interest the students and activate their learning capacities, this will not be the case when they are forced upon them. Since the activities are compulsory, the teacher has to awaken the pupil's interest in them. If he fails to do so, he has no alternative but to enforce discipline. In this way instruction based on teacher-directed activities resembles instruction based on the pupil's attention; that is, both depend on coercion and discipline. Activity resulting from coercion does not lead to the anticipated kind of learning. Despite the theoretical differences between the psychological and epistemological foundations of these two approaches—that based on attention and repetition and that based on dictated activities—there is little difference between them in practice. The type of activity demanded of the pupil by the second approach creates a situation that is no different in principle from the situation created by the activities demanded by the first.

This type of instruction can lead to learning when the pupil discovers how to respond to the secondary motivations it offers him. When the pupil has learned to anticipate the rewards he receives for his activity, he is likely to learn from this activity. He will then, however, demand an additional reward for the learning achievement that results from the activity. It would thus appear that the introduction of directed and dictated activity has caused complications. Whereas in the previous system it was enough to reward the pupil for knowing (remembering) something, it is now necessary to reward him both for acting (writing, reading, and reciting) and for knowing (grades and approval). It is ironic that this results from applying a theory that is supposed to be based on the assumption that to be active is a natural human need. This assumption is soon discovered to be mistaken when teachers and teaching systems take activity to mean occupation. Activity not regulated by the self-motivation of the learner is an occupation unrelated to an inner need of the person so occupied. According to certain educational ideologies, this kind of activity is soon transformed into a ritual occupation performed in schools without any reliance being placed on its results. Thus, for example, the pupil dissects a frog in the school laboratory, but neither he nor his biology teacher expects him to learn anything about the anatomy of the frog from the exercise, which takes place, apparently, for no better reason than to appease the new educational god of activity. After he has performed the dissection, the pupil returns to the textbook or the exercise book from which he has copied whatever the teacher has dictated and learns about the anatomy of the frog from what is written there.

Education involves the initiation of others into worth-while activities. *
The curriculum of a school or university may be operated with a principle
of options, which encourages the individual to choose some activity which
is suitable to his ability, aptitude, and interest; but this choice is between a
range of activities that are thought to be worth passing on. Science, mathe-
matics, history, art, cooking, and carpentry feature on the curriculum, not
bingo, bridge, and billiards. Presumably there must be some reason for this
apart from their utilitarian or vocational value; for it has been argued that
though most of these activities can be viewed instrumentally, to regard
them as having educational value is to rule out such considerations. It
would require, also, a considerable stretching of the concept of "use" to
hold that there was much use in learning poetry if a reason is to be provided
which is somehow extrinsic to the values inherent in the appreciation of
poetry. How then can the pursuit of such activities be justified?

Before tackling the question of the justification of such activities, it is im-
portant to remove certain misunderstandings which often confuse the dis-
cussion of this topic and which load teaching with a quite unnecessary feel-
ing of frustration, guilt, and inadequacy. I am maintaining only that there
must be good reasons for pursuing these sorts of activities rather than
others. This does not imply that there are equally good reasons for saying
that such activities included on a curriculum are more worth-while than
others which are also on a curriculum. It might be possible, for instance, to
show why history and literary appreciation are more worth-while than
bingo and bridge: but it does not follow that there must also be reasons for
saying that history is more worth-while than literary appreciation. Still less
does it follow that the student will grasp what these reasons are before em-
barking on the worth-while pursuit in question and take to it because he
sees the reasons.

I would hazard the guess that such advocacy is pretty ineffective to those
whose view of such activities is an external one. Enthusiasm for them is
caught rather than engendered by argument.

The explanation of this inefficacy of advocacy is not far to seek. The ma-
jority of men are geared to consumption and to the value of anything in
terms of immediate pleasure or as related instrumentally to the satisfaction
of their wants as consumers. When they ask the question "What is there in
this for me?" "Where will this get me?" activities like science and art have a
straightforward appeal. For they offer sweat and struggles rather than im-

---

*R. S. Peters, *Ethics and Education* (Atlanta: Scott, Foresman, 1966), pp. 71 – 72.

mediate delight and their instrumentality to the satisfaction of other wants is difficult to discern.

8.3 Pupil-Initiated Activities

In both previous approaches theoretical assumptions about the psychology of learning lead to a practical question: what must the teacher do to make his pupils learn? In the third approach the assumptions about learning lead to a different question: what must the pupil do in order for learning to take place? It also leads to a different answer: the pupil must act on the basis of his self-motivation and his self-regulation.

The decision in favor of activities resulting from self-motivation and self-regulation is a function of previous decisions regarding such factors as the aims of instruction, the status of the pupil, and the status of knowledge. The teacher who maintains that the aim of instruction is to support self-actualization of the learner, that each pupil is a unique individual whose road to self-actualization differs from that of his fellows, and that the value of knowledge lies in the degree of support it provides for the self-actualization of the learner cannot condone pupils' activities that are controlled by teachers, let alone advocate passive attention as a means of learning. The "natural" activities of infants and small children provide the model of learning appropriate to this approach. A tremendous amount of learning occurs in the first years of childhood; much of it results from the innate drives of the infant himself, with the role of adults restricted to providing opportunities for learning. In this way the child learns to talk and to understand what is being said to him, to walk, and to distinguish relationships existing among himself and various figures in his environment. He learns these and other similar things in order to satisfy his own needs, in his own time, and in a way that is unique to him. This type of learning cannot be advanced in time because it is not possible to arouse the child's needs before growth and maturation give rise to them. As long as adults restrict themselves to providing opportunities for learning, the child will learn and develop as a result of his own inner needs. If they decide to extend their role and attempt to direct the opportunities for learning and development, their interference will block or damage the child's development.

The school could continue the "spontaneous" development of the child. This can be done if his teachers allow him to explore the world, with its objects, ideas, and relationships, and his place in it, by virtue of his innate curiosity and his own interests. The function of the school is to provide the child with a wealth of stimuli; his curiosity will then direct him to those appropriate to his own learning needs. The abundance of stimuli provided by a rich environment and the curiosity of the child (whose development has not been impaired) are the conditions necessary for activity to occur. Under what conditions does this activity lead to learning?

Not all activity leads to learning. Curiosity and interest are necessary, but they are not sufficient to transform activity into learning. An additional factor is the liberation of activity from external rewards and punishments. Rewards and punishments have always been used by teachers to support learning, but the type of learning they support is not the kind anticipated by this logic of instruction. The pupil whose activities are constantly evaluated and always lead to rewards or punishments will learn, of course, to direct his activities into channels that lead to rewards. He will also learn not to act at all if he can expect no reward for his activities. The attempt to encourage spontaneous activity by means of outside rewards achieves, therefore, the opposite of what it sets out to achieve. The only way to support activity that leads to learning as a way of life is by providing stimuli that will, in turn, produce activity that is its own reward.

If a pupil chooses activities because of his interest in them, and if he receives satisfactions or experiences frustrations whose source is the activities themselves, he learns. Satisfaction of this kind differs from the praises or rewards of the teacher in that it reinforces the individual's drive to be active as a means of satisfying his curiosity. The pupil is satisfied because he has succeeded in discovering something or has answered a question that was bothering him. Satisfaction of this kind is also a stage in the crystallization of a method of investigation or, in other words, in the crystallization of an individual style of learning. The learner's frustrations are an inevitable part of learning, but their effect is not the same as the frustrations associated with punishment or censure. A pupil who has not found the solution to a problem that interests him may become apathetic for a certain period of time, but he will not be subject to the teacher's censure for not being able to solve the problem. The teacher's role here differs from that in the two previous conceptions. He does not evaluate his pupil's activities, but rather advises him, shares his doubts, and sometimes helps him. When threat is removed from the teaching situation, the teacher is no longer a judge. He sees himself instead as organizing the teaching situation so that his pupils will become active in it and will derive satisfaction from the activity itself. Then the pupil's activity is likely to be transformed into learning.

"Live and learn" is an old aphorism, and its truth is well known to everyone.* As long as the breath of life is in him, man learns. Every experience provides him with data, every thought provides him with a tool of analysis. From birth, through infancy, youth, maturity, and old age, up to the day of his death, all of life is a revel of learning and self-perfection.

We all know this to be true of ourselves and of others. Why, then, this terrible, anxious preoccupation with learning when people deal with children?

The answer is simple. Most people are not really worried about whether their children are learning. They are worried about whether their children are learning the right things.

There are two sorts of "right things" parents and educators want children to know: the things children "need" to know, and the things children "ought" to know. Let's take these up in turn.

Much time spent by curriculum planners is given over to determining what subjects children need to know in order to function as effective adults in the community. Making such a determination sounds like a fairly straightforward task. One surveys the scene objectively, and one merely isolates the essential basic building blocks. Thus is the core curriculum born.

Unfortunately, what may have been simple in times of stagnation and quiet is no longer simple or even possible. The world today is expanding into new horizons at a dizzying rate, and only a rash man or a fool would venture to predict the shape of things even a decade from now. Can anyone really say what a child of six needs to learn today to be an effective adult twenty years from now? . . . By substituting the educator's judgment for the child's judgment, we are teaching the child something much more far-reaching than a specific subject: we are teaching the child to rely on others for guidance, rather than on his own sense of direction. What a child really

*From *The Crisis in American Education: An Analysis and a Proposal,* pp. 56 – 63. Reprinted by permission of Sudbury Valley School Press.

learns is not the core curriculum—that he may or may not master, depend-
ing on how good a student he is—but rather the idea that it is up to others,
more "expert" than he, to determine what he really needs to know.

The intellectual and emotional needs of each person are different and spe-
cific for that person. No one else can know in advance what they are, and
no one else ought to have the power to enforce his guess as to what they are
on the person concerned.

The question of whether children have learned the things they "ought" to
know is quite a different matter, and goes right to the heart of the larger
question of thought control and censorship. In an authoritarian state, the
powers-that-be determine what everyone ought to know, and that is that.
But in a democratic society, this whole approach is alien and unacceptable.
Who is to say what someone else "ought" to know? Who has that right?
Who has been given that power?

The anxiety about children's learning is entirely unnecessary. They are
always learning, and they are learning—avidly and persistently—what they
want to learn, what they feel they need to learn at any particular time in
life. We do not have to worry that they will not find out what they need to
know, any more than we have to worry that they will not find out when
they are hungry. And we should not be concerning ourselves at all with
what they ought to learn.

What we should be doing, if we believe in what we stand for, is minding
our own business, and getting out of our children's business when it comes
to what is going on in their heads. Let their minds develop as they want
them to develop; place no obstacles in their path towards mastery; the
rewards will be self-motivated, self-regulated children who will know their
minds when they grow to maturity.

It might be worth adding as a postscript that when people are learning
what they want to learn, their rate of absorption and retention as well as
their ability to concentrate are nothing short of phenomenal by comparison
to the externally-forced learning situation. For sheer efficiency, self-
motivated learning has all other forms of learning far, far outstripped.

There are two other concerns about learning worth mentioning. One is
the concern that children will not be exposed to a rich enough variety of
subjects to form the basis for valid self-motivated study unless the schools
force some sort of exposure on them.

It is difficult to take this concern seriously, since it is so completely out of
touch with current realities. On the one hand, the communications revolu-
tion everyone is talking about, with its television, rapid travel, home

movies, etc., etc., has rendered today's three-year-old more "exposed" than the average adult was a mere generation ago. The child entering school today for the first time has picked up, at home and in the street, information about more things, more subjects, more places, more people, and more real issues than all his textbooks and curricula will ever mention. On the other hand, the same communications revolution, and the shrunken world it has brought about, has made us more aware than ever that no matter how much exposure we force in our schools, we can never hope to uncover more than the merest miniscule fraction of the totality of human experience and knowledge. For every subject we painstakingly arrange to have our children exposed to in school, a thousand other subjects lie at hand, ignored by our schools, but no less significant in real life than the few that were somehow selected.

The second concern often voiced has to do with availability of resources. In schools where every child learns what he is interested in, how can we be sure there will be teachers and books and materials to satisfy the interest?

The problem is insoluble if its solution is sought in advance. If we seek from the outset to set up schools that have available at all times all the resources necessary to the full pursuit of every possible subject, we can obviously never dream of succeeding . . . .

The problem is easily solved, however, if we attend to each specific instance as it arises. After all, every possible subject is not in fact in demand all the time; quite the contrary, at any given moment only a few fields are in demand. The school must be prepared to meet all requests for resources as they arise, and not a minute earlier; and it must then be prepared to meet the requests with thoroughness and dispatch . . . .

What a student learns in such a school, he has wanted to learn; and what he wants to learn, he wants to learn well. This has an interesting consequence: in such a school, teachers don't schedule tests and prepare evaluations for unwilling students; instead, students besiege teachers to be tested and criticized, so that they may advance more rapidly to their self-proclaimed goals.

Ninth Dimension:
Leadership

Teaching situations are asymmetrical. On one side are adults with power and authority; on the other are pupils without power and authority. This superiority has a number of sources: power in society is not divided equally among different age groups; adults enjoy institutional support when there is conflict between themselves and the young; adults know more than children. In the school as in the family, the adult is supposed to be right, to know what is correct and what is incorrect, and to have the authority to make decisions.

The asymmetry of teaching situations determines their nature. Teaching situations are created by virtue of authority. In the school, teachers and other adults are those in authority and so are leaders, while pupils are those without or with very little authority and so are led. Though this is the basic teaching situation, it is not usually presented in such naked terms. It is usually wrapped in a rather thick layer of ideology, which disguises the essential fact that teaching situations are authoritarian situations.

These ideologies may be divided into two categories: those that attempt to justify the exercise of authority, and those that repudiate authority.

In the first category are all the beliefs and opinions that consider it "natural" and obvious that children and youths are inexperienced and usually incapable of leading themselves; thus, they should be led by adults. These ideologies are based on authoritarian conceptions that

relate not only to the school but to social relationships in general, such
as the family and the state. Men who are not leaders themselves
should, therefore, be led.

The second category must be further divided into two subgroups.
The first includes ideologies that attempt to disguise the authoritarianism of teaching situations. The second repudiates this authoritarianism. The contradictory though current opinions in education form
the basis for the first subgroup. One holds that authoritarianism is
damaging to the development of pupils. The other states that education is impossible without an authoritarian framework. Basing their
position on these two contradictory assumptions, adherents construct
a position that is, in fact, an attempt to maintain authority without
acknowledging its existence. A bridge between the two contradictory
assumptions is formed by such concepts and slogans as "the pupil is
identified with his teacher," "teachers and pupils are both aiming at
the same thing," and "the teacher should direct his pupil without the
pupil sensing that he is being directed."

The second subdivision consists of ideologies that reject authority
and draw the following practical conclusions from this rejection:
teaching must be reorganized, and the new organization must be
based on forms that are not asymmetrical, that are not based on a
firm division into teacher and taught.

The way in which authority is exercised, which creates the style of
leadership, is the main factor determining the psychological climate
that prevails in the learning group. This psychological climate conditions the products of instruction to no less an extent than the other factors that have been discussed up to now. Indeed, if the only change in
the classroom was the psychological climate, the products of instruction would undergo a radical transformation. The image of aims,
achievements, and the social role of instruction, the status of the
pupil, the teacher, and the contents of knowledge, the preferred types
of motivation and activities — all of these reach the pupil through the
psychological climate in the class. And this climate results primarily
from the nature and style of the teacher's leadership.

Studies of leadership in instruction, which began in the 1940's,
identified characteristics distinguishing the various psychological climates. Most of these studies dichotomize the psychological climates
brought about by different leadership styles. Lippit and White,[43] the
pioneers in this field, distinguished, in fact, three styles of leadership.

One, however, was more a logical possibility than a style of leadership that actually existed among teachers. They termed it "laissez faire" because the teacher simply surrenders his status as leader. Lippit and White's two remaining styles are presented in dichotomous terms: one brings about an authoritarian climate, and the other a democratic climate. All other researchers in this field draw similar distinctions between psychological climates in the classroom. For example, Anderson[44] distinguishes between a dominative and an integrative climate; Gibb[45] between a defensive and a supportive climate; Flanders[46] between a climate created by direct influence and one created by indirect influence.

The ghost haunting these dichotomous distinctions is a reincarnation of the same spirit that inspired generations of pedagogues to search tirelessly for the "right" method of instruction. If one method is right, then the other method must necessarily be wrong. Despite the fact that these distinctions were drawn in the field of empirical research and that their purpose was not evaluative but descriptive, there is no doubt on which side the sympathies of the investigators lie. The integrative (Anderson), supportive (Gibb), and democratic (Lippit and White) climate created by indirect influence (Flanders) is obviously preferable to the dominative, defensive, authoritarian climate created by direct influence. The bias disclosed by these studies in favor of one of the alternatives demonstrates the desire to discover the "right method of teaching." It is perhaps for this reason that the alternatives they describe do not reflect the actual alternatives existing in the classroom; they are instead a product of logical constructions in the minds of their authors.

It is important to draw a distinction, lacking in all these studies, between an autocratic and an authoritative climate. This is the distinction between leadership based on the will, the taste, and the personality of the teacher and leadership based on certain higher principles of which the teacher considers himself the representative. A teacher can be autocratic in any system of instruction, regardless of its ideology. This personality, not his ideology, determines his actions in the classroom and their influence. He can be "democratic" or "supportive" whether or not his ideology is authoritarian, but his leadership style will be different in each case.

All authority involves the exercise of power. In this context, power is defined as the ability of a person to cause another person to do or not to do something according to his will. Authority lies, therefore, with the person who possesses the superior power. What is the source of the teacher's superior power that gives him authority over his pupils?

The teacher's power may be derived from a number of sources. For our purposes, the most suitable discussion of the sources of power is that of French and Raven,[47] who list five such sources.

1. *Reward power.* This power is derived from the ability of one person to reward others, and thereby to impose his will on them. The teacher who evaluates his pupils in terms of grades possesses such power, at least in those school systems where grades are important to the students.

2. *Coercive power.* This is the other side of the coin of reward power. A teacher who has the ability to give bad marks, to censure his pupils in public, to take other such negative actions possesses this type of power.

3. *Legitimate power.* In any formal organization, of which the school is one, there is a hierarchy. The place of the teacher in the hierarchy is higher than that of the pupil. Should a conflict occur between student and teacher, the latter can call upon the power of the institution to back him up. This power can be in the form of interference by the principal, pressure by parents on the pupil, or even expulsion from school.

4. *Expert power.* The person from whom others seek advice or guidance is in the superior position of power. When pupils acknowledge the expertise of the teacher and are interested in his guidance, then he has power over them, and his status is one of authority.

5. *Relevant power.* The source of this type of power lies in the personality of the person who possesses it. Others comply with his will not because they wish to be led by him; his influence is psychological and has nothing to do with rewards or punishment.

Teachers, at least teachers in formal institutions, use all five kinds of power. There are, of course, differences among teachers. These differences are based on the individual preference of the teacher. This preference, involving the choice of a certain pattern of instruction, is a decisive factor in the psychological climate prevalent in the classroom.

This distinction among the various kinds of power used by the teacher makes it possible to distinguish three different types of leadership:

9.1. The autocratic style.

9.2. The authoritative style.

9.3. The permissive style.

9.1 Autocratic Style

The style of leadership based on the teacher's psychological need to impose his will on his pupils is advocated by no educational school of thought. It is, nevertheless, found in the classroom and is supported by a number of factors. First, educational administrators and parents often tend to identify the ability of the teacher to control his class with leadership ability. They do not usually distinguish between the autocratic leadership of a teacher greedy for power and efficient leadership of any other kind; it is important only that the teacher maintain control over the class. Second, a number of teachers favor autocratic leadership because of their own personal needs. As a matter of fact, some choose to teach precisely because of the opportunities it offers for satisfying their drive to dominate and lead others. Up to now teacher-training institutions have done little to make their students aware of their motives. Since a number of educational ideologies justify the imposition of authority on pupils, many teachers believe that by exercising strict control they are serving legitimate educational goals to the best of their ability. This belief is often a rationalization of their drive to dominate.

Teachers of this type depend heavily on reward power, coercive power, and legitimate power. They tend to stress their pupils' dependence on their will. When they successfully lead their classes they are happy to bestow such rewards as are in their power to grant—praise and good marks. When they fail, they exercise coercive power by means of the sanctions available to them—punishment and bad marks. When their authority erodes, they resort to legitimate power—by sending pupils to the principal, demanding their expulsion, and so forth.

It would give an erroneous impression, however, to restrict our discussion of the autocratic style only to the psychological needs of some teachers. While it is true that autocratic teachers can be found in all educational systems, some systems consider the style an indivisible part

of the method as a whole. In this case even those teachers with nonauthoritarian personalities will dominate and subjugate their pupils.
This leadership style was predominant when the school saw as one of
its roles the breaking of the pupils' spirit, whether this was done consciously or unconsciously. For long periods of history the socialization
process was intended to prevent the young from developing as individuals capable of acting according to their own judgment and accepting
responsibility for their acts. These societies wanted their members to
be responsible only to others, to be capable of subjecting themselves to
higher authorities, to surrender their right to decide their actions for
themselves. These aims were well served by the autocratic style of instruction. Autocracy, whether its source is the teacher's personality or
the principles governing certain educational systems, is likely to develop into one of a number of different patterns of leadership. All these
patterns, however, have certain common characteristics.

In the first place, when leadership is autocratic, it must maintain
the external signs of power. Only what the teacher wants, or at least
formally approves, may take place in the classroom. The necessity to
ask the teacher's permission is an external sign of power, and this type
of teacher is very strict about enforcing the rule. A typical expression
of the teacher's sensitivity to the external signs of power is his refusal to
allow his pupils to do anything for which they have not first asked his
permission, even when the content of their actions meets with his full
approval.

A further characteristic of this style of leadership is that the teacher
is not required to explain his decisions to his pupils. "Because I say so"
is a sufficient reason for any demand the teacher makes or any task he
sees fit to impose. Expressions of sympathy, affection, or friendship
are not regarded as stemming from the teacher's actual feelings, but as
favors for which the students should be grateful.

Above all, the relationships created by this approach are characterized by the fact that the pupil faces his teacher in isolation from his
classmates. Members form relationships within the framework of the
class, but these relationships appear not to exist insofar as the school
or the teacher is concerned. In all situations that arise in the class, the
pupil confronts the teacher alone. He is personally responsible for
what he does or fails to do in his schoolwork, his behavior, and his appearance. It is no wonder that the informal relationships among
students often serve the pupil as satisfying his primary social needs, as

a refuge from the formal structure of the class (which is expressed in the relations between pupil and teacher), and as an organizational framework directed against the teacher and the school.

It is paradoxical that this style of leadership creates conditions that are not harmful, but favorable, to certain kinds of pupils. These pupils are usually emotionally secure within their families and are highly intelligent. These characteristics enable them to play the game according to the rules of the school, although they are actually critical of these rules. If these children are aware of the double role they are playing, they may, be these means, differentiate between the essential and the unessential. This experience, although not an easy one even for a well-balanced child, may spur his development. The majority of students, however, are neither sufficiently protected by the emotional support of their parents nor capable of the necessary intellectual differentiation. For these pupils, contact with an autocratic teacher is likely to be a harmful experience that blocks their development.

This style of leadership in instruction is, in fact, an illustration of the self-fulfilling prophecy. The assumption on which this style is justified is that children do not want to learn, either because they are rebellious and disobedient or because they are indifferent and uninterested. Therefore, they need the guidance of a firm hand. When teachers use a firm hand and do not recognize their students' individual needs, some pupils become rebellious, and some become apathetic. Both kinds of pupil, however, lose interest in learning, which was certainly present in some, at least when they started school. The teacher's initial assumptions are thus confirmed, which leads him to increase his autocratic practices, which lead, in turn, to greater rebelliousness or apathy among his pupils. In any event, the activities of the school in this instance do little to advance the development of its pupils.

It is the duty of every school child: *

1. *To acquire knowledge persistently in order to become an educated and cultured citizen and to be of the greatest possible service to his country.*
2. *To study diligently, to be punctual in attendance, and not arrive late for classes.*

*From *Sovietskaya Pedagogica* (October 1943), in Nigel Grant, *Soviet Education* (Harmondsworth, Eng.: Penguin Books, 1964), pp. 48 – 49.

3. To obey the instructions of the school director and the teachers without question.

4. To arrive at school with all the necessary textbooks and writing materials; to have everything ready for the lesson before the teacher arrives.

5. To come to school clean, well groomed, and neatly dressed.

6. To keep his place in the classroom neat and tidy.

7. To enter the classroom and take his place immediately after the bell rings; to enter and leave the classroom during the lesson only with the teacher's permission.

8. To sit upright during the lesson, not leaning on the elbows or slouching; to listen attentively to the teacher's explanation and the other pupils' answers, and not to talk or let his attention wander to other things.

9. To rise when the teacher or director enters or leaves the room.

10. To stand to attention when answering the teacher; to sit down only with the teacher's permission; to raise his hand if he wishes to answer or ask a question.

11. To take accurate notes in his assignment book of homework scheduled for the next lesson, and to show these notes to his parents, and to do all the homework unaided.

12. To be respectful to the school director and teachers; when meeting them, to greet them with a polite bow; boys should also raise their caps.

13. To be polite to his elders, to behave modestly and respectfully in school, in the street, and in public places.

14. Not to use coarse expressions, not to smoke, not to gamble for money or other objects.

15. To protect school property; to be careful of his personal things and the belongings of his comrades.

16. To be attentive and considerate of old people, small children, and the weak and the sick; to give them a seat on the bus or make way for them in the street, being helpful to them in every way.

17. To obey his parents, to help them take care of his small brothers and sisters.

18. To maintain order and cleanliness in rooms; to keep his clothes, shoes, and bed neat and tidy.

19. To carry his student's record book with him always, to guard it carefully, never handing it over to anyone else, and to present it on request of the teacher or school director.

20. To cherish the honour of his school and class and defend it as his own.

9.2 Authoritative Style

One difference between the authoritative style of leadership and the autocratic style is that it rests on an authoritarian philosophy and not on the authoritarian characteristics of the teacher. It is possible, of course, that instruction based on such a philosophy will attract teachers with authoritarian personalities, but even where this is the case, the teacher's behavior is influenced by the way the school's philosophy justifies authoritarianism.

Many systems of ideas, whether religious, political, or social, tend to provide a philosophic basis for authoritarian practices in the school. Such a system of ideas need only claim the status of truth for the education carried out in its name to be authoritarian. When the aim of instruction is to produce people whose opinions, values, and behavior correspond to ideas conceived of as truths, teachers must become the representatives of authority.

The difference between a teacher who represents authority by virtue of a given system of ideas and one who is autocratic by virtue of his own personality traits is demonstrated by the type of power preferred by each. The first kind of teacher prefers to use expert and relevant power instead of reward or coercive or legitimate power. When pupils recognize, even to some degree the ideas the teacher holds, they will turn to the teacher to decide, discriminate, elucidate, and solve problems. This teacher leads his pupils by virtue of his power as an expert.

The use of relevant power—leadership based on the teacher's ability to lead—has a central role in instruction that attempts to mold pupils' personalities. In this case the teacher serves as an example; by identifying with him his pupils internalize the ideas and values of the school's philosophy. The teacher cannot transmit these ideas and values to the pupil simply by means of the authority he claims for himself because of his ability to grant rewards and inflict punishments. In order for pupils to internalize the ideas and values of any religious, political, or social philosophy, they must identify with the figure who represents these values.

This does not mean that the teacher will never use reward or coercive or legitimate power. But he will usually not base his behavior on these types of power; it will be characterized, rather, by expert and relevant power.

The authoritative style of leadership does not conform easily to the institutional structure of the school. Authoritative leadership—which rests mainly on the relevant power of the teacher, on his personal qualities as a leader—is intended to create the conditions by which the pupil can identify with his teacher. By means of this identification he is able to internalize the cultural values or beliefs that the teacher represents. People gifted with leadership qualities do not usually operate in institutionalized frameworks like those according to which the school is organized. When they do so, they tend to take them over. There have been isolated instances in which teachers with charismatic personalities have taken over the leadership of schools for long periods of time. In the majority of cases, however, this kind of leadership is of short duration, and the routine institutionalism of the school soon reasserts itself.

The main power available to teachers who regard themselves as representatives of a higher authority is, therefore, expert power, which is interpreted in this context as knowledgeableness. Teachers who see themselves in this light usually feel that they possess a breadth of knowledge in various subjects. Expert power can be used as the basis for the teacher's leadership, however, only if the pupil acknowledges the value of those subjects in which the teacher is an expert. Thus, students will acknowledge the leadership of a philosophy teacher only if they value a knowledge of philosophy. On the eve of an examination in mathematics, the teacher may find himself endowed with expert power in relation to pupils who suddenly discover that they are in need of his help and guidance. Until that time he has probably relied mainly on reward power, coercive power, and legitimate power in leading his class. That is, he has employed the same sources of power used by the autocratic teacher. These are the factors that constitute the essential weakness of the authoritative style of leadership in teaching. Relevant power is rare, and expert power is sufficient only if pupils place a high enough value on the subjects of the teacher's expertise. For this reason, authoritative leadership often ends up as autocratic leadership—as leadership resting on the power of the teacher to praise, to censure, and to punish.

Even when authoritative leadership is implemented by a charismatic teacher, success is not guaranteed. Leadership of this type may have a repressive influence. A teacher whose pupils identify with him may exploit his domination over them to keep them in subjection for as long as he possibly can. In these cases the influential factor is not the teacher's educational philosophy, but the satisfaction he derives from the response to his leadership.

When authoritative leadership does not degenerate into autocratic leadership on the one hand or into the narcissism of the charismatic leader on the other, it creates a distinctive psychological climate in the class.

In that psychological climate the learning group may develop a strong sense of identity, by means of which the pupil may identify himself as a member of a broader collective — cultural, political, ideological. In elitist education pupils tend to·identify themselves as members of a certain social group, in religious education as members of a certain religious faith, in ideological education as members of a defined political camp. This feeling of belonging to a collective, which in most cases is anonymous to the pupils (since they do not know most of the other members), usually involves a fanatical belief in this one collective and suspicion of other collectives (whose members are also unknown to the pupils). An anonymous collective usually develops a set of norms that are binding inside the group. These norms regulate the relations among the pupils and between the pupils and the teacher.

The content of these norms depends on factors outside the learning group, on values and ideologies of which the teacher is the representative. Thus, for example, in one learning group the pupil is expected to help his classmate, and in another group the opposite is true. In the latter case, the pupil who has worked hard himself will not obtain high marks because he helps his friends. One group places learning achievements at the top of the scale of values, while another considers the behavior and character of the pupil more important. The norm of the learning group will, of course, also be the norm of the teacher. Anyone who disregards these norms will be rejected both by the group and by the teacher.

Despite the connection between the norms of the group and the values represented by the teacher, the teacher is not a member of the group. His status puts him above the group. Though his pupils identify with the teacher and he represents the values they accept, he does not have the same rights and privileges as everyone else. The pupils' identification with these values moderates to a large extent the conflict that this style of leadership creates. Their relations are not, however, free from tension; they are usually formal and ceremonial to a considerable degree, even if only in the classroom. This ambiguity—the teacher as a member of the group because he holds values in common with it and his nonmembership because he represents these values—largely determines the psychological climate in the class. This type of group is always directed, even when the teacher is absent. It always acts in accordance with external direction, whether this direction comes from the teacher himself or from a member of the group who is regarded by his fellows as being closest in spirit to the norms the teacher represents. Group solidarity in this case (unlike the case of autocratic leadership) is not against the teacher and the school, but with them.

By discipline I mean the imposition of external *standards and controls on individual conduct.* Permissiveness, on the other hand, refers to the absence of such standards and controls. To be permissive is to "let alone," to adopt a laissez-faire policy. Authoritarianism is an excessive, arbitrary, and autocratic type of control which is diametrically opposite to permissiveness. Between the extremes of laissez-faire permissiveness and authoritarianism are many varieties and degrees of control. One of these . . . is democratic discipline.*

Discipline is a universal cultural phenomenon which generally serves four important functions in the training of the young. First, it is necessary for socialization—for learning the standards of conduct that are approved and tolerated in any culture. Second, it is necessary for normal personality maturation—for acquiring such adult personality traits as dependability, self-reliance, self-control, persistence, and ability to tolerate frustration. These aspects of maturation do not occur spontaneously, but only in response to sustained social demands and expectations. Third, it is necessary for the internalization of moral standards and obligations or, in other words, for the development of conscience. Standards obviously cannot be internalized unless they also exist in external form; and even after they are effectively internalized, universal cultural experience suggests that external sanctions are still required to insure the stability of the social order. Lastly, discipline is necessary for children's emotional security. Without the guidance provided by unambiguous external controls, the young tend to feel bewildered and apprehensive. Too great a burden is placed on their own limited capacity for self-control.

*D. P. Ausubel, "A New Look at Classroom Discipline," in J. Raths *et al.* (eds.), *Studying Teaching* (Englewood Cliffs, N. J.: Prentice-Hall, 1967), p. 403.

9.3 Permissive Style

Permissiveness is an attitude adopted by those who surrender authority because of values or educational considerations. An admission of pluralism gives birth to permissiveness. When people recognize the right of others to be different and behave differently from themselves and to hold different opinions and beliefs, they admit pluralism. Pluralism promotes an attitude of noninterference in the lives of others, even those who are in a minority in society and even those who are weak. Permissiveness in education, although closely connected with this conception, also has another source: psychological conceptions of the personality current for nearly half a century that are due to the influence of psychoanalysis and its outgrowths. According to these conceptions, permissiveness is an educational strategy that prevents as far as possible society's repressive influence on the development of the individual and his well-being.

The individual is born and grows up in society, which exerts its pressures on him in innumerable ways, both open and hidden. Perhaps the most efficient of these ways is traditional education, which has long repressed the individual. The needs and desires he is forced to repress find new outlets, most of which are destructive both to himself and to society. Aggression, hate, fanaticism, malice, suspicion, hypocrisy, and similar characteristics are the result of suppressed needs and desires. Permissiveness is thus an educational attitude that seeks to relieve society's pressures on the young in order to enable them to actualize their needs and drives. It is assumed that their actualization will prevent the repression of desires over which the individual has no control. As a matter of fact, the advocates of permissiveness feel that the health of society, and not only its individual members, depends to a large extent on the ability of the individual to give free rein to his true desires.

This is, in essence, a new conception of education. It repudiates the views that education is an instrument by which society adapts the individual to existing conditions and that it is an instrument by which culture molds the human personality according to a ready-made model of the "good man." According to this conception, man, by means of education, becomes aware of himself as a being whose existence cannot be comprehended either by society or culture.[48] Development in the spirit of permissiveness is conceived of as a continuous process through which the individual actualizes his personality. At different ages the form and content of the individual's self-actualization change, but the possibilities for experimentation are common at all stages of his development. Experimentation of this kind means a gradual growth of autonomous being. The small child who experiments with choosing for himself according to his own tastes experiences satisfaction at one time and frustration at another. As a result, he learns to make choices, and, what is more important, he learns to trust himself to make choices. Authoritarian education, on the other hand, gives him instead the "good advice" of the adult, who feels that his wisdom and experience entitle him to provide the child with guidance, even against his will. This guidance deprives the child of the opportunity to experiment for himself, and, by doing so, to attain some degree of self-awareness and autonomy.

These assumptions are the points of departure for permissive leadership. Though "permissive leadership" seems a contradiction in terms, the contradiction is only apparent. Teaching situations are, as has been pointed out, asymmetrical situations in which the adults have more power than children. When these adults, because of a specific consciousness of their role as educators, renounce the use of their superior power, permissive leadership results. It continues to be leadership because it is backed by authority, but it uses this authority in order to prevent, so far as possible, outside interference with the development of those for whom it is responsible.

What is the psychological climate created by this style of leadership?

In authoritarian educational frameworks a large part of the pupil's energy is devoted to resisting education. The authoritative style of leadership (let alone the autocratic) interferes with the development of the individual in order to direct it. The pressure intended to direct the individual's development into the "right" channels produces a counterpressure in the individual personality against this direction. In traditional systems of education educators deal with this resistance in one of two ways: they try to suppress it or to circumvent it. Suppression is characteristic of autocratic leadership, circumvention of authoritative leadership. Discipline is the mechanism by which resistance to education is suppressed, and secondary motivation is the mechanism by which it is circumvented. Despite the differences between these two techniques, they have a common denominator. They regard education as a process that begins when resistance to education ceases.* The permissive approach, on the other hand, regards resistance to education as an integral part of the educational process, but leaves it to the pupil to deal with this resistance. Thus, in the absence of any external pressure against which he can direct the resistance aroused in him by education, the pupil is obliged to accept this resistance as his own problem. When he does so, he becomes aware of himself as a changing and developing being. Change that takes place after the individual's resistance to change has been suppressed or circumvented is accompanied by two possible phenomena. One is an inability to admit that such a change has indeed taken place. The other is an inability to resolve the resistance that has been aroused by the change. Both can lead to domination by irrational drives over which individuals have no control. The channel into which these drives flow and where they find release is society. The lack of self-awareness and the need to express suppressed resistance may lead to aggression, to craving for power, or to interference in the lives of others.

Permissiveness also (no less than the various kinds of authoritarianism) exerts pressure on the individual, but this pressure acts in an opposite direction: to make the individual aware of his resistance and to give him the responsibility for overcoming it. An individual educated in this way will have no great need to dominate his fellows, to assert himself at their expense, or to interfere in their lives in order to gain satisfaction for himself. Instead, he will probably want and need to share his problems with them, problems that arise from his awareness of the changes taking place within him. Such an individual needs society because he needs to belong. He is not prepared, however, to sacrifice his selfhood either by surrendering to the aggressiveness of society, or by striving to dominate it. Advocates of permissiveness regard this style of leadership as most appropriate to educate individuals to preserve their individuality. The psychological climate it creates is one in which relations among members of the group do not destroy their individuality and in which participation in the group does not involve denial of self.

---

*I have discussed this problem at greater length in my article "Educational Pressure and Resistance," *Educational Philosophy and Theory*, IV (No. 1, 1972), 55 – 64.

And so I did not wait for José to decide for himself. * *When I thought the time was ripe, I insisted that we begin our lessons. My insistence carried a great deal of weight with him, since for reasons of his own he respected me. Too, his volition, in any event, could arise only from a background in which I myself already figured, with my own interests and my own manifestation of an adult concern he was accustomed to everywhere but in school. He did* not *feel that his own motives were no concern of mine. No child feels this. This belongs to the hang-ups of adolescence and the neuroses of the hippies. To a child, the motives of adults belong quite simply to the environment. They are like icebergs or attractive islands: one navigates between or heads straight for them. The child's own motives are similarly projected outward; they become occasions for dissimulation or closer contact. It is because of this that both affection and straightout conflict come so easily. They come inevitably, and they belong, both together, to the teaching-learning experience.*

My own demands, then, were an important part of José's experience. They were not simply the demands of a teacher, nor of an adult, but belonged to my own way of caring about José. And he sensed this. There was something he prized in the fact that I made demands on him. This became all the more evident once he realized that I wasn't simply processing him, that is, grading, measuring, etc. And when he learned that he could refuse—could refuse altogether, could terminate the lesson, could change its direction, could insist on something else—our mutual interest in his development was taken quite for granted. We became collaborators in the business of life.

Obviously, if I had tried to compel him, none of this would have been possible. And if I had made no demand—had simply waited for him to come to class—I would in some sense have been false to my own motives, my own engagement in the life of the school and the community. In his eyes I would have lost immediacy, would have lost reality, as it were, for I would have seemed more and more like just a teacher. What he prized, after all, was this: that an adult, with a life of his own, was willing to teach him.

How odd it is to have to say this! What a vast perversion of the natural relations of children and adults has been worked by our bureaucratized system of public education! It was important to José that I was not just a teacher, but a writer as well, that I was interested in painting and had

*From *The Lives of Children*, pp. 112 – 114, by George Dennison. Copyright © 1969 by George Dennison. Reprinted by permission of Random House, Inc.

friends who were artists, that I took part in civil rights demonstrations. To the extent that he sensed my life stretching out beyond him into (for him) the unknown, my meaning as an adult was enhanced, and the things I already knew and might teach him gained the luster they really possess in life. This is true for every teacher, every student. No teacher is just a teacher, no student just a student. The life meaning which joins them is the sine qua non *for the process of education, yet precisely this is destroyed in the public schools because everything is standardized and the persons are made to vanish into their roles. This is exactly Sartre's definition of inauthenticity. I am reminded here, too, of how often John Dewey and, in our own time, Paul Goodman and Elliott Shapiro have urged the direct use of the community. The world as it exists is what the young are hungry for; and we give them road maps, mere diagrams of the world at a distance.*

What I have just described of my relations with José might also be said of Mabel, Gloria, and Susan in their relations with the other children. Gloria and Susan were perhaps more demanding than Mabel and I. Nevertheless, all of the children could refuse. They needed a good reason to do it, and they had to stand up to the adults. But they discovered that good reasons were respected. Boredom, for instance, is a good reason. The beautiful days of spring are good reasons. An ardent desire for something else is a good reason. Anxiety is a good reason. So is a headache or a toothache. And there are many things which if they arise during the course of a lesson, deserve and must be given full precedence, such things as considerations of justice, self-respect, friendship. We and the children, in short, were in an on-going experience of attraction and repulsion, of cooperation and conflict. Out of this flexible and many-faceted encounter, the actual structure of our time together evolved. The essential thing was the absence of compulsion. For every child there was always a way out and a way in, and—most important—a Bill of Personal Rights equal to that of the teachers. The children could win, not by availing themselves of an empty foreground of "freedom," but by encountering the adults head-on. It was a noisy school, as should be, though often, as should be, an electrically quiet one.

FOUR   The Cognitive Map of
Instruction

The nine dimensions presented in Chapter Three, when organized in the structures of the three patterns, provide what might be called a cognitive map of instruction. The map sets forth the central problems of instruction (the dimensions) and the archetypal answers to these controversial problems (the patterns).

There are two possible uses for this map. The first would be to employ concepts on the map and their method of organization as instruments in describing theories of instruction, school systems, individual schools, and individual teaching styles, for purposes of comparison and exposition. The second, and most important, use would be to assist the teacher in making choices and decisions regarding the implementation of various activities in the actual process of instruction. When used in this way, the map organizes pedagogical considerations regarding strategies appropriate to the needs of instruction.

The Cognitive Map in Decision Making

The teacher is forced to make decisions in three types of situations: the stage of preparation for instruction; the stage of implementation; and the stage of feedback.

The Stage of Preparation

The institutionalization of teaching situations—fixed curricula, rigid timetables, examinations—has transformed the teacher's prep-

Table 4 – 1

Cognitive map of instruction

Patterns			
Dimensions	Imitation	Molding	Development
1.0 The nature of aims in teaching	1.1 Extrinsic aims	1.2 Extrinsic aims control intrinsic aims	1.3 Intrinsic aims control extrinsic aims
2.0 The nature of desired achievement	2.1 Performing according to given models	2.2 Acting according to given principles	2.3 Discovering new principles and testing them
3.0 The social significance ascribed to teaching	3.1 Socialization	3.2 Acculturation	3.3 Individuation
4.0 The status of the learner	4.1 Homogeneous group member	4.2 Heterogeneous group member	4.3 Unique individual
5.0 The status of the contents	5.1 Utilitarian	5.2 Intrinsically valuable	5.3 Supportive of the learner's capacities
6.0 The status of the teacher	6.1 Employee	6.2 Cultural agent	6.3 Specialist
7.0 The preferred kind of motivation	7.1 Specific teacher's activities	7.2 Means as well as end of education	7.3 Self-motivation and self-regulation
8.0 The preferred kind of activities	8.1 Attention	8.2 Teacher-directed activities	8.3 Pupil-directed activities
9.0 The preferred kind of leadership	9.1 Autocratic	9.2 Authoritative	9.3 Permissive

aration for instruction into a formal and distinctive act. According to this institutional logic, the teacher is supposed to appear in the classroom with a lesson prepared. This demand that the teacher be ready to present his lesson plan before he teaches is the result of a consistent development originating in an administrative-institutional logic that is unrelated to the logic of instruction. In many school systems a contradiction exists. It is acknowledged that there is a need for teachers to respond to the interest aroused in their pupils, to exploit opportunities that may accidentally arise in the classroom, to involve pupils in problems about which the teacher himself has not yet come to any firm decision, and to justify deviations from the syllabus where learning can be achieved by these means. On the other hand, teachers can be required by the school administration to go to their classes with detailed programs of action. This institutional approach results in the teacher's writing down a few sentences about the material he intends to present to his class that have nothing to do with the educational decisions he will be required to make. In some educational systems this approach has gone even further: the teacher is presented with lesson plans prepared in advance by "experts." The teacher's preparation is thus interpreted as learning lesson plans designed by people who have seen neither the pupils (and cannot, therefore, know what they want or are able or need to learn) nor the teacher (and cannot, therefore, know what or how he is able to teach). One cannot deny the inner consistency of this development. If preparing for instruction means drawing up detailed plans of action in advance, outside the classroom, then these plans may as well be designed by individuals with wide experience and subjected to experts in various fields for their approval before being given to the average teacher, with his limited experience and modest expertise, to teach.

It is, however, precisely the consistent development of institutional logic—leading to the institutionalization of the preparation for instruction—that points to the contradiction between this logic and instructional needs. The teacher who knows in advance what action he will take during the course of the lesson is actually less well prepared than the teacher whose preparation is not so specific. There are a number of reasons for this situation. First, the teacher is guided by the lesson plan rather than the immediate needs of his pupils during the lesson itself. Second, preparation is specific, whereas teaching situations are diffuse. It is not the logical structure of any particular learning unit (which is the essence of the lesson plan prepared in advance) that determines the results of instruction; it is, rather, the gaps in logic that make the pupil think, emotional factors that arise during the process of instruction and become involved in it, and unexpected associations resulting from the contact between teaching contents and pupils. All these factors, which are created during the process of instruction, cannot possibly be planned for in advance.

The teacher's preparation for instruction exists on two levels. The first level is diffuse and consists of all the experience, wisdom, intelligence, sensitivity, and will that the teacher can bring to bear on the teaching situation. The main drawback to institutionalized preparation is that it is likely to have a harmful effect on this diffuse preparation. Institutionalized preparation imposes categories of relevance on the teacher. The relevance or irrelevance of the lesson is not determined by the contents of the lesson but by the pupils' learning. The processes of learning cannot be predicted with much accuracy. Rejecting activities, associations, and thoughts as irrelevant to the subject of instruction may mean rejecting actions that are relevant to learning. This level of preparation — diffuse preparation — consists of the totality of thoughts and actions of the teacher who has been trained to examine his experience in the light of his role as a teacher. Reading a book, even one that is unrelated to the subject he teaches, going to a play or a concert, manipulating a tool, reading a newspaper, or talking to a friend may all be equivalent to preparation for instruction, if the teacher's thought has not been influenced by the institutionalization of preparation for a specific lesson according to the logic of relevance and if he does not classify everything according to its relevance to instruction. Everything can, of course, be relevant to instruction, but the teacher must know how to discover its relevance. Since teaching situations are diffuse, the teacher's attitude in the classroom should also be diffuse. He must be more than an expert on the particular subject he is teaching. He is, in fact, always more than this, unless he has deliberately restricted himself to perform the specific role of "teaching something" instead of being ready to maintain a diffuse relationship with his pupils.

This diffuse preparation (which is essentially the experience of the diversity of life) needs, however, a set of categories according to which the teacher can interpret his experience in terms of educational needs. Successful experiences are very persuasive. A teacher who enjoys a hobby or who has been gratified by an activity tends to integrate these experiences into his teaching. Such integration, even if it takes place intuitively, is better than the self-imposed "professional" limitations of the teacher who perceives his role as that of someone who has to "teach something." There is a problem with integrating experiences into instruction: their uncontrolled introduction may lead the teacher into paths he had no intention of taking. Because the teacher is responsible for guiding and helping to develop, he must be able to subject this experience to a set of controls. Preparation for instruction, in this diffuse sense, means that the teacher thinks constantly about his experience as a human being from the point of view of its educational significance.

The second level of preparation for instruction is the specific level; that is, the individual who teaches history or mathematics must prepare himself for instruction in those subjects. Though this preparation is not of great value in itself, without it the teacher is not likely to be successful. Every area of knowledge today has dozens of instructional models available for the teacher to consider. Thus, specific preparation for teaching any particular area of knowledge may take a number of forms. One is strict adherence to an available model. The teacher usually chooses the model according to the dictates of his superiors. The situation is connected with the status of the teacher in the process of instruction. In this case he is not expected to use his own judgment in deciding how to teach. He is expected to teach according to the system that is imposed on him from above and that he makes an effort to understand. However strenuous and honest these efforts are, instruction based on such foundations will inevitably be poor. A teacher in this position does not choose his method either according to the needs of his pupils or according to his own preferences. He merely implements, without taking either himself or his pupils into account, activities that others have decided are appropriate.

Another model of instruction the teacher may select is one in which he uses in every situation methods that reflect the needs of his pupils and his own tastes and inclinations. In this case he must know, evaluate, and use the available methods according to his independent decisions. This is the opposite of teaching according to instructions from above.

This process of decision making may be based on various considerations. One, which seems superficially satisfactory, considers the available research regarding the relative efficiency of the different methods. This is the most inappropriate way of choosing a method of instruction because efficiency is not a self-sufficient concept. Unless we know the particular definition of efficiency, we know little about the method of instruction. The method may be efficient as a means of imparting information, of fostering critical thought, or of developing the ability to use information in concrete situations. Until the teacher decides on his aims, he cannot choose a method of instruction, however "efficient" it may have been proven to be in empirical research.

The teacher must evaluate and classify his diffuse experience and his specific preparation before he can integrate them in one way or another into his teaching. The teacher who is helplessly confronted by two rival methods of teaching illustrates the problem of preparation for instruction. If a teacher can locate a method, idea, or technique on the cognitive map of instruction—if he can classify a particular method or technique as typical of the pattern of imitation or as vacillating between the patterns of molding and development (however he may define these terms)—he will also be able to decide whether that particular method or technique is appropriate to his needs. The teacher who must ask which of two (or ten) ways of teaching arithmetic, grammar, history, or biology is the best demonstrates his lack of the minimal requirements of professional competence. If he is professionally competent, he asks which way is best for imparting information, for developing thinking, or for encouraging creativity. This is precisely how the conceptual scaffoldings of the cognitive map are intended to be used during the preparatory stage, whether on the diffuse or the specific level. Methods, strategies, sequences of action, techniques, and ideas in instruction are constantly changing. The teacher who is expected to put these theories into practice will adopt those that are likely to support his aims. In order to know which innovations are compatible with his aims, however, he needs categories of analysis and classification. If the teacher encountering new textbooks or new techniques for imparting skills knows how to identify their aims, the achievements they desire, and the motivations implicit in their use, then he will also know how to choose among them.

The Stage of Implementation

Decisions concerning instruction should not be final before they are implemented. Instruction that adheres rigidly to decisions taken previously invariably denies the factors present in actual teaching situations and inevitably misses its mark. The teacher who can deviate from the road he has chosen as a result of his sensitivity to factors operating in the classroom will usually attain his aims. Though the teacher must continue to make decisions during the stage of implementation, this process is not identical to the decision making during the stage of preparation. In the implementation stage the teacher is acting under a considerable degree of pressure, and pressure is not usually conducive to making the right professional decisions.

Before entering the classroom, the teacher decides upon a certain course of action. When he begins to teach, he is confronted by a situation in which he must test the validity of his decision. He may find that his decision was justified, but there is always the possibility that it was wrong. The readiness to admit error and the actual admission of it require training in advance. Professional competence is not demonstrated when the teacher admits his mistake only after his pupils exhibit obvious signs of boredom or leave the classroom in protest. This competence is revealed in the teacher's sensitivity to the first indications by his students that his decision was mistaken. Such sensitive teachers conceive of instruction as an exploratory situation in which the right way is not known in advance but must be sought. The search for the right way, if it is not simply a process of trial and error, requires a prior knowledge of existing possibilities. The teacher who knows only one way will be helpless when he discovers that it does not achieve his goal. On the other hand, the teacher who has become familiar with a number of ways and has assessed them in the light of relevant concepts before choosing one will be able to change if his choice turns out to be unsuitable. A teacher may decide, during the preparatory stage, to reject one way of instruction. He may discover during the stage of implementation, however, that the rejected method is approrpriate for his class, or at least for certain members of it. Preparation for instruction, which is an exploration of possibilities, implies the readiness to exchange one way of reaching a goal for another. Decisions regarding a change of method during the implementation stage can be deliberate and considered if they were preceded by an investigation of other available methods and if the teacher was provided with a set of concepts capable of describing the various courses open to him. This is precisely what the cognitive map of instruction supplies.

The Stage of Feedback

While this stage exists in its own right, it is also a return to the stage of preparation and thus closes the circle of instruction. It consists mainly of learning the lessons taught by the stage of implementation. The teacher must evaluate his actions, which is the confrontation of intentions and results. If the evaluation demonstrates that his actions, which mediated between his intentions and his results, need to be modified, he will find himself again at the preparatory stage. This process of feedback and decision making is the only way the teacher can improve instruction and foster his professional growth. Since instruction depends so heavily on the personalities of those who implement it, the only way to improve it is through the individual experience of the teacher. Learning from experience is not, however, as easy as some may think. Many psychological barriers must be overcome before the teacher can learn from his experience. The major difficulty stems from the necessity of the teacher's being able to see his actions as though they were performed by someone else. Only emotional distance makes an objective evaluation possible. The actor must not feel the necessity to defend his self-image. Another barrier to learning from experience, and thus improving performance, is the barrier of the particular. The teacher who can see the results of his actions only in immediate, concrete terms is unable to transcend the specific case of one particular pupil or one particular item of knowledge. The ability to conceptualize the problems of instruction and to see them in abstract terms transforms the individual case into one that represents a particular aspect of a general problem. Without conceptualization, feedback is like a fable without a moral lesson. Objectivization occurs when the teacher translates his concrete experience into explicit concepts within the framework of a theory that gives them meaning. The cognitive map enables the teacher to objectivize his experience at the stage of feedback. Furthermore, the very act of confronting his experience in these terms is likely to help the teacher overcome the emotional barriers to learning the lessons of this experience. The objectivization of experience enables the individual to look at his actions as though he were standing outside of them.

In summary, the cognitive map of instruction does not tell the teacher how to teach a particular subject to a particular grade at a particular time. It can, however, tell him how to prepare to teach a lesson in a number of different ways, without any certainty which will prove successful; how to change tactics during the lesson (which is the very essence of instruction); and how to teach more successfully in the future on the basis of the lessons learned in the present.

FIVE   The Teacher and Instruction

It is a myth that one method of instruction is superior to all others. No drug can cure all illnesses. No political system can ensure happiness for all people in all places at all times. No work of literature, music, or sculpture can express all the possibilities inherent in art. An effective method of instruction advances the development of the individual learner. Since individual learners differ from one another, and since their growth takes place in different circumstances, and at different rates, methods of instruction must also differ if they are to be effective.

The same is true for the teacher. The current idea is that bad teachers are each bad in their own way whereas good teachers are all good in the same way, in accordance with some ideal of the "Good Teacher." But good teachers are not copies of some ideal model; they are human beings with unique characteristics and personalities. They are good only when they succeed—without suppressing their characteristics or subordinating their personalities—in activating all their powers in the process of instruction. This includes diagnosing the needs of their pupils, selecting the means (contents and methods), and implementing instruction that ensures the maximum possible development of their pupils. One of the main factors militating against effective teaching is the constant pressure exerted on the individual to resemble the "Good Teacher," which is nothing more than the image in someone's head of a person who is a good teacher. The fact that success in teaching depends on such qualities as spontaneity, honesty, openness, and subjectivity (the ability to process experience through an inner evaluation center) implies that good teachers cannot all be the same.

The teacher instructs by virtue of the interpersonal relations existing between himself and his pupils. His potential as an educator is not determined solely by his knowledge, values, wisdom, or virtues. He realizes his potential only when he dares to be himself, becomes sensitive to what is happening inside his pupils, is capable of acting according to his emotions, and does not repress his constructive drives. If he is truly open, he is likely to have a profitable educational relationship with his pupils. Such teachers are unique: their truths are different, their feelings are different, and the ways in which they express themselves are different.

A different approach usually dictates the way in which teachers are trained, the way in which their work is evaluated, and the way the public envisages a "Good Teacher." Research in instruction plays a part in maintaining this approach, which actually prevents candidates for teaching positions from becoming good teachers. Good teachers do occasionally emerge. This cannot generally be attributed to the kind of training or guidance they have received; it is due to their strong personal characteristics, which have resisted all the attempts to change them.

Research in instruction and its implementation in teacher-training institutions reduce teaching to techniques and specific behaviors. Thus, a good teacher should speak, react, and organize his material in specific ways. Those responsible for evaluating teachers usually concede that no two teachers are the same. In practice, however, they measure all teachers according to their ideal.

Instruction requires various techniques, but the results are not dictated by them. Two teachers can use the same techniques and achieve different results. It is not the technique that determines the results of instruction, but the manner in which it is used. And the manner in which the technique is used depends on two factors. One is the act of choosing the technique; the other is the attributes possessed by the teacher as teacher.

Before we discuss the factors influencing the way in which techniques are used, it should be stated that the techniques taught at many teacher-training institutions are not worth teaching. These techniques of instruction, as we have already argued, are simply those behaviors employed in all interpersonal relations. There is no need to teach people how to speak, ask questions, and show pictures. They are taught, however, because those responsible for training feel that teachers should speak, ask questions, and show pictures in a way that differs from the one in which these activities are usually performed. This feeling is connected with their image of the ideal teacher, which can distort the personalities of candidates for teaching, pervert their perception of reality, and falsify their reactions. Thus, instruction in techniques represses spontaneity, honesty, openness, and all the other qualities that teachers must have in order to perform their role. A teacher must be capable of choosing, or in many instances, of inventing the technique he considers appropriate to his needs, but he cannot be taught to do this. If he has to be taught it, he will never become a teacher.

The teacher capable of making decisions in all areas of the cognitive map will know how to choose the techniques appropriate to his goals and to the needs of his pupils. This is only one condition for his success. After his initial decisions the success of his actions depends on a number of characteristics that influence the way in which he employs the techniques he has chosen. What are these characteristics?

Psychological research in this area is not sufficiently sophisticated to be able to predict the success or failure of candidates for teaching.[1] Among the factors responsible for the meager results produced by this type of research is the lack of a valid theory according to which the characteristics of a good teacher can be described. The primary factor, however, is related to the type of hypothesis upon which most studies in this field have been based. These hypotheses examine the connections between teaching and various personality types and traits. But these connections have no significance for instruction. Some people belonging to certain personality types succeed in instruction, and others fail. The same is true of personality traits. The reason for failure or success must, therefore, be sought in other factors; our assumption is that it is related to the way in which the individual realizes his personality and characteristics. The extrovert is no more successful than the introvert; nor is the person with one attitude more successful than his colleague with a different attitude. The successful teacher activates his personality in a particular way. Authenticity seems to be one key to effective teaching. A rigid teacher who admits to being

rigid and is thus able to control this trait has more chance of succeeding than a rigid teacher who thinks that teachers should be warm and
friendly and who therefore pretends to be so when he is not.

Through the years the ideal characteristics for a teacher have
changed many times. At the end of the eighteenth century the teacher
was expected to be intelligent, learned, strong willed, clear minded,
and strict.[2] By the beginning of the twentieth century, he was supposed to be tough minded, extroverted, and have leadership ability.[3]
A book published in 1911 lists the following characteristics of a good
teacher: administrative ability, the ability to create the conditions
necessary for instilling good habits, the ability to analyze clearly the
contents of the syllabus, perseverance in drilling, and the ability to
present contents clearly.[4] Since then, of course, these characteristics
have changed.[5] It is interesting to note that different lists often contain completely opposite characteristics. Thus, the characteristics one
generation considers necessary are usually not regarded as desirable by
the next. It is difficult to explain these metamorphoses solely in terms
of social and ideological changes. Images of the good teacher change
more rapidly than social conditions. A more likely explanation is disil-
lusionment with present methods. When it is discovered that certain
characteristics are unrelated to quality in teaching, attempts are made
to replace them with other characteristics.

As has been said, authenticity is one essential condition for success
in teaching. It is not, however, the only condition. As with every other
human activity, teaching demands certain specific attributes of those
who engage in it. The attributes necessary for one occupation are likely to be detrimental in another. An architect needs different attributes
from a doctor in order to succeed in his profession, just as the attributes of a good doctor differ from those of a good administrator.
What we are speaking of here is a special combination of personal
qualities that is appropriate to the structure of a particular profession;
it is not, however, the total combination of qualities that makes up the
total personality. Doctors, teachers, architects, and administrators
may have many qualities in common; these are not necessarily the
characteristics that make them successful in their professions. Certain
attributes, which differ from profession to profession, determine the
quality of performance in the particular profession. These attributes
that profoundly affect the teacher's performance include: involvement
with the objects of instruction; awareness of the aims and objectives of
instruction; operational flexibility; supportive leadership.

Involvement with the Objects of Instruction

There are two objects of instruction: the pupil and the contents of the culture. Involvement is an individual's attitude toward any object that causes him to care about what happens to that object. Involvement with the objects of instruction means, therefore, that the teacher cares what happens to his pupils and to the culture whose contents he is teaching.

As has been said, the teacher is involved with both objects of instruction. In this way his involvement differs from that of parents on the one hand and of creators of culture and scholars on the other. A teacher involved with his pupil in the same way as his parents is not a good teacher; neither is the teacher involved with cultural contents in the same way as a scholar. The teacher should see an active attitude toward cultural contents as a means of advancing the development of his pupils and an active attitude toward his pupils as a way of creating a mutual relationship between them and the contents of their culture. In psychological literature the concept "involvement" or "ego involvement" has many meanings. Two psychologists attempted to examine these meanings on the basis of 170 studies in which the concept was used. They argue that those who use it ascribe to ego involvement the attributes of a motive force that energizes, directs, and sustains activity. Ego involvement also unifies individual reactions; that is, it ensures similar responses to stimuli. In their opinion ego involvement originates in the need to protect self-esteem.[6] There is a connection between ego involvement and effective performance in the area in which the individual is involved. A medium level of ego involvement seems to raise the degree of efficiency in performance, while both a high and a low level of ego involvement lower the degree of efficiency. When a rise in the efficiency of performance cannot be explained by any other factor, it is attributed to the involvement of the subject in his task. When there is a drop in the efficiency of performance, it is explained either by excessive involvement, which interferes with performance, or by lack of involvement, which is essentially lack of motivation.

The involvement of an individual with any object refers to the way in which he relates to that object. Three different types of relationship, originating in three different factors, are all called involvement. This results from an examination of the connection between efficiency and involvement that exists in psychological studies.

Excessive involvement, which interferes with performance and lowers the level of efficiency, apparently originates in the need to pro-tect self-esteem. An individual whose involvement is of this type (anxious involvement) greatly fears that he will lose his self-esteem should he fail. These anxieties contribute to his failure. A low level of involvement (condition apathy) is apparently nothing more than a lack of motivation or interest in any particular object. When there is no motivation, the level of performance is low.

There is a connection between a high level of performance and the interest an individual has in any particular object. When the individ-ual is interested in such an object, his performance is energized, directed, and sustained. We will reserve the term involvement only for this type of relation between the individual and the object of his activity.

The teacher may depart from optimal involvement in two ways. First, he may be involved with the pupil but not with the culture or with the culture but not with the pupil. Second, his involvement with the pupil and the culture may be anxious or apathetic.

On the basis of these two distinctions, we can classify and describe the types of deviation from optimal involvement in instruction. The description of these deviations may help to clarify the characteristics of optimal involvement, which is one of the conditions for successful in-struction. A schematic presentation of the possible combinations be-tween the types of involvement and its objects is given in Figure 5-1.

Figure 5-1

Types of teachers in relation to their involvement with pupil and culture

Involvement with pupil / Involvement with culture	Anxious Involvement	Involvement	Apathy
Anxious involvement	1	2	3
Involvement	4	9	5
Apathy	6	7	8

1. Anxious Involvement with Pupil and Culture

A teacher with a high level of compulsiveness tends to have this characteristic. He is driven by the feeling that a pupil who does not learn proves his failure as a teacher. Since he perceives his success as a teacher as a test of his worth as a person, every pupil who does not make progress in his classes endangers his self-image as a human being. The anxiety that accompanies all his actions drives him from various forms of aggression toward his pupils to attempts to gain their affection in any way possible. Any failure this teacher endures prepares the ground for additional failures. Instruction is, of course, impossible without failures, and so a teacher of this type has no hope of succeeding. In every aspect of involvement this is the worst possible type of teacher.

Pupils who spend a long period of time with such a teacher suffer a fundamental deprivation in the sense that their contact with an adult other than their parents does nothing to balance the anxiety they experience in their relationships with their parents. Furthermore, this kind of teacher does not provide a neutral attitude toward learning and school. Instead the students are exposed to an external, prestige-oriented attitude toward culture: learning is important because ignorant people are not esteemed by others and because learned people are respected. It is unfortunate that this type of teacher behaves in certain ways that please his superiors and sometimes the parents of his pupils. His anxieties are often interpreted as true concern for his pupils and for the standard of instruction. His aggression is seen as a sense of responsibility. His ingratiation is regarded as a readiness to be lenient when circumstances demand it. The more extreme manifestations of this type of involvement, however, may instill in the pupils exposed to them a lastingly negative attitude toward learning.

2. Anxious Involvement with Culture and Involvement with Pupil

This type of teacher is involved with his pupils to the extent that he feels their needs and tries to satisfy them. He is concerned for their welfare without being anxious that his self-image depends on his successful relationship to them. Though he feels affection for his pupils, this affection does not impair the logic of his actions. He wants all his pupils to make progress, but is able to accept an occasional failure, which does not arouse his aggression toward them.

His relationship to cultural contents is different. In this his attitude — anxious involvement — is the same as that of the previous teacher. He deeply believes that it is the duty of people to learn. His self-image is connected with what he himself has learned and with his achievements in learning.

These two contradictory approaches are in constant conflict. Sometimes the balanced, mature attitude toward the pupil becomes ascendant; at other times the uncontrolled anxiety about his self-image dominates. The compromise between these two attitudes often takes the form of preaching. Thus the teacher finds an outlet for his affection for his pupils and for his morbid anxieties with regard to culture. He does so by talking a great deal about the importance of learning and by appealing to the intelligence and conscience of his pupils in order to get them to study.

3. Anxious Involvement with Culture and Apathy toward Pupil

Though this type of teacher takes no interest in his pupils and their learning, he is filled with anxiety about everything concerning his status as a person who knows (or is supposed to know) about any given area of knowledge. One thing that arouses his anxiety is the fear that new research will bring about changes in the field he teaches. He is actually hostile to research because it may upset his fragile security in his subject. His defense against this danger is an attitude of contempt toward all modern "innovations." His admiration is reserved for what he was taught as a student; all subsequent developments are of no importance. He demands that his pupils adapt themselves to him, to his method of teaching, and to the contents he considers important. When his pupils challenge his expert knowledge, he is no longer apathetic toward them. Their demands for change in content or method of instruction are likely to lead to outbreaks of hostility or aggression toward them.

In any case, however, he regards his pupils as a necessary evil; they are an inevitable part of the business of teaching, but he need not concern himself about them unduly.

4. Involvement with Culture and Anxious Involvement with Pupil

If the anxious involvement with culture characteristic of the three types of teacher described above is the distinguishing mark of the pseudocultured person, then the optimal involvement in culture is characteristic of the truly cultured person. This kind of person is vital-ly interested in the area of knowledge with which he deals and enjoys working in it. The gratifications he derives are not dependent on prestige—on the attitudes of others; they are intrinsic gratifications. In situations of conflict between the demands of his field of interest and other obligations he will unhesitatingly choose the former, even if he must pay a price for doing so. This person may never contribute anything original in his field, but is sustained by an authentic experience and a living interest in it.

This attitude may exist alongside one of anxious involvement with pupils. In this case the teacher will be extremely anxious about his pupils' attitude concerning him. Every manifestation of positive feelings will raise his spirits, and every negative manifestation will depress him. Though contact with cultural contents sustains him and keeps his personality in a state of constant growth, contact with pupils is a continuing source of anxiety to him. These anxieties may, of course, limit his capacity to derive all possible satisfactions from the particular field of knowledge in which he is interested.

5. Involvement with Culture and Apathy toward Pupil

In his attitude toward culture this teacher resembles his predecessor, but in his relations with his pupils he is apathetic and indifferent. This type of person should have been a scholar or a creative thinker. As a teacher he is benefiting neither himself nor his pupils. Despite his positive qualities in his field of specialization, his teaching is poor because he is not motivated to teach. Even though he derives pleasure from his field, he is unable to teach what he knows to others, and perhaps even less to involve himself in the problems of those pupils who encounter difficulties in learning his subject. It is likely that those pupils who are talented and interested in his field will derive at least some benefit from his instruction.

6. Apathy toward Culture and Anxious Involvement with Pupil

This combination is largely the consequence of the social mobility that has led many people into teaching in the hope of improving their social status. They have obtained the necessary qualifications at teacher-training institutions, but their learning experience is usually dependent on secondary motivations. They learned not because they were curious to know, not because of any interest in the subjects of instruction, not even because they wished to identify themselves with the figure of a learned or educated man. They learned in order to receive a diploma that would gain them entrance to an institution of higher learning that would, in turn, open the doors to a lucrative or respectable profession for them. They know what they learned at the level on which they mastered it, and they have shown no further interest in study since they received their teaching certificates. In the classroom they are motivated mainly by the fear of failure. Entry into the teaching profession is for many of them the greatest achievement of their lives, and they are afraid of losing it. This fear places them in a constantly defensive position toward their pupils, since undisciplined behavior or poor results are capable of endangering their hard-won position. Teachers of this type often tend to become friendly with their students, hoping thus to gain security. If popularity means relinquishing any particular goal of instruction, this does not seem to them too high a price to pay, since their attitude toward culture imposes no real obligations on them.

7. Apathy toward Culture and Involvement with Pupil

The difference between this teacher and the one above lies in his honest attitude toward his pupils and his sensitivity toward their problems. His goodwill, understanding, and concern are not put on in order to ingratiate himself with his students, and they are not dictated by the need to protect his self-esteem. His style of operation is similar to that of a nursemaid who loves children or an intelligent social worker who has the good of his clients at heart. His apathetic attitude toward culture helps him to perform his role in this spirit because the demands implicit in the exacting instruction of any subject do not stand between him and his pupils.

8. Apathy toward Both Culture and Pupil

This teacher lacks motivation of any type. He performs his role as would an official in a bureaucratic institution. Without understanding exactly what the purpose of his actions is and without attributing any special importance to them, he does what he imagines is expected of him. Though he is less efficient than the teacher whose involvement with his pupils and with culture is one of anxiety, he is also less dangerous. His apathy toward the objects of instruction usually will not lead to aggression because he is not particularly interested in the success of his pupils or in his own success as a teacher. He is a bad teacher, but, of all bad teachers, he is the least harmful.

9. Involvement with Both Culture and Pupil

This combination endows the teacher with one of the four attributes necessary for success in his professional role. First, this attribute — involvement with culture and pupils — is a motivating force. The teacher of this type seeks opportunities to teach and to experience different teaching situations because he derives satisfaction from them. Second, this attribute contains mechanisms for directing instruction during its implementation. The teacher who is involved with his pupils senses intuitively what he should and, perhaps even more often, what he should not do. Because of his dual involvement, he is able to strike a balance. His involvement with culture provides him with a means of controlling his involvement with his pupils and vice versa. Although the dual involvement keeps the teacher in a constant state of tension, the tension is different from that of the teacher who is anxiously involved with one or the other or both of the objects of instruction. It is tension experienced by a mature person. It involves things that are incompatible by nature. In order to make them compatible, the teacher must act. Sometimes he restrains his involvement with the culture and sometimes with the pupil. His actions are not, however, dictated merely by the desire to assert himself in his own or his pupils' eyes (although there is no reason why he should completely deny his drive to assert himself). As a matter of fact, with a minimum of self-assertion, this teacher is able to perceive intuitively the needs of his pupils and the claims of the culture and to resolve conflicts between them.

To some extent, involvement of this type prevents the teacher from becoming stale. There is always the danger that after a number of years the teacher will simply repeat the formulas of previous years. If he is interested in his pupils, that interest is renewed every year because his pupils change. When he is involved in the subject he teaches, he constantly renews his interest by keeping abreast of changes and new developments in it. Involvement with his field and with his pupils is to the teacher what the drive to write is to the writer, what curiosity is to the scientist, or what the drive to power is to the politician. Without it a person can teach, but his performance will resemble that of the writer who has no inner urge to express himself, the scientist who lacks inquisitiveness, or the politican who is not interested in power.

Involvement constitutes the emotional and willed element in the teacher's functioning. It is, however, only one essential factor. Emotions and the will to act may lead the teacher into conduct that is unrelated to the aims of instruction. Without aims, instruction is impossible, but they, too, are only one essential factor.

The second attribute that profoundly affects performance, "awareness of the aims and objectives of instruction," besides its specific function in the process of instruction, also controls involvement.

Awareness of the Aims and Objectives of Instruction

Awareness is a general term for the various processes by which the individual knows what he knows. In this sense awareness includes perception, memory, imagination, judgment, evaluation, and, of course, thinking in all its facets. Thus, awareness is the cognitive aspect of individual existence, whose other aspect is the emotions and the will.

Instruction is composed of specific actions whose meaning is derived from the aims for which they are undertaken. A teacher tells a story. The instructional meaning of this act derives not only from its contents and its literary value, but from the teacher's goal in telling the particular story. A teacher who knows the contents of a story and is endowed with narrative gifts may sometimes achieve something valuable by telling a story even if he does not know exactly why he is telling it. But this is an occurrence that belongs in the realm of chance. A teacher who does not know why he is telling a particular story, even if his story is excellent and he relates it effectively, is not teaching. Sometimes he merely enjoys performing (which is, in itself, not a bad thing), and sometimes he simply can think of nothing else to do. Instruction is not based on such factors. It is, of course, desirable that the teacher enjoy what he is doing, but only on condition that what he is doing is directed toward the aims of instruction. Awareness in instruction thus means awareness of aims and awareness of the specific acts—the objectives—that lead to these aims. This awareness is not identical with the knowledge of the subjects the teacher teaches. Awareness of the aims and objectives of instruction includes such knowledge, but it alone is meaningless insofar as instruction is concerned. The role of historian and the role of teacher of history or the role of mathematician and the role of teacher of mathematics demand utterly different personality structures. The mathematician may also be able to teach. He will not, however, be a teacher because of his mastery of mathematics but because of certain attributes that make him competent to teach the subject. Awareness of the aims and objectives in any particular field of instruction, such as mathematics, means a number of things: understanding the connection between the teaching of mathematics and the pupil's learning mathematics, including the possibility that some pupils will not learn it; understanding the connection between specific acts and the possible aims in the light of which the subject can be taught. Anyone who understands all these things may not be a mathematician, but he is a teacher. If he knows enough mathematics to adapt its contents to the needs of different pupils, and if he understands the possible contribution of mathematics to the intellectual development of his pupils,· he is a good teacher of mathematics.

Both the knowledge of a subject and the pedagogic awareness necessary to use this knowledge in the process of instruction can be realized in a number of ways and at various levels. A teacher's knowledge of his subject can be restricted to familiarity (at different levels) with its contents. A teacher of history, for example, may be at the level of repeating the information, factual or evaluative, available to him in books. Obviously, this level can be higher or lower, but its common denominator is its reproductive character. Some teachers of this type will know many facts and interpretations; others will know fewer. A teacher's knowledge of his subject may be manifested in a way that is different from familiarity with facts, although there is of course no necessary contradiction between the two. The other manifestation of knowledge is knowing its structural foundations, its principles, its methodology, in short, knowing its spirit rather than the bodies of knowledge from which it is composed. Despite the widespread opinion held by many who have a mastery of the subject's contents, it is possible to know the principles of a subject without having a full mastery of its substance. A philosopher of science, despite the fact that he is not a physicist or a chemist, knows more about physics and chemistry than many physicists and chemists, whose specialization consists of knowing physics or chemistry. What is possible at the level of philosophical generalization is also possible in a number of other ways. A person may have an intuitive feeling for literature without being a scholar of literature or have an intuitive grasp of history without being a historian. The scholar in all these fields must master a large amount of information, without which there is little chance of his being able to broaden the area of knowledge in his field. It is doubtful, on the other hand, if he needs to be aware of the structural foundations of his subject (except methodology). If he achieves anything, it will be the task of the philosophers of science to explain the principles that were implicit in his research, but of which he himself need not have been aware. This is not true of the teacher. Awareness of structures in the areas of knowledge he teaches is incomparably more important to his work than familiarity with contents. Such awareness can grow out of a systematic study of the structural foundations of his subject — from a study of the theory of literature for the teacher of literature, of historiography for the teacher of history, or of the philosophy of science for the teacher of physics, biology, or chemistry. But it can also grow from creative interaction with selected contents of the subject matter — from firsthand experience of creative writing, for example, or from a close study of any period of history, which is motivated by an impulse unconnected with scientific research, such as a religious or ideological-political impulse. It can also come from fascination with the philosophical problems of knowledge connected with scientific research. The source of the awareness is not important. But the teacher who is to any degree aware of the structural foundations of a given area of knowledge knows something that his colleague who is only familiar with its contents does not know: how to distinguish the essential from the unessential. Awareness of this kind develops a sense of what is important. The teacher who can distinguish between what is important in his subject and what is secondary is in a far better position to decide what to do in the classroom than the teacher who simply knows the contents of the subject, however impressive his familiarity with the facts may be.

These distinctions between various levels of familiarity with contents and awareness of structural foundations are obviously made only for the purpose of analysis. In reality, teachers are distinguished from one another by a mixture of familiarity with contents at various levels and of awareness of structural foundations at various levels.

This is also true of didactic awareness (awareness of the ways by which pupils internalize the principles of the subjects of instruction and learn their contents). The concepts that link the level of awareness in this area to the processes of instruction indicate aims at various levels. A teacher may be aware only of objectives, how to teach a defined, concrete unit of the curriculum. He may be aware of goals as well as objectives; he may be able to derive techniques of instruction regarding the defined and concrete unit from an overall view of any given subject or area of knowledge. He may be aware of objectives, goals, and also aims; that is, he may know how to connect techniques to sequences of actions and how to relate these to the general aims of instruction. The main difference among these levels of awareness lies in the degree of flexibility they bestow on the teacher. A teacher who is familiar with only techniques (objectives) is a prisoner of rigid procedures. He knows, probably very well, how to teach a particular poem or problem in mathematics, but he does not know why he teaches it thus. When his way fails, he is incapable of choosing another on the basis of his own professional knowledge. A teacher who is aware of goals as well as objectives is more flexible. He is aware of the purpose of instruction in an entire field. Should a particular technique fail him, he is likely to find an alternative without deviating from his goals. The most comprehensive awareness is that which applies to all the aims of instruction and enables the teacher to choose by their means both goals and objectives.

Didactic awareness is sustained by the knowledge of the structures and principles of the field in which the teacher specializes, as well as by the knowledge of the processes by means of which the pupil internalizes these structures and principles. A teacher who only can employ a certain type of exercise lacks didactic awareness, as does a teacher who knows how to describe or analyze the principles of his subject, but cannot make his pupils understand and use these principles. The didactic awareness characteristic of a good teacher combines the knowledge of the structures, principles, and methods of the subject with the ways in which to impart these to his pupils. The way the teacher thinks about the aims of instruction at their different levels manifests this awareness. He can think about objectives only, about objectives as derived from goals, or about these as derived from aims. But he can also think about each of these levels as though it exhausted his intentions in instruction, as though it was sufficient in itself.

For purposes of simplification we shall restrict our discussion to only two levels—aims and objectives. With the help of these two concepts, we shall describe the deviations from good teaching in the subject being discussed here. As in the description of the previous attribute, the concepts will indicate only points on a continuum; they are not intended to describe isolated phenomena.

Figure 5-2

Types of teachers in relation to their awareness to aims and
objectives of instruction

Objectives / Aims	Optimal awareness	Limited awareness	Minimal awareness
Optimal awareness	1	4	7
Limited awareness	2	5	8
Minimal awareness	3	6	9

1. Optimal Awareness of Both Aims and Objectives

A teacher of this kind has everything that could be asked for in this area. He knows both his subject and the realm of meaning in which the principles of that subject have crystallized.[7] He knows not only a group of techniques by which he can teach his subject, but also how to obtain guidance in choosing the appropriate techniques. Because his mastery of instruction is rational, he is able to control his involvement with the objects of instruction. Involvement provides motivation, and awareness provides direction.

2. Limited Awareness of Aims and Optimal Awareness of Objectives

A teacher with these characteristics directs the process of instruction partly by rationality and partly by habit and routine. When his awareness of aims is limited, his decisions will rely on ready-made, un-controlled, and usually standard opinions. In this group are teachers whose actions are likely to be surprising, in accordance with the extent to which their awareness of aims is limited. Some generally act in ac-cordance with rational considerations, but may suddenly find them-selves in situations in which they behave completely irrationally. Others usually behave in a way that does not appear to be particularly rational or considered, but change when an isolated incident causes them to act in a manner that seems to be totally rational.

3. Minimal Awareness of Aims and Optimal Awareness of Objectives

This teacher's behavior has apparently been subjected to what is known as instrumental fixation.[8] Because of a particular type of training or because of his individual characteristics, this kind of teacher has absorbed techniques of instruction and learned to use them successfully. If his techniques are appropriate to many of his pupils, he may even have a measure of success in instructing them. Success is rare, however, because a teacher of this type can never respond to all the frequent changes, transitions, and situations in the classroom. At best, his instruction will never be more than a standardized treatment of both pupils and contents that he may be able to implement with a relative degree of success. But his chances of failure are great.

4. Optimal Awareness of Aims and Minimal Awareness of Objectives

Usually this is an individual who might have been a good teacher but whose training was deficient. Someone who can absorb the essence of an area of knowledge and the process of instruction (which is what optimal awareness of aims implies) is also able to master the various objectives of instruction. If his awareness in this field is limited, it may be assumed that his training was lacking. Even in these circumstances, however, his performance in the classroom is likely to be superior to that of the teacher who is aware of objectives but whose awareness of aims is limited.

5. Limited Awareness of Both Aims and Objectives

Habit dictates the actions of this type of teacher, but his routine does not include any behavior that is inadmissible. He adheres to a particular way of implementing instruction, justifies it on the basis of arguments that are not particularly consistent, and does not attempt to solve problems that transcend day-to-day requirements. Awareness at this level can be calamitous when it is accompanied by other negative attributes, such as lack of involvement in culture. It can, however, be partially remedied when such positive attributes as involvement with pupils are present.

6. Minimal Awareness of Aims and Limited Awareness of Objectives

Though this teacher resembles the previous one, the differences in habit and routine may lead to patterns of behavior that are inadmissible in any teaching situation. For this reason there is little chance that positive attributes will make any significant difference in the situation.

7. Optimal Awareness of Aims and Minimal Awareness of Objectives

Belonging to this group are teachers whose intellectual interest in instruction is greater than their interest in its implementation. Deficient training cannot be held responsible for their lack of awareness of objectives. A person capable of reaching a high level of awareness of aims can also do the same with objectives. If he fails to do so, some aspect of his personality must be the cause. Such a teacher is interested in the theory of instruction, but he is neither concerned with nor capable of actually teaching.

8. Limited Awareness of Aims and Minimal Awareness of Objectives

This individual is similar to the teacher with minimal awareness of aims and limited awareness of objectives. Both are dominated by a routine that chooses the line of least resistance. Neither can be expected to produce creative thinking in instruction, or even intelligent behavior guided by relevant professional considerations.

9. Minimal Awareness of Both Aims and Objectives

Such an individual is a teacher by mistake, either his own or those who appointed him.

Awareness of aims and objectives as an attribute of the good teacher is derived from the essential nature of instruction, which is a goal-directed activity. These goals are not, however, given in advance. The teacher must decide among rival aims, and the necessity to make such decisions is ever present in all his activities. He must decide what is important and what is not regarding each unit of instruction (even when the unit has been imposed on him from above). But this decision alone does not exhaust the relations between the teacher and the contents of the culture. Since the good teacher instructs by means of contents — not contents in themselves — he must know how to transform the contents of culture into part of the personality of the learner. Without an awareness of aims and objectives the teacher cannot know this.

Operational Flexibility

Awareness of aims and objectives can never be complete. So many factors influence instruction that changing objectives and sometimes even changing aims are basic needs of effective instruction. But awareness of aims and objectives would seem, on the contrary, to lead to adherence to them. A teacher who has come to certain considered conclusions regarding the aims of instruction and the measures he should adopt in order to achieve them tends to stick to these conclusions. His independent judgment is on trial (Were his conclusions wrong?) as is his curiosity (Were his conclusions right?). A teacher who considers alternatives and makes decisions on the basis of them may ignore the facts of a situation when they conflict with his decisions. This is why controls are needed on awareness of aims, which is in itself a control on involvement.

Operational flexibility controls awareness. Thus, if the teacher is flexible, he is willing to change his technique when he feels it is not working. Flexibility is a personality trait about which opinions are divided, both in regard to its nature and the reasons for its presence or absence.[9] It is not our function to prescribe how this attribute can be acquired. What is almost certain, however, is that teacher-training institutions can contribute very little in this area, and so a measure of flexibility should be one of the criteria by which candidates for teaching are selected.

But flexibility, or the readiness to change aims and techniques, is not always compatible with good teaching. Just as rigid adherence to goals conflicts with the demands stemming from the nature of instruction, so too are certain types of readiness to change them inappropriate. A teacher who changes because he enjoys change for its own sake and one who alters his aims every time he runs into difficulty are both being flexible, but their flexibility is not appropriate to the needs of instruction. Flexibility as a necessary attribute of the good teacher is best described by means of the concept of feedback.

If the teaching situation is defined as a system, feedback is the situation in which the teacher receives information from his class on what is happening in it as he teaches and proceeds to act in accordance with this information. This information is not, of course, anything such as a written report from a class representative. The teacher receives and interprets messages, verbal or nonverbal, that reach him as he teaches and adapts his actions to the meaning implicit in them. A teacher who is able to receive feedback knows when his pupils are bored, even if they do not yawn in his face; he knows when they do not understand, even when they do not announce it; and, he knows when they are satisfied, even if they do not applaud. The teacher may have a number of reactions to feedback, but they can all be classified into three groups.

First, the teacher can receive information from his class and not react to it. There is nothing, in fact, that distinguishes this teacher from the one who fails to receive the messages sent by his class. Both continue to teach in the same way, either according to plan or to habit. Second, the teacher may receive information and respond positively to its implications. Realizing the unit is boring, he stops teaching it. This is termed positive feedback.[10] Disintegration of the system is the result of positive feedback, which works in the following way. Because the teacher thinks a unit is important, he decides to teach it. When he notices his pupils are bored, he stops teaching it. Thus the particular system of instruction breaks down.

Positive feedback, or the disintegration of a system, can also occur in another way. The teacher may realize that his pupils are bored and reacts by intensifying the boredom. For example, the teacher drills his pupils in an arithmetic problem. He senses they are bored to a state of near stupor and responds by giving them additional exercises. His reaction may be triggered by frustration or by a conscious conviction that pupils must overcome their lack of interest in certain units of learning and acquire this necessary knowledge by an effort of the will. In any case, it is to be expected that the pupils will stop learning. They may rebel openly, by not doing the things the teacher tells them to do, or they may pretend to carry on their activities. In both instances, however, they will have effectively detached themselves from the project in which they are supposedly engaged. Thus, the system is destroyed. Positive feedback is, therefore, incompatible with the needs of instruction and, indeed, prevents it from taking place.

A different type of reaction is negative feedback, which occurs when the teacher receives information from his class and reacts to its implications, but continues to concern himself with the maintenance of the system. (The term "negative" is derived from the theory of cybernetics. According to this theory, all systems strive for self-destruction and self-extinction. Positive feedback is positive in these terms since it supports this tendency of the system. Negative feedback is negative since it counteracts the inherent tendency of the system to destroy itself.) When the teacher senses that his pupils are bored but tries to teach what he has been teaching up to then in a way that is not boring, he is acting according to negative feedback. The class remains a class, instruction remains instruction, and the teacher strives to keep the system going by new means because he has found that the previous means are failing.

Negative feedback can also occur when the teacher abandons his previous goals and changes his actions to achieve new goals. In this case the teacher learns by feedback that his goal is faulty and that in order to achieve more comprehensive aims he must abandon his previous, partial ones.

These three reactions to feedback—lack of reaction, positive feedback, and negative feedback—affect every aspect of the teacher's functioning, including his teaching, because he brings his personality into the classroom with him. For purposes of simplification, however, this discussion will be restricted to those aspects that directly affect his classroom behavior.

All teachers, like all human beings, make mistakes, but they differ in the way in which they relate to their mistakes. A teacher who does not receive feedback consistently repeats his mistakes. He is blind to the lessons implicit in his mistakes, he is insensitive to his pupils' reactions, and he does not feel he should analyze his actions once they are completed. A teacher who reacts positively to feedback tends to rationalize his mistakes. He will make excuses for them. According to him, his mistakes only seem to be mistakes; in fact, he did what he did on purpose. Though the feedback from his class indicates that he made a mistake, he does not admit it. In most cases he not only repeats the same mistake but intensifies it. Only the teacher who reacts negatively to feedback will learn from his mistakes. Because he senses and analyzes his mistake, he is unlikely to repeat it.

Teaching is an activity that can be successfully performed only after a process of trial and error. An effective teacher is one who has found a way of relating the principles of instruction to his own personal characteristics. This way cannot be arrived at in advance. It must result from the teacher's trying a number of ways before finding the one that suits his personality. The crucial stage in training a teacher is the one at which he learns from his own mistakes. This should occur when the individual is a student. In this case teaching resembles the arts. Academies of painting or sculpture teach principles, but the road from these principles to the point at which the student becomes an artist is paved with many experiments in which these principles are put to use, and each failure is a step toward greater mastery of color, form, or composition. Like the artist who learns to create by making mistakes, the teacher finds his teaching style by profiting by his errors. Thus a person who does not learn from his mistakes has little chance of becoming any sort of teacher, let alone a good teacher. A good teacher improves his performance by being sensitive to feedback and ready to change his behavior according to what he learns from it. A bad teacher continues to tread his accustomed paths, blind and deaf to the lessons of experience.

The description of these three different behaviors is intended to demonstrate the connection between the teacher's ability to receive feedback and his utilization of it. This connection is apparent in every aspect of his activities, not only in his reaction to his mistakes. A teacher who does not receive feedback does not sense his pupils' difficulties, or the changes taking place within them, either as individuals or as a group. In addition, he has no grasp of the connection between the changes taking place in the social environment of the school and what happens inside it. He is mainly sensitive to physical disturbance: rebellious behavior by his pupils or a refusal to comply with his requests by his superiors. In such circumstances he attempts to return to a situation in which he can act without being disturbed by the environment. He always seeks a situation in which he can teach without the necessity of paying attention to what is occurring in the learning group and its environment.

The teacher who reacts positively to feedback does sense the difficulties of his pupils and the changes taking place within them as individuals or as a group. But his reactions reinforce the causes of failure and the sources of disturbance in the process of instruction. This teacher strives stubbornly to attain his goals, and when he learns from his pupils' reactions that these goals are inappropriate or unattainable, he intensifies his efforts to reach them and justifies himself in terms of rationalizations. In order to achieve his goals, he is prepared to use almost any means from sermonizing to punishment. His sensitivity to what is happening in the class, which is a condition for good teaching, becomes a curse. As a matter of fact, a teacher who lacks this sensitivity is preferable, since this lack at least does not cause him to increase his failure.

Obtaining feedback in the classroom is not a rational process; sometimes it is not even a conscious one. Absorbing information concerning classroom activity is essentially emotional. Reaction to the information, on the other hand, can be either emotional (in which case it will consist mainly of the activiation of defense mechanisms to protect the teacher's self-image and beliefs) or rational (in which case it will consist mainly of considerations relevant to the teacher's actions and their goals). The difference between positive and negative feedback lies in the difference between emotional and rational reactions. A teacher sensitive to what is going on in his class and in each of his pupils, who senses the changes taking place in the intensity of their learning, in their feelings of satisfaction, and in their shifting moods, and who is able to relate to these things as data relevant to his professional considerations regarding what he should do next is acting on the basis of negative feedback — the condition for operational flexibility in the classroom.

What has been said up to now has implied that the source of such operational flexibility lies in the individual personality traits of the teacher. But this is not the complete story. Many educational ideologies have, in fact, suggested consistency as the teacher's most desirable attribute. A teacher's actions are often guided by these ideologies. Thus, the individual may have a personality that would permit operational flexibility, but would sublimate that flexibility because of the conviction that consistency is desirable. Not all manifestations of rigidity in instruction result, therefore, from rigidity in the teacher's personality; there is also a rigidity in teaching that is in opposition to the personal characteristics of the teachers. Rigidity of this type is produced by a certain type of teacher training and can be avoided by training of a different sort.

Consistency and rigidity in instruction are the same thing. The teacher who is not ready to change his techniques, and, when necessary his aims, is consistent; and the behavioral expression of this consistency is rigidity. In teaching, rigidity means perseverance in using means even when they arouse pupils' resistance and in striving for ends even when they are unattainable. There are no means or ends in instruction that are "good" or "right" in themselves. Means that pupils reject are bad means, whatever their theoretical justification. And aims toward which pupils refuse to work are pseudoaims, whatever their philosophical basis. A flexible teacher can adapt himself to his pupils' reactions by changing means and aims. When theories of instruction persuade this teacher that he must adhere to his goals and that he should never give in to his pupils, his ability to be flexible will be wasted.

Not all theories of instruction, however, advocate rigidity. Some, usually those influenced by the child-centered approach to education, consider, explicitly or implicitly, the changing reactions and situations of the pupil. These ideologies attach the highest importance to the teacher's flexibility.

All this leads to a confrontation between the contents of teachers' cognition (educational ideologies) and their personality traits. This encounter provides the basis for a typological distribution of teachers with regard to operational flexibility or rigidity (see Figure 5-3). The first dimension shows the three possible behaviors with regard to feedback: lack of feedback, positive feedback, negative feedback. The second dimension demonstrates the two existing attitudes in instruction: consistency, which includes all the opinions justifying rigid behavior; and "responsiveness," which includes all the opinions justifying flexible behavior.

Figure 5-3

Types of teachers in relation to their operational flexibility

Feedback / Attitude	Lack of feedback	Positive feedback	Negative feedback
Consistency	1	3	5
Responsiveness	2	4	6

1. Lack of Feedback and Attitude of Consistency

This combination characterizes the most rigid of teachers. He is insensitive to feedback from his class and believes that a teacher should strive to attain the goals he set at some time in the past. If he is exceptionally knowledgeable and his pupils are exceedingly interested in learning, then they, or at least the most gifted among them, may be able to overcome his rigidity and benefit from his instruction. In most cases, however, only failure and frustration result from instruction implemented by a teacher of this type.

2. Lack of Feedback and Attitude of Responsiveness

There is little difference between this type of teacher and the preceding one. Their actions produce similar results because both are insensitive to their students' evaluations. Unlike his predecessor, this teacher believes that he should respond to his pupils' needs, but is incapable of doing so because he does not receive the messages telling him what these needs are. We are, however, dealing with attributes that exist in varying degrees. Thus, when the students convey their frustration strongly enough, this teacher admits the need to reexamine and correct his actions. In crisis situations this teacher is more effective than the previous one, who usually feels that situations of stress and disintegration call for a firmer hand and more repressive measures than usual. With the exception, therefore, of unusually obvious circumstances he behaves in the same way as his predecessor, even though he believes that teachers should act differently.

3. Positive Feedback and Attitude of Consistency

From the viewpoint of instructional needs, this combination produces the worst possible behavior. A teacher of this type wants to behave in a consistent manner while at the same time receiving feedback from his class. His reactions to this feedback tend to destroy the system, that is, to increase the causes of failure. Because of his desire to be consistent, he uses the same techniques and strives for the same goals as in the past, usually with increasing zeal. When a student fails to perform a task, the teacher normally doubles the task. A pupil who fails to copy a passage will be told to copy two passages, a pupil who is unable to understand the teacher's explanation will be made to do more exercises on the problem he has not grasped than those who understand it, a pupil who lacks interest in a subject will be given extra work in that subject rather than in any other. If the first pupil's failure to copy the passage is not simply accidental, then increasing the pressure on him is likely to make him withdraw even further from school. The same is true for the pupil who cannot understand and the one who is not interested. This teacher refuses to ask himself why one student does not do his homework or why another does not understand the explanation. Though he senses his students' situations, he perpetuates rather than changes them.

4. Positive Feedback and Attitude of Responsiveness

A teacher with this combination is sensitive to what is happening among his pupils as a group and as individuals and recognizes the necessity for guiding his own actions according to their needs. Everything he does, however, aggravates problems where they already exist and creates them where they do not. He attributes his interference with his students to affection and concern. He explains the increasing pressure he exerts on them as stemming from the requirements of a method or a principle of teaching. Though his intentions are always good and he tries answering his students' needs, everything he does results in increased resistance to learning.

5. Negative Feedback and Attitude of Consistency

This combination produces opposite behavior to the preceding one. The teacher's consistency originates in ideology. On the basis of some educational theory, he believes that he must be consistent in his actions. But an incomparably more powerful factor than this belief—negative feedback—balances his behavior. Though he wants to be consistent, he cannot be. The feedback he receives forces him to adjust his attitudes. Even when he does manage to remain consistent, however, his interpretation of consistency enables him to adapt himself to the changes taking place among his students. He is thus able to change techniques when that becomes necessary while remaining consistent with regard to goals. He can even change goals if the reactions of his pupils indicate that is required.

6. Negative Feedback and Attitude of Responsiveness

According to the schematic description in Figure 5-3, this is the most successful of all possible combinations. We should remember, however, that the description is schematic and that both feedback and responsiveness have varying degrees of intensity in different situations. Sometimes a teacher reacts negatively to feedback from his class but not from himself, from his class but not from his colleagues, or from his colleagues but not from his class. His responsiveness to his pupils' needs may be great in one area and lacking in another. The typology outlined here is a presentation of "pure" types that do not exist in reality. We intend only to establish criteria for describing the behavior of teachers in defined situations. When a teacher is able to react negatively to feedback and when the theories of instruction in which he believes oblige him to respond to his pupils' needs by changing tactics and aims, then we have a teacher who is the best suited to instruction as a process intended to support his pupils' development. It might be helpful to describe the behavior expected of this teacher on the basis of the above combination of attributes, as compared to behavior that might be anticipated as a result of other possible combinations. This will be done by means of examples.

A teacher explains some new material. By asking a few questions he discovers that a large number of students have failed to understand the explanation. Teachers' reactions to this common situation differ radically. Some teachers ignore the situation or do not sense it. Others become angry, and their anger may be accompanied by accusations against their pupils. A few explain again, using a different method the second time. Most, however, repeat the same explanation.

Ignoring the students' incomprehension shows lack of feedback. Anger and blame are characteristic of positive feedback, as is the repetition of the same explanation that was not understood before. A teacher incapable of admitting that his presentations and explanations are defective is angered by pupils who are having difficulties with them. An angry response does not help the student understand what was previously incomprehensible to him; nor does it explain to the teacher the students' initial difficulties.

Repetition of the previous explanation is a mechanical reaction, and the assumption underlying it is that the pupils were not paying attention to the teacher and therefore did not understand what he said. Such things, of course, do happen. In most cases, however, it is inconceivable to the teacher that the pupils did pay attention and nevertheless failed to understand.

The other possible reaction — explaining in a different way — is the flexible behavior of the teacher who is guided by negative feedback. His pupils did not reach the desired destination by taking the road he mapped out for them. Therefore, he tries a new road. That is, he changes his tactics as soon as he realizes that those he is using are not successful.

A pupil consistently fails to do his homework. There are a number of possible reactions by the teacher: ignore it; reprimand the pupil and sometimes punish him; attempt to find a way to get him to do his homework. When the teacher regards the act of doing homework as a goal in itself, this must be taken as a sign that the teacher has lost sight of the true aims of instruction. If, however, he regards homework as a means in the process of instruction, he may conclude that he should give the pupil less homework for a time. This does not mean that he has decided to ignore the situation. It is, rather, a strategic measure designed to change the situation. The teacher first seeks to arouse his pupil's interest in learning in the hope that this will gradually lead to his doing his homework. At the same time he will not dismiss two other possible developments. One is that he will not succeed in arousing the pupil's interest; in this case there will be no point in forcing him to do his homework. The use of such means would probably be more harmful than beneficial. The other possibility is that he will succeed in arousing his pupil's interest in learning without that interest leading him to prepare his homework. In this case pressure exerted on the pupil to prepare his homework might destroy the interest, and so he will refrain from exerting it.

A pupil or a class exhibits indifference or even resistance toward certain teaching material. The teacher has tried a number of different approaches and has failed in all of them. This is a common occurrence, and one in which instruction is fundamentally distorted. In this situation many teachers lose rational control over their behavior. They disregard their pupils' reactions until they are too strong to ignore, and at that point they use all the means of coercion and persuasion at their command. It is unfortunate that this behavior eventually affects the teacher's style in those areas of instruction where his pupils might perhaps have wished to learn if he had behaved differently.

The teacher behaves in this manner for many reasons. One stems from institutional pressure. Curricula imposed from above, external examinations, and administrative procedures place the teacher in a difficult position. He must teach certain things even if his pupils reject them, even if he is indifferent to them or is insufficiently familiar with them, or even if he is convinced that there is no justification for teaching them. Another reason originates in the belief held by many teachers that pupils do not know what is good for them. Yet another reason results from the teacher's anxiety about his leadership; he feels that his students have no right to tell him what to teach.

It is impossible to predict the behavior of the teacher who is guided by negative feedback and an attitude of responsiveness toward his pupils' needs because of the very nature of these attributes. Since he senses these needs, the nuances and subtleties of the situation will influence his decision. It is possible, however, to surmise some courses of action he might adopt. One possibility is that, despite the institutional pressure, he will abandon the material. He will make every effort to teach it, but, if he does not find the right way, he will not lose control because of feelings of humiliation, frustration, or anxiety. It is not that he is immune to such feelings. He will, no doubt, be disappointed when he fails to achieve his goals. Because he knows that these feelings lead to the distortion of the process of instruction and of his role as a teacher, he is capable of controlling them. Thus, he stands up for his pupils against the institutional pressure and takes the responsibility on himself. As a matter of fact, the teacher's readiness to accept responsibility for his decisions is one of the important factors in determining his relations with his pupils. Some teachers abandon the material that cannot be taught, blaming their students for not being able to understand it. Such a feeling on the part of the teacher must influence in some fashion the way in which he sees his pupils. The first teacher, on the other hand, admits that he is not going to teach the material because he has decided not to do so. If any blame is involved, it is his.

Another possible reaction of the responsive teacher is to involve the students in the problem. He may concede that he feels the same way about the material as they do, but convinces them that they need to learn it in order to pass a required examination. In this case the teacher does not pretend to be a representative of the culture that has deemed the material in question vital to the education of its young. Nor does he adopt coercive measures or blandishments. He and his pupils share the responsibility with complete honesty.

The teacher might react to the same situation by telling his superiors that he has attempted to teach the material in a number of ways, but has been unsuccessful in all of them. Going further, he might state that he and his students feel the same way about the material and that it could prove beneficial for someone else to teach it. By handling the situation in this manner, the teacher demonstrates to his superiors that his attitude concerning the material is not an admission of failure owing to professional incompetence. But this teacher is taking a risk. He wants to give meaningful instruction that is based on his pupils' wishes to learn. This may conflict with his recognition that certain material, which he feels cannot be meaningfully taught, at least by him, must nevertheless be taught, even if the reasons for teaching it have nothing to do with education.

It is impossible to present a comprehensive picture of the behavioral style of the teacher with operational flexibility. Only in day-to-day instruction is operational flexibility fully expressed. A teacher of this type is capable of abandoning a goal or a technique during the course of instruction and substituting another for it. He never loses sight of the role instruction is supposed to play in his pupils' development, and his actions are guided by their reactions, whether overt or covert, to what he does.

Supportive Leadership Ability

The difference between the way leadership ability is discussed here and the way it was presented on the cognitive map of learning is the difference between the description of an attribute in operation and the examination of a concept for the purpose of clarifying its meaning. A teacher may believe in authoritarian leadership in terms of his general outlook and, nevertheless, lead his pupils in a way that is supportive of their development.

Most leadership studies have assumed that the school is a closed system and that its dominant leadership styles are produced by the decisions and personalities of the teachers (in certain cases even of the decision and personality of the individual teacher) whose actions determine what kind of psychological climate will prevail in the class.

But the psychological climate in the classroom is never the sole product of the teacher's leadership. A permissive teacher who behaves in the same manner in a group of middle-class children, of culturally deprived children, of children who grew up in a patriarchal culture creates a different psychological climate in each of them. Classroom activity results not only from the teacher's actions but from the pupils' reactions, which have their source outside the classroom and even outside the school. These reactions depend largely on the culture in which the children grow up and on the social climate of the school of which the class is a part. These factors influence the psychological climate in the classroom even before the teacher begins to operate. Thus, the teacher's actions take place against a background of the cultural patterns of the pupils' home environment and the institutional patterns of the school.

The psychological climate in the classroom is, therefore, the result of the meeting between the teacher's leadership style and the situation that existed before he began to act upon it. One must concede, nevertheless, whatever the resulting psychological climate in the classroom — authoritarian or permissive to varying degrees — that the teacher's actions can still either support or repress his pupils' development.

At this point it is necessary to distinguish between the nature of the climate and the leadership style. The school functions, as does any other institution, according to a pattern of relatively structured relationships (climate). The climate in the classroom, which is the result of the culture in which the school exists and the traditions of the school, can be either authoritarian or permissive to varying degrees. Instruction, however, even if it needs the institutional structure within which it takes place, is always a web of interpersonal relationships. These relationships can help the pupil grow, or they can direct his development into channels that are not necessarily compatible with his individual needs.

It is paradoxical that the more repressive the climate in the school, the easier it is for the teacher to be supportive. A single sympathetic gesture toward the pupil has supportive significance in a climate in which sympathy for pupils is rare. In a sympathetic climate much more will be demanded of the teacher in order to support the development of his pupils. We are, of course, speaking here of relative supportive power. A teacher gifted with supportive leadership ability operating in a repressive framework will be able to counteract, to some extent, the repressive effect of the institution. Though this is a form of support, it is more in the nature of the prevention of negative influences than the exertion of positive ones. On the other hand, a teacher operating in an institutional framework geared to support the development of pupils will have to work hard to find a way in which to support the individual development of each pupil. Supportive leadership is not an automatic function of a permissive framework, just as a repressive framework does not oblige the teacher to be repressive in all his actions. Interpersonal contact between teacher and pupil exists largely as an independent factor operating side by side with the other factors present in teaching situations. This contact can support, at varying degrees of intensity, tendencies toward repression or liberation present in the school. Its influence can also be so weak as to give all the real power to other factors, chiefly the climate prevailing in the school.

In describing the characteristics of the teacher whose leadership supports the development of his pupils, we shall, therefore, ignore the climate in the school. These characteristics will, of course, be more in demand in an institution that supports pupils' development than in one that directs, or even represses, this development. Apart from the extent to which such characteristics are seen as desirable by the school and are independent of the climate prevailing in it, there are certain traits in teachers that enable them to give supportive leadership to their pupils.

The first supportive trait is the teacher's ability to respect the child as a person.[11] Respect entails recognition of the child's twofold right: to be a child and to be himself. Many adults, including a number of teachers, regard the child as deficient. The conventional school usually makes no attempt to grant the child adult status and regards his childish state as a weakness, an inability to bear responsibility, and a justification for keeping him in perpetual dependence. The fact that the child is not an adult is interpreted by the school as a justification for constantly suspecting him, his acts, and his intentions. Because he is always in the position of being a suspect, the child soon learns to defend himself by deceit.[12] For an adult it is sufficient to explain that he did not read an article recommended by a friend because he could not find the time. The child at school must say that he had a headache. The adult excuses himself and leaves the room; the child at school has to ask permission to go to the lavatory. The lowest level of respect for the child is that which enables him to give up deceit for purposes of self-defense. This level can be attained by any teacher, in any normal school, and in any educational system. Though this is not much, in the atmosphere prevailing in many schools today, one teacher acting in this way may be able to restore some degree of his students' self-respect.

A higher level of respect for the child involves recognition and encouragement of individual differences. The behavior of a teacher guided by a recognition of the uniqueness of each pupil will largely depend on the climate of the school in which he teaches. Every institutional framework does not allow the same scope to the teacher who wishes to encourage individual differences. Even in the most repressive schools, however, there are some teachers whose leadership style enables pupils to manifest their unique individuality. They exist side by side with other teachers who repress such manifestations. Recognition and encouragement of difference take on a number of forms in the school. In modest forms they are admitted today even in the most traditional schools. This usually consists of recognizing the student's right to demonstrate individuality outside school hours. In social activities, school parties, and even recesses the pupil is permitted, sometimes even encouraged, to exhibit his individuality. At the other end of the spectrum are schools that encourage individual difference in the area of learning as well, by introducing differentiated curricula and by abolishing procedures intended to exert pressure or encourage competition for similar achievements. Recognition of difference or denial of it is at least as dependent on the kind of relationship existing between the teacher and his pupils as on the institutional organization of the school. By his actions the teacher can accept manifestations of individual difference with encouragement or with resignation or not accept them at all. The fact that the interpersonal relations between teacher and pupil can counteract the influence of the institutional structure of the school is strikingly evident here. In a school that exerts pressure to conform, a teacher who recognizes and encourages difference protects the healthy development of his pupils. This behavior may, of course, bring the teacher into conflict with the school administration. But the conflict will be no more severe than that in which he will find himself if he seeks to add his pressure to the pressure already existing in the school to make pupils repress their individuality. Every teacher must ultimately decide if he is loyal to the institution or to the pupil. Whatever decision he makes, he will find himself in a conflict. Thus, he must decide which conflict he prefers.

The behavioral manifestation of the recognition and encouragement of difference originates in the principle of acceptance. In this context, acceptance is the rejection of any prior condition that might influence the relations between the teacher and his pupil. The teacher can recognize difference only if he accepts each of his pupils as he is. Success in learning is no more a reason for a favorable attitude on the part of the teacher than failure is a reason for a chilly attitude. "Good" behavior does not bring him closer nor "bad" behavior alienate him. Acceptance in this sense exists by virtue of the psychological advantage that the teacher has over his pupils and entails at the same time the use to which he puts it. As a style of leadership, acceptance is directed toward supporting the development of the pupil. A teacher who accepts his pupils as they are does not give up hope of changing them. His style of leadership is such that the change it anticipates comes about not as a result of pressure exerted by the teacher, but as a result of the maturing powers of the pupil living and acting in an educational environment. One of the characteristics of such an environment is the acceptance of the pupil by his teachers. Thus a pupil need not invest much energy in fighting for his right to be what he is; he can, instead, invest it in growing.

The level at which the teacher accepts his pupils can be measured by the extent to which he must use corrective action. One can see the proportion among the number of comments intended to "correct" the pupil's behavior, the degree of praise and condemnation, the amount of evaluation of characteristics, and the degree of acceptance or rejection. Instead of assuming the position of a judge or a critic, the teacher of this type will want to be a member of the group and to share in its life. In this, too, he acts by virtue of his authority over his pupils. But this use of authority is in the nature of educational leadership, which is intended to help the pupil know himself by means of his actions. The pupil's desire to be a member of the group originates in his need to belong. The teacher's motive in participating in the life of the group does not derive from this same need because he gets his satisfaction from belonging to other groups. It derives, rather, from his need to lead the group. This need can result in either domination of the group or in supportive leadership. The teacher's self-awareness largely determines the direction of his participation in the life of the class.

Self-awareness is the most decisive factor in the teacher's ability to give his pupils supportive leadership. A teacher who is unaware of the sources of his excessive sensitivity to order, cleanliness, and politeness is unable to accept his pupils if they are disorderly, casual about cleanliness, and impolite. A teacher who is unaware of his need to dominate others will be unable to give them freedom to grow. A teacher who is unaware of his motives will be unable to control them. Increasing the teacher's self-awareness can improve his supportive leadership ability.

There are two ways of classifying teachers according to supportive leadership ability: the situations in which they can act and their level of support. Some teachers are able to function as supportive leaders in interpersonal relations with their pupils so long as their schoolwork is not at stake. Others can do so in the area of learning, but cannot participate in their pupils' personal affairs. Still others are able to provide supportive leadership both in the area of learning and of their sudents' personal lives. In each case the level of support is of varying degrees of intensity.

The four attributes of the teacher described above complement and correct each other. A teacher with supportive leadership ability needs an awareness of the aims of instruction in order to control this ability. Supportive leadership alone can become a kind of psychotherapy for pupils, a role that does not exhaust the functions that the teacher is expected to perform. An awareness of aims alone, on the other hand, can harden the teacher's attitude as he strives to attain these aims.

Thus, awareness of aims must be controlled by operational flexibility, which, in turn, is likely to deflect the teacher's actions from their proper goals. Consequently, it needs to be controlled by an awareness of aims.

We must conclude, therefore, that any one of these attributes, even if it exists in the teacher to the fullest possible degree, will not compensate for the lack of any other requisite attribute. Only the combination of all four attributes produces the necessary conditions for behavior in accordance with the needs of instruction. Since each of these attributes can be manifested at different levels of intensity and realized in different ways, and since they may be present in all the different combinations possible, the number of ways in which teachers can actually perform their professional role on the operational level is exceedingly great. This is true both of performance assessed as good and performance assessed as bad. What we have here is a spectrum. At one end is the best possible combination of attributes. At the other is the lack of all the attributes necessary for effective teaching. Every teacher can be placed at some point on this spectrum according to the type and intensity of his involvement, the type and extent of his awareness of aims, the degree and extent of his ability to receive feedback, and the depth of his self-awareness, which determines his supportive leadership ability.

In conclusion, the three components of instruction are graphically represented in Figure 5-4.

Figure 5-4

The three components of instruction

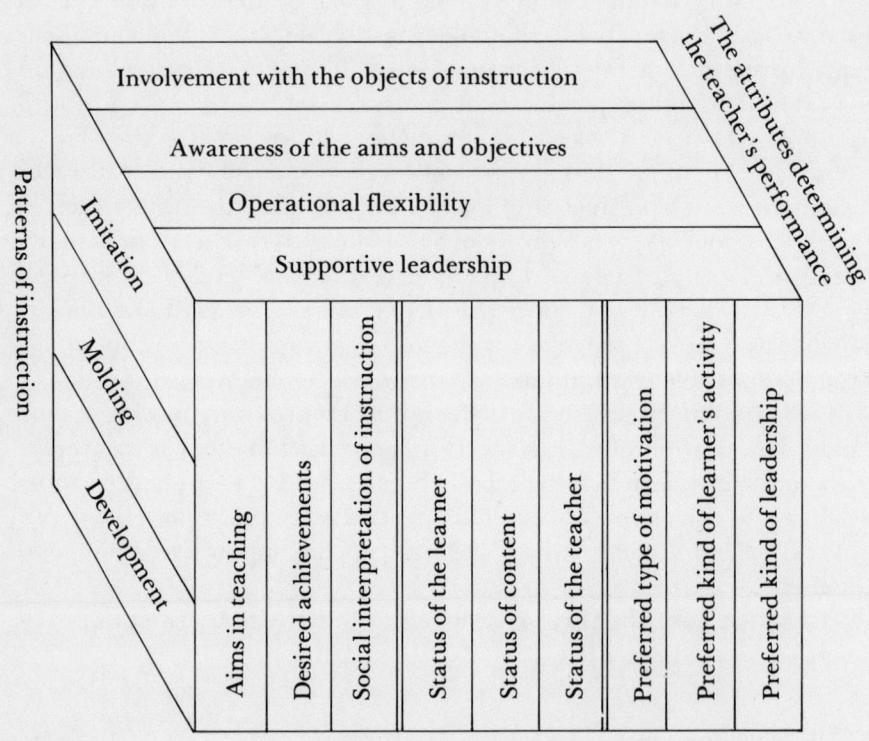

Dimensions of the cognitive map of instruction

NOTES

Chapter One

1. Arno A. Bellack *et al., The Language of the Classroom* (New York: Teachers College Press, 1966).

2. J. Hoetker and W. P. Ahlbrand, Jr., "The Persistence of Recitation," *American Educational Research Journal,* VI (No. 2, 1966), 163.

3. M. Gibbons, "What Is Individualized Instruction?" *Interchange,* I (No. 2, 1970), 28.

4. H. Read, *Education for Peace* (New York: Charles Scribner's Sons, 1949), pp. 81 – 82.

5. Everett Reimer, *School Is Dead,* Anchor Book (New York: Doubleday, 1972).

6. Ph. Aries, "Le XIX siècle et la révolution des moeurs familiales," in R. Prigent, *Renouveau des idées sur la famille* (Paris: n.p., 1954), p. 116.

7. J. H. van den Berg, *The Changing Nature of Man,* Delta Book (New York: Dell, 1964).

8. See Reimer, *School Is Dead,* p. 161.

9. See Margaret Mead, *The School in American Culture* (Cambridge, Mass.: Harvard University Press, 1959), pp. 33 – 34.

10. Jean Piaget, *Science of Education and the Psychology of the Child* (New York: Viking Press, 1971), p. 10.

11. *Ibid.,* p. 66.

12. Paulo Freire, *Pedagogy of the Oppressed* (New York: Herder and Herder, 1971), p. 58.

13. Neil Postman and Charles Weingartner, *Teaching as a Subversive Activity* (New York: Delacorte Press, 1970), p. 27.

14. Jean Paul Sartre, "Une idée fundamentale de la phenomenologie de Husserl," *Situations* (Paris), 1 (1947).

15. Nathaniel Cantor, *The Teaching-Learning Process* (New York: Holt, Rinehart and Winston, 1953), pp. 59 – 71.

16. Aristotle, *Politics,* tr. Benjamin Jowett (Oxford, Eng.: Clarendon Press, 1905), Book VIII.

17. For example, see H. I. Marrow, *A History of Education in Antiquity* (New York: Sheed and Ward, 1956).

18. B. Bandman and R. S. Gutchen (eds.), *Philosophical Essays on Teaching* (Philadelphia: Lippincott, 1969).

19. *General Education in a Free Society,* Report of the Harvard Committee (Cambridge, Mass.: Harvard University Press, 1945).

20. *Ibid.,* pp. 54 – 65.

21. *Ibid.,* p. 65.

22. *Ibid.,* p. 65.

23. *Ibid.,* p. 67.

24. *Ibid.,* p. 68.

25. *Ibid.,* pp. 69 – 70.

26. *Ibid.,* p. 71.

27. See A. H. Maslow, "Psychological Data and Value Theory," in A. H. Maslow (ed.), *New Knowledge in Human Values* (New York: Harper and Row, 1959), p. 130.

28. L. A. Cremin, *The Transformation of the School,* Vintage Book (New York: Random House, 1961).

29. A. S. Neill, *Summerhill* (New York: Hart, 1960).

30. A list of the schools operating on radical principles in the United States at the beginning of the 1970's is to be found in *The Modern Utopian Alternatives Foundation* (San Francisco: Alternatives Foundation, 1971), pp. 173 – 175. Several schools of this type are described in Satu Repo (ed.), *This Book Is about Schools,* Vintage Book (New York: Random House, 1970), pp. 167 – 354.

31. Descriptions of these reforms are to be found in many books about primary schools in England. For example, J. Blackie, *Inside the Primary School* (London: Her Majesty's Stationery Office, 1967); J. Featherstone, "Revolution in the Primary Schools," "A New Kind of Schooling," and "Experiments in Learning," *New Republic* (August 10, September 2, September 9, 1967; March 2, December 21, 1968); Vincent Rogers, *Teaching in the British Primary School* (New York: Macmillan, 1970).

32. R. S. Barth, "Open Education—Assumptions about Learning," *Educational Philosophy and Theory,* I (1969), 29 – 39.

Chapter Two

1. John Dewey, *Democracy and Education* (New York: Free Press, 1966).

2. J. A. Comenius, *Didactica Magna Universale Omnes Omnia* (1657).

3. J. H. Pestalozzi, *How Gertrude Teaches Her Children,* tr. L.E. Holland and F. C. Turner (London: Swan Sonnenschein, 1938).

4. See J. W. Getzels and P. W. Jackson, "The Teacher's Personality and Characteristics," in N. L. Gage (ed.), *Handbook of Research on Teaching* (Chicago: Rand McNally, 1963), pp. 506 – 582.

5. *Ibid.,* p. 574.

6. See R. M. Gagné, *Conditions of Learning* (New York: Holt, Rinehart and Winston, 1965).

7. J. S. Bruner, *Toward a Theory of Instruction* (Cambridge: Mass.: Harvard University Press, 1966).

8. H. Anderson and E. Brever, *Studies in Teachers' Classroom Personalities. II: Effects of Teachers' Dominative and Integrative Contacts on Children's Classroom Behavior,* Applied Psychology Monographs, No. 6 (Washington, D.C.: American Psychological Association, 1946).

9. R. Lippit and R. K. White, "The 'Social Climate' of Children's Groups," in R. G. Barker *et al.* (eds.), *Child Behavior and Development* (New York: McGraw-Hill, 1943), pp. 458 – 508.

10. J. R. Gibb, "Sociopsychological Process of Group Instruction," in P. Bradford (ed.), *Human Forces in Teaching and Learning* (Washington, D. C.: National Education Association, 1961).

11. N. A. Flanders *et al., Helping Teachers Change Their Behavior* (Ann Arbor: University of Michigan, School of Education, 1963, mimeo).

12. M. Hughes, *Development of the Means for an Assessment of the Quality of Teaching in Elementary Schools* (Salt Lake City: University of Utah Press, 1959).

13. M. K. Openshaw, *Development of a Taxonomy for the Classification of Teachers' Classroom Behavior* (Columbus: Ohio State University Research Foundation, 1966, mimeo).

14. B. O. Smith, "A Concept of Teaching," *Teachers College Record,* LXI (1960).

15. J. Wilson, "Education and Indoctrination," in T. H. B. Hollins (ed.), *Aims in Education* (New York: Humanities Press, 1966).

16. See H. J. Rousseau, "The Impact of Educational Theory on Teachers," *British Journal of Educational Studies,* XVI (No. 1, 1968), 60 – 71.

17. See B. J. Biddle *et al., Contemporary Research on Teachers' Effectiveness* (New York: Holt, Rinehart and Winston, 1964).

18. Most of the textbooks on teaching intended for use in teacher-training institutes are written in the spirit of this approach. See A. D. Woodruff, *Basic Concepts of Teaching* (San Francisco: Chandler, 1961); L. N. Nelson (ed.), *The Nature of Teaching* (Waltham, Mass.: Blaisdell, 1969).

19. Reductive compositions written from the point of view of imitation are mainly found in literature on programmed instruction. See R. F. Mager, *Preparing Instructional Objectives* (Belmont, Calif.: Fearon, 1962). Reductive compositions from the point of view of molding may be illustrated by *General Education in a Free Society,* Report of the Harvard Committee (Cambridge, Mass.: Harvard University Press, 1945). Reductive compositions from the point of view of development may be illustrated by C. R. Rogers, *Freedom to Learn* (Columbus, Ohio: C. E. Merrill, 1969).

20. The homeostatic approach is represented by J. Piaget, *Six Psychological Studies* (New York: Random House, 1967), ch. 4. The other approach is represented by A. H. Maslow, *Toward a Psychology of Being* (Princeton, N. J.: Van Nostrand, 1962), ch. 4.

21. See I. Scheffler, "Philosophical Models of Teaching," *Harvard Educational Review,* XXXV (No. 2, 1965), 131 – 143.

Chapter Three

1. See G. McLure, "Growth as an Educational Aim: A Reply to R. S. Peters," *Studies in Philosophy and Education,* III (No. 3, 1964), 259 – 270.

2. See R. Bourne, *Untimely Papers* (New York: Viking Press, 1919), p. 21.

3. D. H. Wrong, "The Oversocialized Conception of Man in Modern Sociology," *American Sociological Review,* XXVI (No. 26, 1961), 183 – 193.

4. For example, R. S. Peters, *The Concept of Education* (London: Routledge and Kegan Paul, 1968); H. H. Horne, *The Democratic Philosophy of Education* (New York: Macmillan, 1935); R. M. Hutchins, *The Conflict in Education in a Democratic Society* (Westport, Conn.: Greenwood, 1953).

5. See A. H. Maslow, *Toward a Psychology of Being* (Princeton, N. J.: Van Nostrand, 1962); G. Allport, *Becoming* (New Haven, Conn.: Yale University Press, 1955); C. Rogers, *On Becoming a Person* (Boston: Houghton Mifflin, 1961).

6. See Sigmund Freud, *The Future of an Illusion* (Edinburgh: Horace Liveright, 1928); A. H. Maslow, "Psychological Data and Value Theory," in A. H. Maslow *et al.* (eds.), *New Knowledge in Human Values* (New York: Harper and Brothers, 1959).

7. See C. R. Rogers, "Toward a Theory of Creativity," in S. J. Parnes and H. F. Harding (eds.), *A Source Book for Creative Thinking* (New York: Charles Scribner's, 1962).

8. See Milton Rokeach, *The Open and Closed Mind* (New York: Basic Books, 1960).

9. See A. Inkeles, "Social Structure and the Socialization of Competence," *Harvard Educational Review*, XXXVI (No. 3, 1966), 265 – 283; K. Mannheim and W. A. C. Stewart, *An Introduction to the Sociology of Education* (London: Routledge and Kegan Paul, 1962).

10. P. Goodman, "The Present Movement in Education," *New York Review of Books*, April 10, 1969.

11. See R. Dreeben, "The Contribution of Schooling to the Learning of Norms," *Harvard Educational Review*, XXXVII (No. 2, 1967), 211 – 237.

12. See F. M. Keesing, "Memorandum for the Study of Acculturation," *American Anthropologist*, XXXVIII (1936).

13. See A. L. Kroeber and C. Kluckhohn, *Culture*, Vintage Book (New York: Random House, 1952), p. 357.

14. See T. S. Eliot, *Notes towards the Definition of Culture* (London: Faber and Faber, 1948), p.21.

15. See R. S. Peters, *Education as Initiation* (London: Evans, 1965).

16. Jolande Jacobi, *The Way of Individuation* (New York: Harcourt, Brace and World, 1965), p.13.

17. Maslow, "Psychological Data and Value Theory," pp. 130 – 131.

18. Erich Fromm, *Escape from Freedom* (New York: Holt, Rinehart and Winston, 1941), p.24.

19. See Erich Fromm, *The Sane Society* (Greenwich, Conn.: Fawcett, 1955).

20. Freud, *The Future of an Illusion*.

21. H. Read, "Pragmatic Anarchism," *Encounter*, XXX (January 1968), 58.

22. Maslow *et al.* (eds.), *New Knowledge in Human Values*, p. 129.

23. A. Neumann, *Depth Psychology and a New Ethic* (London: Hodder and Stoughton, 1969), p. 38.

24. See Georg Kerschensteiner, *Das Grundaxiom des Bildungsprozesses und seine Folgerungen für Schulorganisation* (Berlin: Deutsche Union Verlag, 1917).

25. This approach is illustrated by A. N. Whiteheard, *The Aims of Education* (New York: Macmillan, 1929).

26. H. Read, *The Redemption of a Robot* (New York: Trident Press, 1966), pp. 26 – 27.

27. Herbert Spencer, *Education: Intellectual, Moral and Physical* (first edition, 1861; New York: D. Appleton, 1900).

28. See R. J. Hutchins, "The Great Conversation: The Substance of Liberal Education," in *Encyclopaedia Britannica* (Chicago: Encyclopaedia Britannica, Inc., 1955); A. E. Bestor, *The Restoration of Learning* (New York: Knopf, 1955); H. G. Rickover, *Education and Freedom* (New York: Dutton, 1959).

29. See Clifton Johnson, *Old-Time Schools and Schoolbooks* (New York: Dover, 1963).

30. See Erich Fromm, "Values, Psychology and Human Existence," in Maslow *et al.* (eds.), *New Knowledge in Human Values*, p. 163.

31. See Herbert Read, *To Hell with Culture* (New York: Schocken Books, 1963); Jules Henry, *Culture against Man* (New York: Random House, 1963); D. Cooper (ed.), *Dialectics of Liberation* (Baltimore: Penguin Books, 1968).

32. See Maxine Green, *Existential Encounters for Teachers* (New York: Random House, 1967), especially the chapter entitled "Knowing" (pp. 66 – 96).

33. See W. Waller, *The Sociology of Teaching* (New York: Wiley, 1965), especially ch. 5, "What Teaching Does to Teachers" (pp. 375 – 404).

34. See P. M. Symonds, "Education and Psychotherapy," *Journal of Educational Psychology*, XL (January 1949), 1 – 32.

35. F. Blättner, *Geschichte der Pädagogik* (Heidelberg: Quelle and Meyer, 1961), pp. 210 – 218.

36. See Johnson, *Old-Time Schools and Schoolbooks*.

37. See Maslow, *Toward a Psychology of Being*, p. 25.

38. R. W. White, "Motivation Reconsidered," *Psychological Review*, LXVI (No. 5, 1959), 297 – 333.

39. K. Bühler, *Die geistige Entwicklung des Kindes* (Jena: Gustav Fischer, 1924).

40. John Holt, *How Children Fail* (New York: Pittman, 1964), p.168.

41. William James, "Psychology and the Teaching Art," in *Talks to Teachers* (New York: Norton, 1958), p. 21.

42. T. P. Green, "A Topology of the Teaching Concept," *Studies in Philosophy and Education*, III (No. 4, 1964 – 65), 284 – 319.

43. R. Lippit and R. K. White, "The 'Social Climate' of Children's Groups," in R. G. Barker *et al.* (eds.), *Child Behavior and Development* (New York: McGraw-Hill, 1943), pp. 458 – 508.

44. H. Anderson and E. Brever, *Studies in Teachers' Classroom Personalities. II: Effects of Teachers' Dominative and Integrative Contacts on Children's Classroom Behavior*, Applied Psychology Monographs, No. 6 (Washington, D.C.: American Psychological Association, 1946).

45. J. R. Gibb, "Sociopsychological Process of Group Instruction," in P. Bradford (ed.), *Human Forces in Teaching and Learning* (Washington, D.C.: National Education Association, 1961).

46. N. A. Flanders *et al.*, *Helping Teachers Change Their Behavior* (Ann Arbor: University of Michigan, School of Education, 1965, mimeo).

47. J. R. P. French and B. Raven, "The Bases of Social Power," in Darwin Cartwright and Alvin Zender (eds.), *Group Dynamics* (New York: Harper and Row, 1953), pp. 607 – 623.

48. Neumann, *Depth Psychology and a New Ethic*.

Chapter Five

1. See J. W. Getzels and P. W. Jackson, "The Teacher's Personality and Characteristics," in N. L. Gage (ed.), *Handbook of Research on Teaching* (Chicago: Rand McNally, 1963), pp. 506 – 582.

2. J. Sully, *The Teacher's Handbook of Psychology* (London: Longmans, 1886).

3. J. Welton and F. G. Blandford, *Principles and Methods of Moral Training* (London: London University Press, 1909).

4. See C. M. Fleming, *Teaching, A Psychological Analysis* (London: Methuen, 1958), p. 15.

5. Those interested in the characteristics attributed to the good teacher should consult "Teaching Competencies," in W. S. Monroe (ed.), *Encyclopedia of Educational Research* (New York: Macmillan, 1950).

6. M. A. Iverson and M. E. Render, "Ego-Involvement as Experimental Variable," *Psychological Reports*, II (No. 2, 1956), 147 – 181.

7. See Ph. H. Phenix, *Realms of Meaning* (New York: McGraw-Hill, 1964).

8. Instrumental fixation is a term indicating the automatization of reactions in any given action, which prevents those subjected to it from changing their behavior.

9. See E. Sorren and G. Thompson, "Problem Solving, Rigidity and Personality Structure," *Journal of Abnormal Psychology*, XLVI (No. 2, 1951), 165 – 176; N. C. Foster *et al.*, "Flexibility and Rigidity in a Variety of Problem Situations," *ibid.*, L (No. 2, 1955), 211 – 216; C. Frankenstein, *The Roots of the Ego* (Baltimore: Williams and Wilkins, 1966).

10. See W. Ross Ashby, *An Introduction to Cybernetics* (London: Chapman and Hall, 1958), ch. 1.

11. An attitude of respect for the pupil as the starting point of any educational activity is much discussed in the literature of the new radical approach to education. See C. R. Rogers, *Freedom to Learn* (Columbus, Ohio: Charles E. Merrill, 1969); Paulo Freire, *Pedagogy of the Oppressed* (New York: Herder and Herder, 1971). One of the first to stress this problem, and, indeed, to make it the main theme of his writing, was the educator Janusz Korczak, whose work is, unfortunately, little known in the West.

12. See H. Hartshorn and M. A. May, *Studies in Deceit* (New York: Macmillan, 1928).